Whiterstein Series in Software Agent Technologies

Series Editors:
Marius Walliser
Stefan Brantschen
Monique Calisti
Stefan Göller

This series reports new developments in agent-based software technologies and agent-oriented software engineering methodologies, with particular emphasis on applications in various scientific and industrial areas. It includes research level monographs, polished notes arising from research and industrial projects, outstanding PhD theses,and proceedings of focused meetings and conferences. The series aims at promoting advanced research as well as at facilitating know-how transfer to industrial use.

About Whitestein Technologies

Whitestein Technologies AG was founded in 1999 with the mission to become a leading provider of advanced software agent technologies, products, solutions, and services for various applications and industries. Whitestein Technologies strongly believes that software agent technologies, in combination with other leading-edge technologies like web services and mobile wireless computing, will enable attractive opportunities for the design and the implementation of a new generation of distributed information systems and network infrastructures.

www.whitestein.com

Dissertation, genehmigt von der Fakultät für Wirtschaftswissenschaften der Universität Fridericiana zu Karlsruhe, 3. August 2006
Dissertation approved by the faculty of Economics and Business Engineering at the Universität Fridericiana Karlsruhe, Germany, August, 3rd 2006
First Reviewer :   Prof. Dr. Christof Weinhardt
Second Reviewer :   Prof. Dr. Detlef Seese
Examiner :   Prof. Dr. Andreas Geyer-Schulz
Chair of Commission :   Prof. Dr. Hagen Lindstädt

Clemens van Dinther

Adaptive Bidding in Single-Sided Auctions Under Uncertainty

An Agent-based Approach in Market Engineering

Birkhäuser Verlag
Basel · Boston · Berlin

Author:

Clemens van Dinther (born Czernohous)
Research Center for Information Technologies
Haid-und-Neu-Str. 10-14
D-76131 Karlsruhe
Germany

2000 Mathematical Subject Classification 91A15, 60J20, 68Txx, 00A72

Library of Congress Control Number: 2006934675

Bibliographic information published by Die Deutsche Bibliothek
Die Deutsche Bibliothek lists this publication in the Deutsche Nationalbibliografie;
detailed bibliographic data is available in the Internet at <http://dnb.ddb.de>.

ISBN 978-3-7643-8094-6 Birkhäuser Verlag, Basel – Boston – Berlin

© 2007 Birkhäuser Verlag, P.O. Box 133, CH-4010 Basel, Switzerland
Part of Springer Science+Business Media
Cover design: Micha Lotrovsky, Therwil Switzerland
Printed on acid-free paper produced from chlorine-free pulp. TCF ∞
Printed in Germany
ISBN-10: 3-7643-8094-2   e-ISBN-10: 3-7643-8113-2
ISBN-13: 978-3-7643-8094-6   e-ISBN-13: 978-3-7643-8113-4

9 8 7 6 5 4 3 2 1   www.birkhauser.ch

Foreword

Technical innovation has changed the way of doing business in recent years. In many developed countries the majority of the households has access to and make use of the Internet. In 2004, for example, German consumers have brought up a volume of approx. 11 Billion Euros for buying goods on the Internet. The Internet auction platforms of eBay and Amazon have established a strong position in online markets. Finance industry revolutionized securities trading systems on stock exchanges during the last decades - not only by increasing trading speed and extending trading hours - this industry even calls for more innovations and services like high frequent information services, algorithmic trading and flexible market institutions.

Industry and science are interested in understanding the impact of new market institutions and services on the market outcome. Thus, the interest in studying electronic markets has significantly increased during the last five years. In fact, auctions have been subject to research before the rise of the electronic trading, but it was noticed in recent years that human participants not always behave as predicted in theory. Nobel prize laureates Reinhard Selten and Vernon Smith stated recently that economists need to better understand and consider human behaviour within their analysis. There is a need to complement theory with other analysis techniques as experimental and computational approaches.

This book picks up the issue of using software agents for economic simulations. Clemens van Dinther gives an overview on the fundamental theory of electronic markets, Market Engineering and computational economics. The idea of a structured approach for designing electronic markets including perspectives from economics, computer science and law came into being as Market Engineering at the Institute for Information Systems and Management in 2004. This book briefly summarizes this design approach and puts the focus on the evaluation of electronic markets by agent-based computational means. In order to facilitate the implementation of electronic markets and to give customers the opportunity to design their own market the flexible electronic trading platform meet2trade was developed. It allows to easily design, create and test various electronic market mechanisms for different application domains and is presented as a first step towards Computer Aided Market Engineering.

The idea of using software agents for simulation became known as Agent-based Computational Economics. So far, agents have been used to simulate different kinds of (economic) problems such as social issues, economic growth, stock exchanges, market economies, or logistics. However, main criticism on agent-based research is that it has not established a consistent methodology. Clemens van Dinther draws attention to this lack and presents a brief overview on some methods that show interrelations to economic approaches. This is a significant step forward to understand and properly apply agent-based methods in economics. Several software packages are available to build multi-agent systems and simulations. The author evaluates available software tools and presents the five most popular packages in more depth. JADE is a multi-agent middleware that is widely-used in science for building multi-agent systems. His System AMASE was developed as an extension to JADE to enable agent-based simulations, where agents represent various participants or group of participants, respectively, who can easily participate in these kind of simulations. Thus, AMASE assists market engineers to build and run multi-agent systems for simulation purposes.

When participating in electronic auctions the most important issue is to determine one's own valuation. This is especially difficult if not all information is available and/or considered. Therefore, bidders might be uncertain about their own valuation of a distinct good and in consequence might bid below or above their true valuation. Bidders can reduce their risk of overbidding by acquiring additional information. In his work, Clemens van Dinther addresses this issue of valuating this type of uncertainty. He develops an agent-based economic model to simulate the strategic implications on the bidding behaviour and, hence, is able to show the impact of increasing information acquisition costs on the bidding behaviour. The results are consistent with theory which simultaneously shows the appropriateness of the agent-based simulation model.

The present work is an excellent example for interdisciplinary research. Such research requires methodological knowledge in both, economics and computer science. Therefore, I wish the reader will benefit and learn from the present illustrations.

This work developed during the project electronic Financial Trading (e-FIT) which was conducted in cooperation with Reuters, the brse-stuttgart, and the spin-off company trading fair. The industrial interest shows the high relevance of electronic market research in practice.

Therefore, I wish best success for its publication, for its author, and for the readers who might hopefully better understand electronic markets and agent-based simulations.

Karlsruhe, Germany   Christof Weinhardt
September 2006

Acknowledgements

Many people contributed in one way or the other to finish this book. This dissertation would not have been possible without the guidance of my advisor Prof. Dr. Christof Weinhardt at Universität Karlsruhe (TH). He faced me with new challenges, gave critical comments to enrich the scientific work, and encouraged me to finish the thesis. Thanks are also due to the examination board, namely Prof. Dr. Detlef Seese as second reviewer, Prof. Dr. Andreas Geyer-Schulz as examiner, and Prof. Dr. Hagen Lindstädt as chair of the commission.

The dissertation was developed during my work at the Institute of Information Systems and Management (IISM) and at the Research Center for Information Science, both at Universität Karlsruhe (TH). The fruitful discussions during the doctoral seminars as well as the countless discussions with both research groups built an tremendous input. Therefore, I am grateful to the whole team for their support. Thanks are due in particular to Dr. Henner Gimpel, Dr. Daniel Rolli, Dr. Stefan Seifert, and Ilka Weber who contributed through their critical comments, discussions and ideas. Additionally, I thank Carsten Block, Matthias Burghardt, Xin Chen, Björn Schnizler, Stephan Stathel, and PD Dr. Daniel Veit for proofreading and commenting the work. I am also indepted to Marc Schleyer of the Institute for Conveying Technology and Logistics for his mathematical assistance as well as to Matthias Schwaiger of the Control Systems Laboratory for his help in technical problems.

I thank the German Federal Ministry for Education and Research, Börse Stuttgart AG, Reuters AG, trading fair AG, and the Institute of Information Systems and Management (IISM) for funding the work under the Grant number 01HW0148.

Personally, I am grateful to my parents, Christa and Walter Czernohous, who always supported my decisions and made my education possible. The person I thank the most is my wife, Silke van Dinther, who showed remarkable patience for my work on weekends, encouraged me in finding solutions and helped me to structure my ideas.

Karlsruhe, Germany   Clemens van Dinther
August 2006

Contents

List of Figures

List of Tables

Part I

Motivation and Fundamentals

Chapter 1

Introduction

Auctions have been used for centuries to efficiently allocate goods and determine prices. During the recent decade also electronic versions of auctions became more and more popular. The motivation for the use of auctions is manifold. Auctions are applied in procurement in expectation of lower prices due to increased competition and transparency. Individuals discovered that online-auctions are a profitable way to trade used items. Both sides, buyers and sellers, expect to benefit from electronic auctions. On the one hand sellers expect high prices for used goods, whereas on the other hand buyers hope to find a good at a reasonable price. This illustrates one conflict of goals in the context of auctions.

The interest in studies on auctions has increased in the recent years, since the technical evolution and increasing interest in the internet has led to a renaissance of classical and new auction mechanisms on the new electronic media. It is not a surprise that the different auction mechanisms produce different effects in varying environments, but still there are many open questions left. Economists are able to theoretically study auctions under strict assumptions such as rational behaviour of the participants. But the behaviour of the participants in reciprocity to the auction rules is one crucial point for the analysis of auctions. E.g. Ockenfels and Roth [2005] have studied the effects of fixed and soft end online auctions.[1] It is found that bidders in auctions with hard end tend to bid late in comparison to auctions with a soft end. This effect was not expected during auction design, since theory assumes that it makes no difference when to place a bid during an auction as long as all valuations are fix and all participants bid their full valuation at some stage. In that case the bidder with the highest valuation would win the auction. But in the auctions studied by Ockenfels and Roth [2005] a positive probability exists that a bid placed in the last n seconds of a hard end auction is not accepted by the system due to technical reasons (e.g. network delay, processing time). This is just one example for effects caused by auction design and bidders' behaviour.

---

[1]In auctions with hard end, the auction is terminated at a predefined time, whereas auctions with soft end continue until no additional bid has been send during a certain time period.

During the same time of the internet evolution, science made progress in the use of software agents within different areas. At the one hand the artificial intelligence community has to be mentioned that studies and develops distributed intelligent systems that are able to imitate human behaviour. The effort ranges from autonomous software objects to avatars – software programs with a human like visualization that are often used to provide help services on web sites or other applications. On the other hand, intelligent agents are more and more used in other sciences, e.g. in biology to simulate the evolution of certain animal populations or a part of the ecosystem. Software agents have also found their way in the research of social science. The idea of using computer simulation for studying social phenomena dates back to Schelling [1969] but was not intensively pursuit in those years due to the low computing capacity. During the last decade the use of software agents for simulating problems of social science became more and more popular. The Santa Fee artificial stock market [Arthur et al., 1996] is to be cited as one of the precursors for simulating economic problems. Tesfatsion [2002] coined the term "Agent-based Computational Economics" (ACE) and provides an introduction to the field. The present work concentrates on bringing together the work

Advantage of simulation	Disadvantage of simulation
• Test at low costs in comparison to experiments • Simulations follow a normative approach in order to understand *why* (by manipulating parameters) • Possibility to model time (e.g. long/ short simulation runs) • Opportunity to explore the possibilities of the model • Identification of problems and constraints (e.g. load tests with large number of users) • Simulation can be used for training	• Model building is difficult • Approach might not be correct and thus, produces wrong results • Results may be difficult to interpret (e.g. large amount of data) • Model building, simulation, and/or analysis may be time consuming • Simulations may be used inappropriately (manipulate the simulation in order to produce the wanted data)

Table 1.1: Advantage and Disadvantage of simulations

of both fields, electronic market research and intelligent software agents for evaluating markets. Simulations bear the advantage to study markets in a controlled environment, i.e. the researcher is in control of the environmental parameters, and thus, able to isolate effects through variation of the parameters. Compared to experiments, simulations are conducted at lower costs since no payment to subjects is necessary, but on the other hand the development of simulation models is difficult and more time intensive. There is also the risk of having constructed a wrong model that appears correct but produces incorrect data. Table 1.1 depicts the advantages and disadvantages of simulation according to Banks [1998, p. 10-13]. One of the greatest difficulties in simulation is to build a correct model. Simulation results can not be taken for granted unless the data can be validated on appropriate data such as empiric data or theory. Moreover, it is essential to scrutinise the applied methodology since not all methods are applicable in any case. Unfortunately, researchers have neither agreed upon a common standard for identifying and selecting appropriate methods, nor for analysing and publishing results. The present work discusses the methodological approaches and applies agent-based computational simulation on an economic research problem in electronic markets. The following section presents the problems discussed in the present work.

1.1 Problem Description and Research Questions

The present work combines the economic question of the impact of uncertainty on the market outcome and methodological issues of agent-based simulation for the evaluation of electronic markets.

Auction theory often assumes rational bidders being certain on their valuation, but in reality effects can be observed that are not allegeable with standard theory. The determination of one's own valuation of a particular product is difficult and is formed upon one's own preferences and upon the information available on that product. In theory this valuation is expressed in one explicit value. It is obvious that rational bidders would never bid higher than their private valuation; otherwise they could receive a loss.

In practice, it is more difficult to determine one explicit value than a value range unless one possesses perfect information. It is not to be expected that all bidders are perfectly informed in reality. Rather, people acquire additional information over time in order to determine their valuation more precisely. This process of information acquisition is associated with costs, and thus, the timing for the information acquisition becomes important. The question whether to buy information early or late during an auction certainly depends on several environmental factors such as the amount of costs, the quality of available information, and the behaviour of the competitors within the auction.

Consider the following brief example for the described problem. A used car is to be auctioned. Two persons are interested in buying the car. Person A wants to buy the car, has inspected the car allready and has a distinct valuation of 1050 Euros. Person B also likes the car but lives farer away and thus, has not inspected the car. She is uncertain of how much to spend in the range of 1040 ± 50 Euros. Let us assume that additional information is available for bidder B at cost of 30 Euros, e.g. she can spend 30 Euros on travel costs in order to inspect the car. Let us further assume that this inspection would consolidate B's valuation at 1090

Euros if B will spend the money. If B does not acquire the additional information, it would be rational for B to bid the expected valuation of 1040 Euros. In this case bidder A wins the auction by bidding the valuation of 1050 Euros. Alternatively, B can spend the money on inspecting and determines the own valuation at 1090 Euros. Consequently, B wins the auction.

The described example poses several economic questions such as finding the best bidder behaviour in case of uncertainty. Some studies were conducted for better understanding the problem but most of the research requires strong assumptions and only copes with two bidders. In the present work an agent-based simulation approach is applied that allows for manipulating several model parameters. As such, a comprehensive analysis is possible. The application of simulations always raises questions on the appropriateness of the methodological approaches for the specific problem. The central economic and methodological issues of this work are summarised in the following:

1. *How to conduct valid agent-based market simulations?*
   The application of an agent-based simulation approach for economic models implies the question if the methodology is appropriate. So far, agent-based simulations follow different methodological approaches that are more or less theoretically founded. Many economists still doubt the validity of agent-based simulation results since simulation results are often published without scrutinizing the underlying theoretical simulation model. First approaches have been made to link agent-based methods to economic theory. The main agent-based approaches and the link to corresponding economic theory are summarized in this work. This is an important basis for valid economic simulation models. One of the studied agent-based methods is developed, implemented, and applied to the described economic problem of valuation uncertainty in auctions.

2. *What is the impact of uncertainty about one's own valuation on the bidding strategies?*
   The strategy of a bidder is understood as the sequence of the bidder's actions during one auction. A bidder with uncertain valuation faces the decision, whether and when to buy information. Either bidder, being certain or uncertain about the valuation, has to decide when to bid how much. This decision might depend on the competitor's actions, the costs for information acquisition, or the number of competitors.

3. *How do sealed-bid auctions perform under valuation uncertainty in comparison to open-cry ascending auctions?*
   In theory, second price sealed-bid auctions and ascending open-cry (first price) auctions are revenue equivalent assuming that bidders are rational and know their valuation. It is not expected that revenues are equivalent under valuation uncertainty for bounded rational agents. Therefore, it is studied, how different auction types perform in case that bidders participate who are

uncertain about their valuation. The bidders' payoffs, the auctioneer's profit, and the social welfare are compared.

The structure of the present work is outlined in the following section.

1.2   Organization of the Book

The work is organized in four parts which are subdivided into eight chapters. The overall structure is depicted in Figure 1.1. After the introduction, Part I starts with the fundamental economic theory on markets and an overview on agent-based computational economics. Both, Part II and Part III, build upon the fundamentals of Part I. The methodological approaches of agent-based simulation are discussed in

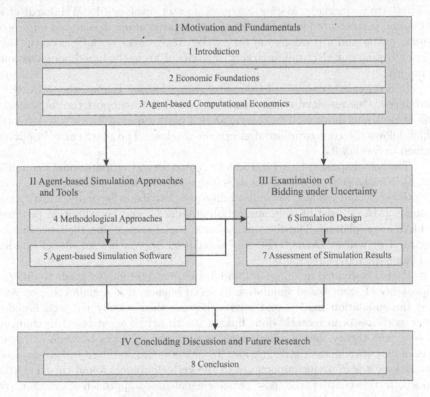

Figure 1.1: Organisation of the book

Part II. Additionally, a requirement analysis is applied to agent-based simulation software. The results motivate the development of the Agent-based Market Simulation Environment (AMASE). In Part III, the discussed methodology and tool of Part II is applied to model and analyse valuation uncertainty. Finally, the main results of the work are summarised and an outlook is given in Part IV.

Part I is structured in three chapters, starting with the introduction. In the second chapter, this work's underlying economic theory is introduced and the basic terms are defined. Chapter 2 is organised in three sections. An overview on markets in general and electronic markets in particular is provided. A market framework is introduced on which the basic understanding of markets in this work is built on. Different market institution types and auctions are presented in more detail on a market microstructure level. For a common understanding of markets, the fundamental definitions of the term *market* are given. Furthermore, the basic auction types are introduced. The chapter closes with an introduction to bidding in auctions, and gives a literature review on strategic bidding under uncertainty.

Section 2.2 presents Market Engineering as a structured design approach to build electronic markets. Market Engineering was developed by Weinhardt et al. [2003] and is structured in the four stages *test clarification*, *design and implementation*, *testing*, and *introduction of the market*. The present work focus on the third stage *"Testing"* of electronic markets on basis of an agent-based computational approach.

In Section 2.3, the idea of Computer Aided Market Engineering (CAME) is introduced. One essential requirement for CAME is to support the implementation of electronic markets. The generic market platform meet2trade was developed which allows the configuration of electronic markets. The platform is briefly described in Section 2.3.

The last chapter of Part I introduced Agent-based Computational Economics (ACE). Firstly, general definitions of software agents, their characteristics, agent architectures, and agents' learning ability are described. Secondly, Multi Agent Systems (MAS), existing communication standards, and coordination processes in MAS are explained. Thirdly, simulation in social science and their benefits are discussed as well as characteristics of simulation approaches for model building and simulation are introduced.

Part II is divided in Chapter 4 and 5. Chapter 4 provides a guide to different approaches of agent-based simulation in social science. It is a main critic on ACE that the simulation models and approaches are theoretically not well founded. Some work has been recently done linking the theory of agent-based mechanisms to economic theory, but a comprehensive overview on links between computer science and economics is still missing. To enhance the credibility of agent-based simulations it is of major importance to theoretically better found the simulation models. In this chapter, the most popular agent-based approaches and their corresponding economic theory are presented. This overview can help to build more appropriate models in the future.

Since there is a great variety of agent-based simulation software available but none of them was specifically designed for simulating electronic market, requirements for agent-based market simulations are discussed in the first section of Chapter 5. On the basis of the defined requirements a set of 36 agent-based simulation frameworks is reviewed. In order to match the requirements, an extension of the JADE framework is proposed and implemented as agent-based market simulation environment (AMASE). The JADE framework is described in Section 5.2 and AMASE is introduced in Section 5.3.

Having introduced the methodology and the simulation tool, Part III evaluates the described problem of valuation uncertainty and the implications on the bidding strategy as well as on the auction outcome. Since the theoretic analysis of the problem is complex and only partially solvable, an agent-based simulation approach is applied. Part III is subdivided in Chapter 6 that describes the developed simulation model, and Chapter 7 presenting the analysis of the simulation results.

Chapter 6 begins with the description of the simulation model, including the bidding process, the possible agents' actions, the agent types, and the model's environment as well as the adaptive behaviour of the agents modelled by an artificial learning approach. The initial parameter values of the simulation model and different simulation settings are explained. At the end of the chapter, an analysis of the theoretically expected results is conducted and hypotheses for the evaluation of the simulation are derived. The presented simulation model combines artificial learning and economic games, and successfully applies multi-agent learning in a competitive environment.

In Chapter 7 the simulation results are evaluated. The first section presents the results for a two-player and five-player environment under fixed costs comparing the auction outcome of a sealed-bid auction with an ascending open-cry auction. It is found that agents receive higher payoffs in sealed-bid auctions compared to ascending open-cry auctions, whereas the auctioneer gains a higher revenue in the ascending open-cry auctions. Section 7.2 scrutinises the outcome and bidder behaviour for the two-agent and five-agent case under different information acquisition costs. Increasing costs result in less and later information acquisition. The findings are summarised in Section 7.3.

The final Part of this book (Part IV) provides a concluding discussion of the contribution of this research, summarises the main results of the simulation, and also discusses limitations of this approach. Finally, an outlook on further research is given.

Appendix A depicts the mathematical proofs that are used in Part III. These theoretical solutions serve as benchmark for the evaluation of the simulation. It comprises the expected social welfare, the auctioneer's expected revenue, the certain and uncertain bidders' expected payoffs, and the valuation functions. Appendix B contains tables and figures to which it is referred to in Part III and which are helpful for the understanding of the results. The bibliography and used abbreviations are found at the end of this book.

Chapter 2

Economic Foundations

This chapter introduces the economic research areas of the present work, electronic markets and Market Engineering (ME). As one step towards Computer Aided Market Engineering (CAME) it presents the electronic market platform meet2trade as a tool for modelling, operating, and testing of electronic markets.

Section 2.1 starts with the theory of markets in general and electronic markets in particular. It gives a brief historical excursus on markets, introduces the microeconomic system framework of Smith [1982] and concludes with a section about market institutions and classic auction types.

Electronic market theory builds the basis for Section 2.2 on Market Engineering as a structured approach for the development of electronic markets. This section is subdivided into an explanation of the structured (engineering) process of electronic markets and the idea of electronically assisting this process by Computer Aided Market Engineering (CAME).

2.1 Electronic Markets and Strategic Bidding

During the last decades developments in Computer Technology, electronic information processing, and the Internet has pushed the transformation of traditional trading mechanisms into the electronic world. Various electronic market types are applied e.g. for procurement, in stock exchanges, for trading new or used items on Internet auction platforms such as eBay,[1] Amazon,[2] or Yahoo!,[3] or even for the allocation of the national wireless frequency spectrum for UMTS telephony in countries of the European Union.

All these examples describe auctions as market mechanisms for the exchange of commodities or property rights among several participants. Thus, markets serve

---

[1] http://www.ebay.com
[2] http://www.amazon.com
[3] http://www.yahoo.com

as an instrument for coordinating exchange and for information revelation. Co-ordination of information and asset allocation is the main function of markets in general. So, *what are the characteristics and differences of markets and auctions respectively? How can an auction or market be defined? What types of markets exist?* The present section answers these questions by giving a brief introduction into the theory and history of markets in general. Section 2.1.2 presents a framework for markets as it is used throughout this book and which is based on the microeconomic systems framework of Vernon Smith [1982]. In the following Section 2.1.3 a classification of market institutions is explained and auctions are addressed in more detail presenting some of the main auction mechanisms.

2.1.1   Historical Background of Markets

There are many views on the term *market* in economic literature. It can be generally stated that a market coordinates the exchange of goods, information, services, (property) rights and/or money. It provides a mechanism to match demand and supply (resource allocation) and determines a market (or clearing) price. This mechanism can be either defined explicitly as e.g. in an English auction, or it can evolve during a negotiation process. Markets are understood as one form of coordination in economic interaction. In contrast to coordination by markets, Coase [1937] discusses hierarchical coordination as it is known from the organisation of firms where the coordination of tasks and resources takes place through delegation and control. In their purest form, neither hierarchies, nor markets involve cooperation throughout the coordination process, although in reality mixed forms occur.[4] These two main forms of economic coordination span a continuum where many mixed forms for cooperation lay in between.

The market coordination can take place at a physical location such as the trading floor of a stock exchange, where individuals trade directly with each other, or at a virtual place such as an electronic auction platform on the Internet. Thus, *location* as a single characteristic for markets is ambiguous, as the term *market* also subsumes physically or virtually distributed markets that are additionally characterised by time and products: e.g. the world's *financial market* consists of (distributed) national financial markets for each country, and each national market again consists of specific product markets for e.g. stocks, bonds or money.

This is a macroeconomic view on markets. From such a high level perspective, the term *market* is merely understood as the business area of specific branches or industries and involves analysis of aggregated demand and supply, or the development of specific marketing strategies rather than the determination of sophisticated resource allocation mechanisms as noted earlier.

While discussing the term market from a management perspective, Holtmann [2004, p. 8] alludes to the industrial organization theory that assess competition

---

[4]Strategic alliances are a well established cooperation in e.g. the airlines industry. Airlines cooperate on selected routes but remain competitors on the other flight routes.

in industries by following the Bain/Mason Industrial Organization paradigm for the interdependency of industry structure, the conduct (the firm's strategy) and the collective performance of companies (see Porter [1981] referring to Bain [1968], Mason [1953]).

From a neoclassical view, markets are frictionless places for exchanging goods. Adam Smith [1776] first described the coordination capability of markets governed by the *invisible hand* – meaning the interplay of supply and demand. Walras [1874] studied the relation of demand and supply and postulates the existence of a general market equilibrium that matches demand and supply at a certain price. In his microeconomic model, he introduces an auctioneer (known as the Walrasian Auctioneer) who determines the equilibrium price during a so-called *tâtonnement process* which is a special auctioneering procedure. The main focus of neoclassical theory is on studying the existence and stability of equilibria.

But the absence of transaction costs is a central point of criticism on neoclassical theory. Several subsequently developed economic theories pick up the question of transaction and coordination cost, e.g. the new theorem on institutional economics.[5] Hayek [1945] points out that it is the price system that summarizes (and thus coordinates) all necessary information in case of imperfect information. Based on his work, researchers started studying markets and especially the process of decision making (resource allocation) under more realistic assumptions [c.p. Strecker, 2004, p. 28]. Decision making is subject to (institutional) rules and individual behaviour of the market participants.

From an economic perspective, the study of markets is coined by the question, to which extent markets contribute (and can be optimized) to economic coordination. Smith [1982] developed the *Microeconomic System Framework* that clearly defines the core concepts of a market system. Foregoing work on that issue was accomplished by Hurwicz [1960, 1969, 1973] and Reiter [1977]. The microeconomic system framework is presented in more detail in the next section.

2.1.2 Markets as an Economic System

The previous section gave a brief overview on different perceptions of markets. This section presents the definition of markets as it is used in the work at hand. Markets are understood as economic systems that, basically spoken, consist of three main components, (i) *economic agents* acting in the market, (ii) *commodities* being exchanged (at least one), and (iii) a *set of rules* defining the *market institution*. This definition is mainly based on the microeconomic system framework introduced by Smith [1982] and extensions suggested by Weinhardt et al. [2003], Holtmann [2004] and Neumann [2004]. The presented definition also provides the basis for the development of the electronic trading platform meet2trade, which is described in more detail in Section 2.3. Thus, this section also discusses terms from the field of electronic commerce.

---

[5] Holtmann [2004, p. 8] gives a brief introduction on this aspect of new institutional economics.

Before introducing the basic terms and definitions, it should be noted that there occurs an overlapping usage of the terms *market* and *(trade) negotiation* in literature. Both, markets and (trade) negotiations, deal with the allocation of goods or services. As such, trade negotiations can constitute a market, and on the other hand markets can be perceived as negotiations. The difference of these two terms will be clarified within the present section by determining the concept of economic agents, commodities, microeconomic system environment, and market institution. Examples for concrete market institutions and a taxonomy for markets is discussed in Section 2.1.3.

Economic agents are the participants in an economy and can be defined as follows:

Definition 2.1.1. Economic Agent
An economic agent is a human or judicial person acting in the economy by producing and/or exchanging goods and/or services.

In the context of markets, examples for economic agents are buyers, sellers and auctioneers. It has to be noted that this work strictly distinguishes economic and software agents. A precise definition of software agents is provided in Section 3.1.

The second integral part of markets are the commodities traded on it. In the following a definition for commodities is given:

Definition 2.1.2. Commodities
Commodities are either goods/products, resources, services or property rights that are described by at least one distinct attribute.

Examples for commodities[6] are consumer products like computers, natural resources like oil and gas, services like the development of software, or property rights like licences for the usage of distinct telephone frequency spectrum. These commodities have certain attributes which might by themselves be subject to negotiation. Crude oil for example is found with different ingredients dependent on the region of exploitation. The ingredients of the oil determine the processing costs and thus, have a price impact.

Smith [1982] describes economic agents and commodities more precisely and subsumes them in the term *microeconomic environment*, which is determined by the commodities to be traded, the economic agents participating in the market, and the characteristics of each agent. Hurwicz [1973, p. 16] states that *"more generally, the environment is defined as the set of circumstances that cannot be changed either by the designer of the mechanism, or the agents (participants)."* Smith [1982, p. 924] provides a definition of the economic environment which is summarized in the following:

---

[6]In contrast to the definition provided above financial markets understand commodities as resources like oil, gold or silver, or goods like grain or butter. Nevertheless, the above definition of commodities for the present work also includes other financial products such as bonds or stocks.

Definition 2.1.3. Microeconomic system environment
The environment of the microeconomic systems is constituted by

(1) a list of $K+1$ commodities $\{0,\dots,K\}$,

(2) a list of N economic agents $\{1,\dots,N\}$, and

(3) the characteristics of each economic agent i described by

- *a utility function u^i,*
- *the technology (knowledge) endowment T^i, and*
- *the commodity endowment ω^i.*

Thus, the (private) vector $e^i = (u^i, T^i, \omega^i)$ characterizes agent i. The components are defined in the $K+1$ commodity space R^{K+1}. The collection of characteristics $e = (e^1,\dots,e^N)$ defines the microeconomic environment.

Smith explicitly remarks that this definition also includes learning that can be understood as changes in the agent's preferences or technology. Consequently, it is necessary to determine limitations for the search opportunities within the environment.

The *market institution* is the third element of the economic system and defines rules on how the economic agents are allowed to interact (e.g. the starting, transition and stopping rules) and how the price is determined. A simple example for such a rule is the posted price offer, e.g. on the Internet or in supermarkets where the seller labels the products with a fixed price and the agent is left with the choice either to take it or leave it. The market institution also defines how processes takes place in a sense that it determines which kind of messages the agents are allowed to exchange. McAfee and McMillan [1987, p. 701] amend that the institution contains an *"explicit set of rules determining resource allocation and prices"*. As such, the institution defines all rules on the interaction of the economic agents. More formally, Smith [1982, p. 924 f] gives a definition which can be summarized to:

Definition 2.1.4. Market institution
The market institution administrates and sets the rules for the communication, exchange of commodities, and/or transformation of commodities. Thus, it defines

(1) a language $M = (M^1,\dots,M^N)$ consisting of messages[7] $m = (m^1,\dots,m^N)$ and $m^i \in M^i$, with M^i being the set of messages of agent i,

(2) the allocation rules $H = (h^1(m),\dots,h^N(m))$,

(3) the cost imputation rules $C = (c^1(m),\dots,c^N(m))$, determining the cost for communication, and

(4) the adjustment process rules $G = (g^1(t_0,t,T),\dots,g^N(t_0,t,T))$ with starting rule t_0, the transition rule t, and the stopping rule T.

---

[7] m^i might be a bid, offer, or acceptance

The language together with the rules defines the property rights I^i of each agent i:

$$I^i = (M^i, h^i(m), c^i(m), g^i(t_0, t, T))$$

Thus, the institution is the collection of all private property rights $I = (I^1, \ldots, I^N)$.

A system environment together with a market institution defines a market as a microeconomic system. The market (system) consists of actors (economic agents), their characteristics, commodities, a language for communication, and some sets of distinct rules for the organization of the system. Consequently, a formal definition for markets can be given by:

Definition 2.1.5. Markets as a Microeconomic System
A market is understood as a microeconomic system S that consists of the environment e and the institution I: $S = (e, I)$

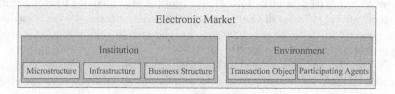

Figure 2.1: An electronic market as a microeconomic system.

The microeconomic system framework was introduced to describe markets in general. Neumann [2004] points out that with respect to electronic markets the framework has to be extended. He suggests the *electronic market system framework* which is based on Smith's microeconomic system framework. Particularly, it is remarked that electronic markets use an explicit (electronic) infrastructure as part of the market institution. Incidentally, non-electronic markets also need an infrastructure like a physical place or additional resources such as electricity. Electronic infrastructure has to be administrated (hardware configuration, software development). The administrative aspect is partially also true for common (non-electronic) markets. This supply of infrastructure is understood as a service. Since the provision of services is an economic action associated with production costs, electronic (and physical) markets are typically operated by firms (or governmental organisations), and hence, charge service fees. Considering these circumstances, Weinhardt et al. [2003], Holtmann [2004], and Neumann [2004] extend the institutional view on the market institution to the IT-infrastructure and business structure perspective leading to the following definition of electronic markets, which is also depicted in Figure 2.1.

Definition 2.1.6. Electronic market
An electronic market consists of

1. *the environment e,*

2. *the extended market institution I consisting of*

   - *the microstructure (collection of private property rights as defined earlier),*

   - *the infrastructure, and*

   - *the business structure.*

A precise definition of markets in general and electronic markets in particular was provided. Nevertheless, it is necessary to further distinguish certain market components that otherwise might be confusing, especially in software development if not explicitly defined.

A software object that comprises the processing rules of electronic markets such as the order processing, the start and stop rules, the allocation rules, or the fees describes a market's microstructure and business structure. A concrete instance of this object running on an electronic platform can be understood as a market institution since it contains the microstructure as well as the business structure and is part of the market infrastructure itself. Throughout this work, a platform is understood as framework on which software can run. From a software engineering point of view it is easy to provide several instances of the same object on one platform. Consequently, each of the object instances is an electronic market institution and together with a commodity and two or more economic agents, it constitutes an electronic market. The collection of electronic markets of *one* provider builds an electronic *marketplace*.

The internet auction company eBay[8] may serve as an example for the given explanation. Thousands of products are offered for sale on eBay, each linked to one specific instance of a market institution (software) object comprising the rules for an ascending auction or a posted price. Since each item is offered by one unique seller (economic agent), each of the auctions/posted price offers running on eBay are understood as one electronic market. These electronic markets together build an electronic marketplace. Consequently, eBay can be classified as a marketplace.

An electronic market platform has to be capable of running several market institution instances in parallel, and thus, to operate a marketplace. It was defined earlier that a marketplace is the collection of market instances of one provider. A market platform provides the hardware and software environment to run the software objects of at least one provider. It is also cogitable that a market platform operates the marketplaces of several providers.

Let us suppose to transfer this taxonomy to real world markets using a farmer's market as an example. Each farmer has his own stall where he offers

---

[8]http://www.ebay.de/

his products. Each farmer defines his own market rules such as a fixed price per weight of a certain vegetable. But especially at the end of the day, he might lower the prices in order to sell those products which could not be stored any more, and his willingness to bargain on these products probable increases. As such, each farmer's stall constitutes a market. The collection of stalls builds the marketplace. The platform consists of the provided resources, e.g. electricity, and the physical space. There might be more than one location in the city, where farmers are allowed to settle their stall. Thus, a city can operate more than one marketplace on its market platform. Table 2.1 summarizes this comparison. Having introduced the

Term	Physical Market	Electronic Market
Market object instance	Stall of individual merchant	Running software instance
Marketplace	Collection of stalls in one location	Collection of market instances of one provider
Market platform	Collection of physical locations and additional services of one platform operator (e.g. a city)	Hardware and software framework to run collections of market instances of several marketplace providers

Table 2.1: Comparison of the terminology for physical and electronic markets

framework for markets in general and electronic markets in particular, the next sections deals with market institutions and auctions in more detail.

2.1.3 Market Institution Types and Auctions

In the following the market microstructure is discussed in more detail. Note that the terms *Microstructure*, market/auction format and *Market Model* are used synonymously. Schmid and Lindemann [1998], and Schmid [1998] presented the Media Reference Model (MRM) for electronic markets identifying the four phases *Knowledge*, *Intention*, *Agreement*, and *Settlement*. Gomber [2000] suggested that the micro structure consists of structural parameters describing the institutional rules and distinguishes between phase specific structural parameters[9] and phase spanning parameters.[10] The main difficulty is the determination of these parameters, and the identification of parameter sets.

Ströbel and Weinhardt [2003] present criteria within the Montreal Taxonomy (MT) to describe electronic markets. This taxonomy distinguishes between *explicit* and *implicit* criteria as well as *endogenous* and *exogenous* criteria. Explicit criteria can be clearly determined whereas implicit criteria describe certain circumstances without being directly measurable. Exogenous criteria cannot be influenced by a

---

[9]For example the matching rule.

[10]Parameters considering the information revelation

market designer but are given by the environment, whereas endogenous criteria can be adapted explicitly in order to ensure that traders or the auctioneer on this market yield the expected outcome. Examples for these criteria are given in Table 2.2.

	Exogenous criteria	**Endogenous criteria**
Explicit criteria	Constitution	Business Rules
	Business Conduct	Trading Rules
	Negotiation Situation	
Implicit criteria	Culture	Revenue
	Social Norms	Efficiency
	Strategic Goals	

Table 2.2: Criteria of the Montreal Taxonomy [Ströbel and Weinhardt, 2003]

A market designer can determine the endogenous explicit criteria. This includes parameters such as the number of rounds, product attributes, bid thresholds or starting and stopping rules. Still, the determination of parameters itself is not sufficient for the distinct determination of electronic markets. These criteria are structured using the generic market process introduced in the MRM. Ströbel and Weinhardt [2003] extend the MRM market process by introducing additional sub phases for the intention and agreement phase.

The intention phase is characterized by the offer (i) specification, (ii) submission and (iii) analysis. It has to be remarked that the offer specification is accomplished by the user (e.g. in a browser or some other Graphical User Interface (GUI)), whereas the analysis takes place within the market institution. Hence, this is a first reference for market structure parameters defining the offer specification and the analysis. The agreement phase consists of the processes (i) offer matching, (ii) allocation, and (iii) acceptance. In general, all possible trade combinations of orders are computed during the offer matching. The allocation determines the definite order pairs for trading. In many markets, matching and allocation are performed at once, since usually the objective is to find only the best solution and not all possible solutions. The differentiation into these two phases is derived from a point of view, which also covers negotiation systems within that framework. The understanding of negotiations in literature is controversial; in this work the description of Bichler et al. [2003, p. 316] is adopted:

Definition 2.1.7. Trade Negotiation
A negotiation is "an iterative communication and decision making process between two or more agents. The situation is characterized in that agents (i) cannot achieve their objectives through unilateral actions, (ii) exchange information in form of offers, counter-offers and arguments, (iii) deal with interdependent tasks, and (iv) search for a consensus which is a compromise decision."
A negotiation protocol defines rules including (i) the place/location (of negotiation), (ii) the specification of the negotiated issue, (iii) the decision making rules,

and (iv) the rules of communication (message exchange).
Negotiations can be further divided into

1. *unstructured negotiations that do not follow and specify any protocol,*

2. *semi-structured negotiations that follow, but do not fully specify a protocol, and*

3. *structured negotiations that follow a fully defined protocol.*

Following this definition, negotiations concerning the allocation of goods or services constitute a market institution. In other words if one goal of the negotiation is to accomplish an agreement on the exchange of goods (satisfy supply and demand), negotiation can be perceived as a market. Note that not all negotiations establish a market since just trade negotiations are concerned with the allocation of goods/services.

The separation of matching and allocation as suggested in the MT allows the construction of complex market structures. It is assumes that it is helpful in negotiations to find out possible matches of offers and counter-offers and lets the agent choose which offers to focus on in a subsequent stage.

The identified criteria of the MT are a helpful step towards the classification of market institutions. Still, the presented criteria are too general for an unambiguous determination of electronic markets. Thus, there is a need for a more detailed classification of microstructure parameters.

Having discussed the idea of parametrization of market institutions, the focus will now shift to design issues regarding the operability of market rules. If a market designer defines and implements one distinct market institution (microstructure and business structure implemented in one software object), the designed (software) object can be instantiated several times with each instance representing a market on its own as discussed in the last subsection.

Market Model Types

A market model which consists of the smallest possible set of parameters is called *Atomic Market Model (AMM)*. Such an atomic market model can be extended and combined by additional further structural parameters. Rolli et al. [2004] introduce a Minimal Market Model which can be understood as an AMM. Gomber [2000] also notes that parameter settings can change over time. A market model is called *static market model* if its constituting parameters do not change over time. It is possible to combine static market models. A simple English auction is an example for a static market model.

A sequential combination of market parameters is called *Flexible Market Model (FMM)*, i.e. the structural parameters of a flexible market model change over time. Stock exchanges e.g. often use a call market to start trading and switch to a continuous double auction after a certain opening period. This sequential change of market rules is an example for a dynamic market model.

The parallel execution of market models *(XOR combination)*, where users have to choose either of the offered market models, is called *Dynamic Market Model (DMM)*. Let's again use eBay as an example: offers can be submitted according to the rule's of an ascending second price proxy auction,[11] but additionally a *BuyItNowPrice* option[12] is offered. The BuyItNowPrice option is removed as soon as the first bidder chooses the auction market model by submitting a bid. Thus, the bidder has the choice of either taking the BuyItNowPrice or starting an auction. Seifert [2005] has studied economic implications of this choice at length.

A *Cascading Market Model (CMM)* is a parallel combination of market parameters *(AND combination)* where bidders cannot choose between the combined models but have to submit bids to all market models. Nevertheless, the order is executed just on one market. On some stock exchanges, a Market-Maker Market (MMM) is combined with a Continuous Double Auction (CDA), and orders submitted to that market can either be executed on the CDA or on the MMM. This is an example for an CMM.

The *Cascading Dynamic Market Model (CDMM)* is the parallel combination *(OR combination)* of market models, meaning that agents have the choice between different market models or the combination of them. Amazon, for example, offers to set up an ascending auction and simultaneously offer a *BuyPrice* that remains visible during the whole duration of the auction. The BuyPrice will not be removed if the auction is started.

Auctions

An *auction* is a specific type of market. Auctions are known as one of the oldest forms of trading used already at 500 B.C. in Babylon (see Strecker [2004, p. 34] referring to Cassady [1967]). Nowadays, auctions are mainly used for three reasons: (i) speed of sale, (ii) information revelation of buyers' valuation, and (iii) prevention of dishonest dealing between the sellers and buyers [Wolfstetter, 1999]. In auctions economic agents compete against each other on settling a trade by submitting bids representing their willingness to pay. Bertsekas [2001, p. 1] states that auctions are an *"intuitive method for solving the classical assignment problem."* The auction rules determine the way of bidding (e.g. amount of bids, increments, start, end), the winner (and thus, the allocation of the good), and the price to pay. McAfee and McMillan [1987, p. 701] define auctions as follows:

Definition 2.1.8. Auction
"An auction is a market institution with an explicit set of rules determining resource allocation and prices on the basis of bids from the market participants."

---

[11] A bidder submits the maximum bid to the proxy. As long as the actual highest bid is smaller than the proxy-valuation , the proxy rises the bid to a value which is one increment above the highest valuation of the competitors. This also happens if an additional competing bid arrives which is lower than the proxy-valuation.

[12] The BuyItNowPrice is a posted price offer that the buyer can either accept or ignore. If the BuyItNowPrice is chosen, the market is immediately closed.

Bids can be specified in several ways, e.g. by raising the hand when an auctioneer calls a certain price, or explicitly in written form. Wolfstetter [1999] points to the information problem in economic trade, where an individual has incomplete information about the competitors' valuations. This is one of the main issues in auction theory and leads to the question of how to design auctions in order to reveal this information. There is no general answer to this questions, since it depends on several factors. Therefore, auction need to be analysed in the given context. Part III, for example, compares two auction models in different environments.

Since auctions explicitly define rules for exchanging information (bidding) and determining resource allocations and prices, the definition also suffices the definition of negotiations. Therefore, in literature auctions are often understood as (structured) negotiations [Bichler et al., 2003].

There are various auction formats depending e.g. on whether one single unit or multiple units are to be traded and whether there are single or multiple sellers or buyers. Auctions with just one seller and multiple buyers (or vice versa) are called single sided auctions. Double sided auctions have multiple buyers and sellers. Klemperer [2004] names four standard single sided auction types: (i) ascending (e.g. English auction), (ii) descending (e.g. Dutch auction), (iii) first price sealed-bid, and (iv) second price sealed-bid (e.g. Vickrey auction). Wurman et al. [2000] propose a classification of five classic auctions by differentiating the attributes (i) single vs. double sided, (ii) open (cry) vs. sealed, and (iii) ascending vs. descending. This classification is also depicted in Figure 2.2.

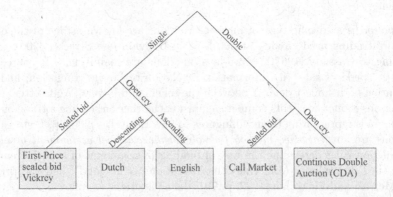

Figure 2.2: A classification of classic auction types, Source: Wurman et al. [2000, p. 4]

The English auction is one of the classic standard auctions. As the sealed-bid and the Dutch auction it is a single sided auction, meaning that there is just one seller and multiple buyers in the forward case and vice versa in the reverse case.[13]

---

[13] Reverse auction formats are common in procurement auctions.

The bids are publicly announced (open outcry) and have to be ascending in the sense that a new bid must be higher than the current highest bid in the forward case. When the auction terminates the current highest bidder wins the auction and pays the price as it is determined in the institutional rules. The standard English auction is a pay-as-bid auction, i.e. the highest bidder pays the price equal to his last bid. The use of the term *English Auction* is ambiguous in literature since it is often used synonymously for ascending single sided auctions in general.

An alternative to pay-as-bid auctions is to use a "k-price" rule:[14] for $k = 1$ it is a pay-as-bid auction, for $k = 2$ the winner pays the price of the second highest bid, etc. The first case is also known as first price auction, the second case is known as second price auction.

In a first price sealed-bid auction the each bidder submit one sealed-bid. Thus, in contrast to the English auction, the bidders do not know the bids of the competitors. The bidder with the highest bid is awarded the item or service at the price of the highest bid (his own bid). The Vickrey auction is an example for a sealed-bid second price auction, where the winner is awarded the good or service at the price of the second highest bid.

A Dutch auction is of descending type. An auctioneer starts announcing prices and lowers the price until the first bidder signals his willingness to buy.

The classic double sided auction formats are the Continuous Double Auction (CDA), and the Call Market. In both auction types multiple buyers and multiple sellers participate. The bids either comprise offers to buy or offers to sell. Bids in double sided auctions are also called "*order*". Orders are collected in an order book. The order book has two sides, one for the buy orders and one for the sell orders. In the case of a CDA, each incoming order is either matched with the best possible order on the opposite side[15] of the order book, or it is put into the order book. The order book can be open, which means that all (or at least a specified number of) orders currently outstanding are displayed. The classic case of a Call Market (CM) works with a closed order book. All incoming orders are put into the order book until the matching process starts. The price determination in both cases depends on the ex ante defined institutional rules. Double sided auctions are commonly used in stock exchanges. Beside the described auction formats there are various other subtypes, extensions or additional auctions formats, but it is not in the scope of this work to discuss all auction types.

Basic auction models are build on the assumption of asymmetric information, meaning that participants do not possess equal information. In this context economists usually distinguish between the independent-private-values model and the (pure) common-values model. McAfee and McMillan [1987, p. 704f] provide following definition:

---

[14]This form was introduced to simplify implementation of ascending auctions in the market platform meet2trade which is described in Section 2.3.

[15]E.g. a buy order at the price of 30 EUR for stock (a) arrives in the system. If there is at least one sell order on the opposite side of the order book that sells for equal or less than 30 EUR, a match is possible and a trade occurs immediately.

Definition 2.1.9. Independent-Private-Values

"[...] each bidder knows precisely how highly he values the item; he has no doubt about the true value of the item to him. He does not know anyone else's valuation of the item; instead, he perceives any other bidder's valuation as a draw from some probability distribution. Similarly, he knows that the other bidders (and the seller) regard his own valuation as being drawn from some probability distribution. Differences among the bidders' evaluation reflect actual differences in tastes. More precisely, for bidder $i, i = 1, \ldots, n$, there is some probability distribution F_i from which he draws his valuation v_i. Only the bidder observes his own valuation v_i, but all other bidders as well as the seller know the distribution F_i. Any one bidder's valuation is statistically independent from any other bidder's valuation."

One example are collectors of stamps, art paintings or other items, who develop different and thus, private valuations for certain products. Another example are the production costs of goods that differ from firm to firm. The valuations of the product are dependent on the company's costs. The same applies to the determination of the value of a company, e.g. in take-over bidding. Let us assume two competitors that are bidding on the acquisition of a supplier. Competitor A may be able to integrate the supplier and would thereby realise greater synergies than competitor B. Therefore, competitor A values the acquisition higher than competitor B and both competitors have different (and independent) private values concerning that issue. In contrast to the private-values model, the common-values model is defined as follows:

Definition 2.1.10. Common-values

In the common-values model a good has the single true valuation which is the same for every agent, but this value is not known. Agents may have access to different information, or may have "different guesses about how much the item is objectively worth. If V is the unobserved true value, then the bidders' perceived values $v_i, i = 1, \ldots, n$, are independent draws from some probability distribution $H(v_i|V)$. All agents know the distribution H" [McAfee and McMillan, 1987, p. 705]. *Bids carry information about the bidder's valuation and thus, can influence other bidders expectations.*

The exploitation right for oil is a typical example for a common value good. The potential earnings from selling the oil is the same for every agent and depends only on the size of the oil field and its quality.

The described valuation models mark two extremes in economic theory that span a continuum. In reality, there will more often occur mixed cases with common and private valuation components. Nevertheless, the two extremes are an important assumption for the economic analysis of different auction formats that has a great impact on the bidder behaviour and the auction outcome. Recall that a submitted bid carries information on the bidder's valuation. In common-values settings this is information on the bidder's guess concerning the common but unknown value. Thus, it is of strategic importance to decide *when* and *how much* to bid. A high preemptive bid might deter competitors from bidding. On the other hand if the bids are submitted late, the competitors might not be able to consider the price information for their decision.

The bidding behaviour depends not solely on the valuations model, but as well on the market rules and environmental factors (e.g. the number of competitors). It has an impact on the auction outcome as well. Both, bidding behaviour and auction outcome, are of main interest for economist who search for optimal strategies and market equilibria. This work studies the impact of uncertainty about one's own private valuation on the bidder behaviour and the auction outcome. The following section summarizes the related work on bidding under uncertainty.

2.1.4 Bidding in Auctions under Uncertainty

The problem of uncertainty about the own valuation is known in literature in the context of merger and acquisitions where more than one company is potentially willing to takeover one competitor. Takeover bidding with more than one bidder is characterised as pay-as-bid auctions. The challenge during takeover bidding is to determine the true value of the target. This value is different among bidders, since synergy effects, economies of scale or the costs for integration vary. Nevertheless, it is difficult for outsiders to determine a value for the company, without in-depth knowledge of the internal organisation and processes. The costs for external consultancy that provides a well founded analysis of the target's value cannot be neglected. Assume two companies, B_1, B_2, are willing to takeover a target T. Further assume that B_1 has determined a certain value for the target and B_2 has not decided whether to bid or not. In such a situation it might be advantageous for B_1 to submit a preemptive bid, so that B_2 abandons the possibility of acquiring costly information, and looses interest in entering the takeover bidding process.

In economics, it is distinguished between *risk* and *uncertainty*. In both cases, a decision-maker is faced with a situation of randomness. Knight [1921, p. 20, Ch. 7] introduces the interpretation of risk as situations in which the decision-maker is able to assign mathematical probabilities to the randomness. In situations of uncertainty, it is not possible for the decision-maker to determine mathematical probabilities. In the following, it is assumed that agents are faced with situations of uncertainty while determining their valuations, e.g. agents are not able to assign probabilities to the error of estimating the valuation.

In order to understand the problem of bidding under uncertainty, it is first necessary to analyse the bidding strategy in second price auctions under certainty. According to Krishna [2002, p. 15], it is a weakly dominant strategy to bid the full valuation in a second price auction. Assume the highest competing bid in the auction is b^{2nd} and bidder 1 has a valuation of v_1. If bidder 1 submits a bid b_1 while $v_1 > b^{2nd} > b_1$, bidder 1 looses the auction, although bidder 1 has the highest valuation and could have earned positive payoff. If $v_1 > b_1 > b^{2nd}$, bidder 1 wins the auction and makes a profit of $v_1 - b^{2nd}$. The profit is still the same if bidder 1 bids $b_1 = v_1 > b^{2nd}$. This examples shows that bidding less than v_1 does not increase the profit of bidder 1 but increases the risk of losing the auction if bidding less than the best competing bid b^{2nd}.

Bidders who are uncertain[16] about their own valuation face a more complex decision. If it is possible for them to acquire additional information about the valuation of the auctioneered product during the course of the auction, uncertain bidders have to decide *if* and *when* to buy information. Some authors have investigated the issue of bidding under uncertainty. The following an overview on the related literature is given.

Compte and Jehiel [2000] assess the bidding strategy of one uncertain bidder competing with $\{2, \ldots, n\}$ certain bidders during sealed-bid (2nd price) and ascending price auctions. The information can be discovered instantaneously and the number of bidders still participating in the ascending auction is publicly known. They find that it is advantageous for an uncertain bidder to stay in the ascending auction until the auction price reaches the uncertain agent's expected valuation. If there is just one competitor left, the uncertain bidder acquires information, or drops out of the auction otherwise. If the number of bidders is large enough, the uncertain bidder will not acquire information in a sealed-bid auction, since the probability is fairly low for getting a higher payoff in case of value discovery compared to the payoff without value discovery. They also found out that in such a scenario, ascending price auctions induce higher expected welfare than a sealed-bid auction. The findings hold for the described auction types with one uncertain bidder participating. The model cannot fully explain real world observations, since in electronic auctions it is often unknown how many bidders participate. The authors also suggest further research for cases with more than one uncertain bidder.

Among the first researchers analysing bidding under uncertainty were Schweizer and von Ungern-Sternberg [1983] who analysed a symmetric auction game in a common value setting. Agents in this game are uncertain about their true valuations and draw estimates from probability distribution defined on an interval centred around the true value. The authors don't find a closed form solution and thus, compute samples for a two-player game. The analysed model suggests that the aggregated expected bidders' profits decrease with the quality of information available increasing. The authors also found out that a bidder's bidding strategy *"will be affected by the quality of the information available to his competitors"* [Schweizer and von Ungern-Sternberg, 1983]. While the results from this paper cannot be generalized, since the assumptions were quite restrictive, they build a starting point for further research.

Kolstad and Guzman [1997] study the question of how much to expend in narrowing uncertainty. Therefore, they develop a model in which agents are not certain on their true valuation. Agents can either spend the amount c_i to discover their true valuation and formulate an optimal bid, or formulate an optimal bid on an estimate. The expected value of the distribution is known to each agent. The

---

[16]In the following, bidders who are uncertain about their own valuation are called *uncertain bidders*. Similarly, bidders who know their own valuation for sure are called *certain bidders*.

information costs are modelled as a random variable with a common distribution. The authors develop some propositions on the effects of the number of bidders and changes in the distribution of information costs and valuations, which they are able to proof with comparative statics. They find, e.g. that an increase in the number of bidders implies an increase in the expected value of the winning bid and a greater number of informed bidders, but no larger proportion of bidders that buy information. Furthermore, the authors state that the decision of whether or not to acquire information depends simply on the relation between the value of information (e.g. positive amount of expected gross profit) and the costs of information acquisition.

Milgrom and Weber [1982] analyse strategic bidding in ascending auctions in general. They form the prediction that under uncertainty, English and Sealed Bid auctions are not equivalent, since ascending auctions scrutinize concurrent bids. This information carried by the competing bids weakens the winners curse and leads to more aggressive bidding that results in larger expected prices in English auctions. They build a general symmetric model with affiliated values, i.e. the valuations are dependent. The authors propose that for affiliated values second price auctions generate higher average prices.

Fishman [1988] studies a model for preemptive takeover bidding within a context of asymmetric and costly information. He is interested in the interrelation of the first bid that carries information about the first bidder's valuation and the decision of the second bidder whether or not to acquire information. The model shows that in equilibrium a first bidder may submit a high-premium initial offer above the current market price to deter a second bidder from competing. In this case, the expected target price is higher under the assumption that the bidder with the highest valuation is the first bidder and submits the preemptive bid respectively. Accordingly, Fishman shows that the expected first bidder's profit is higher while submitting an initial premium bid. An increasing number of bidders causes a higher target price. It has to be remarked that it is not the premium bid itself that deters the second bidder from bidding but rather the information conveyed by the first bid.

The problem of information acquisition in first and second price auctions in an affiliated values setting was studied by Persico [1996a,b, 2000]. The papers analyse how bidders' information acquisition behaviour varies across auction formats. In an affiliated value setting, first price auctions are more risk-sensitive than second-price auctions, and therefore, information is more valuable in a first price auction. This results in a higher incentive to acquire information in a first-price auction.

The bidder behaviour in first-, second- and third-price auctions with varying number of bidders was experimentally studied by Kagel and Levin [1993] in order to compare the results to the underlying theory. The paper finds discrepancies between theory and experimentally observed behaviour, but supports Nash equilibrium bidding theory as the main strategic force of the underlying behaviour. In first price auctions a majority of the subjects bids below valuation, whereas in third price auction a majority bids above the valuation. In second price auctions only a minority submits bids equal to their valuations. This study is a good example for human behaviour deviating from theoretically expected rational behaviour.

The paper of Bajari and Hortacsu [2000] studies empirical data from eBay and compares it to theory. The eBay mechanisms are designed for private value auctions, but the analysis supports a better fit of the eBay auction to a common values framework. The authors also investigate the *"winner's curse effect"* dependent on the number of bidders and study the effect of entry that seems to play a very important role in determining revenues. That is, a high initial bid *"reduces the incentive to spend time and effort to enter the auction"*[p. 37]. The work does not consider uncertainty on the valuation, but it incorporates the effect of entry and investigates it empirically. Preemptive bidding under uncertainty is studied by Fishman [1988] and Hirshleifer and Png [1989].

Hirshleifer and Png [1989] pick up Fishman's model [Fishman, 1988] of corporate acquisitions to study the bidding behaviour of the participants and the impact of preemptive bids on the expected price of a takeover target. The difference to Fishman's model is that the authors assume bids not to be costless. The basic models assumes that each bidder is allowed to send a single bid and in an advanced model costly bidding is introduced. Costly bidding leads to an equilibrium expected price that *"[...] may differ markedly from that of the standard English-auction model [...]"* [Hirshleifer and Png, 1989, p. 602]. In the English-auction model the expected takeover price is the minimum of the valuation of the two bidders. In this case the takeover price is maximized if the costs for information acquisition are minimized. In the author's model with costly information, the first bidder's willingness to incur the acquisition costs may result in a high signal that deters competing bidders, and thus, avoids costly counterbidding. This might lead to a takeover price below the minimum of the two valuations also in cases where both bidders make offers. It is remarkable that the analysis for costly bidding shows a lower price under competitive bidding than with one deterring bid. Furthermore, it is shown that an increase in the costs for investigation may raise expected social welfare.

Rasmusen [2005] analyses strategic implications of uncertainty over one's own private valuation in ascending price auctions with fixed and soft end. The two-player model is used to explain sniping in auctions with fixed end and analyses the bidding behaviour in the two bidder case with one uncertain bidder. The uncertain bidder cannot discover the valuation instantaneously, but after paying c_i and waiting for a time period δ. The author found out that in second price sealed-bid auctions the uncertain bidder benefits from knowing the competitors value. This means that the uncertain bidder profits from learning the competitors valuations before deciding whether to discover her own valuation (which is only possible in open-cry auctions). Furthermore, the certain bidder receives a higher expected payoff if the uninformed bidder discovers her own valuation right at the beginning of the auction. Rasmusen also proposes that the auctioneer has a preference for bidders not knowing their valuation at the beginning of an auction.

In open-cry ascending auctions there is an incentive for both, certain and uncertain agents, to bid early in order to stimulate value discovery. The uncertain bidder wants to discover the certain bidders value before optionally acquiring information, whereas the certain bidder might submit a preemptive bid in order to stimulate value discovery of the uncertain agent, who might leave the auction afterwards.

The review of the literature breeds some general propositions that are valid for the particular model. All models make restrictive assumptions, e.g. discuss two-bidder cases that make it difficult to generalize the findings or to compare them with reality. Furthermore, all studies have in common that they apply comparative statics, i.e. mostly ambiguous situations are discussed. The authors derive propositions for the discussed cases under strict assumptions. The most general of them are summarized in the following:

(P1) It is advantageous for uncertain bidders to wait for competing bids conveying information about the competitors valuations before deciding on information acquisition [Compte and Jehiel, 2000].

(P2) The certain bidder profits from uncertain bidders that acquire information early in an auction [Rasmusen, 2005].

(P3) The auctioneer profits from bidders being uncertain [Rasmusen, 2005].

(P4) Early bidding is likely to stimulate value discovery [Rasmusen, 2005]

(P5) Increasing information costs may reduce social welfare [Hirshleifer and Png, 1989].

(P6) Under uncertainty, English auctions[17] lead to higher expected prices compared to sealed-bid second price auctions [Milgrom and Weber, 1982].

(P7) First-price auctions induce a higher incentive to acquire information than second price auctions [Persico, 2000].

So far, there is no study known that analyses bidding under uncertainty under more general settings, or that studies the dynamics of an auction game. It is possible to determine optimal policies for distinct cases, but there is no study on the agents' behaviour in dynamic environments. It is of interest to answer the raised questions for different environmental settings, e.g. for auctions with two and more bidders. Therefore, this work applies an agent-based simulation approach with adaptive agents. This method offers the possibility to study auction dynamics in particular environmental frameworks and to model bounded rational behaviour. The focus of the present model is on sealed-bid and ascending price auctions with fix end under instantaneous value discovery and different information acquisition cost. Bidding under uncertainty in two and five player settings is modelled and evaluated in Part III (Chapters 6 and 7).

An other main issue is to study the outcome of an auction which can be influenced by several criteria as presented in the MT and explained at the beginning of

---

[17]Here, the term English auction is understood as an open-cry ascending first price auction.

Section 2.1.3. The basic research questions on auctions arise from this dependency of criteria and outcome. In order to design appropriate auction mechanisms it is essential to study the impact of explicit criteria. The structured development of auctions and the evaluation of auction mechanisms has become known as Market Engineering, which is presented in the next section.

2.2   Market Engineering

Searching an appropriate structure for an economic system is not a new question for economists. But the optimal design of such a system is often unknown. Hurwicz [1973, p. 1] argues on the question in what respect the structure of an economic system is unknown:

"Typically that of finding a system that would be, in a sense to be specified, superior to the existing one. The idea of searching for a better system is at least as ancient as Plato's Republic, but it is only recently that tools have become available for a systematic, analytical approach to such search procedures."

The interest in studying electronic markets has increased in the last few years. It can be observed that the market outcome not only depends on the market participants and their valuations, but also on the market structure which stimulates strategic behaviour of the participants. Holtmann [2004] and Neumann [2004] distinguish three components in market structure: (i) market micro structure (the market rules), (ii) IT-infrastructure and (iii) business structure. Even small changes in the market micro structure can result in enormous effects on the market outcome. Ockenfels and Roth [2005] have studied experimentally an English auction with a fixed closing time versus an English auction with soft end. Their experimental results show differences in the bidding behaviour: sniping is applied much more frequently in auctions with hard end. Seifert and Ehrhart [2005] analysed the design of the third generation spectrum auction in the UK and in Germany. Results show that the bidder surplus is lower in the German auction but revenue is higher compared to the UK design. Weber [2005] studies the influence of a first bidder discount in on-line auctions. First analysis show that such a discount does not lead to higher revenues as assumed by some on-line auction houses.

Electronic markets become more and more an essential mechanism within daily business. Still, there is little knowledge about the effects of market structure on the market outcome. Presently, electronic markets are mainly used by human agents, but in the future more and more artificial agents will represent human principals. It might even be possible that certain markets are used by artificial agents only. The market structure and the IT-infrastructure must be able to deal with requirements of human and artificial agents. The study of electronic markets and the interdependency of the participants' behaviour is an essential basis for the design of new electronic markets. Additionally, electronic markets have to satisfy individual and situation driven needs of the participants – buyers and sellers. For example, to satisfy the demand for immediate execution eBay offers the "BuyItNow" option as explained in the previous section. Electronic markets underlie no evolving process like other negotiation mechanisms that change due to the interaction of economic agents and social or institutional rules. Instead, electronic markets are explicitly designed and implemented by humans that have less or no knowledge about specific effects of market rules. This has too often led to the development of electronic markets based on arbitrariness or trial and error which in turn make later adaptations necessary. Holtmann [2004, p. 120] claimed that the failure of NASDAQ Germany or JIWAY are two prominent examples, but it has to be analysed to what extent the market structure or the participants' behaviour were the reasons for this failure. Many electronic markets failed, because the developers were not aware of specific market and/or user requirements, or of the interdependency of market structure and market participants. Thus, Neumann [2004] points out that the development of electronic markets is a wicked problem [Rittel and Webber, 1973] that has the following characteristics:

- Requirements can be contradicting

- The problem may change over time

- Uncertainty exists, whether the reached agreed solution is optimal, or whether a solution exists at all

Since there is still little knowledge on the interdependence of market structure rules, characteristics of the trading object and agents behaviour, it is necessary to study electronic markets comprehensively and apply the gathered knowledge during the designing phase of new markets.

A structured approach on how to design and implement markets is introduced as Market Engineering and is presented in the next section. Section 2.3 presents a computer aided approach to Market Engineering. Finally, Section 2.3.1 and 2.3.2 present the generic market platform meet2trade.

2.2.1 Structured Design Approach

It has been more and more called for scientific support in designing and developing electronic markets [Roth, 2002, Varian, 2002]. One approach for the design of markets has been introduced by Weinhardt et al. [2003] as *Market Engineering (ME)*. Holtmann [2004, p. 121] remarks that it were McCabe et al. [1993] who used the term Market Engineering for the first time, but since then the term was only used a few times. Therefore, Weinhardt et al. [2003] picked up this term and provided a comprehensive definition of ME as a service oriented design approach to the development of electronic markets. An electronic market can be perceived as a service which enables electronic trading and which is provided by either a non-profit organization or profit oriented company. Holtmann [2004] and Neumann [2004] describe the idea of ME comprehensively. Hence, the present section is based on their work.

The terms *market design* and *mechanism design* are often used in economic literature to describe the conceptual development of market rules as defined in Section 2.1.2 by Smith [1982] comprising the information exchange rules (the language), adjustment process rules, allocation rules, and cost imputation rules. For electronic markets such mechanisms have to be implemented and operated on an Information Technology (IT) infrastructure. The operator of an electronic market can be understood as a service provider for economic trades. This service concept includes also some kind of fee in order to cover at least the costs for service providing. These additional requirements for designing electronic markets are picked up by the ME methodology and lead to the following definition, which summarises the work of Neumann [2004, p. 154-176].

Definition 2.2.1. Market Engineering
Market Engineering subsumes the systematic approach to development, analysis and design of electronic market services integrating theory from the scientific areas of economics, business administration, computer science and law. ME focuses on the three core activities (1) design, (2) operation, and (3) research of electronic markets.

In order to appropriately design electronic markets, it is essential to base the design on research results of electronic markets and to study new mechanisms comprehensively. There is also a need for successful business models and powerful technologies. The ME process includes these different aspects according to the service engineering process and engineering design approaches and is described in the following. Figure 2.3 depicts this approach.

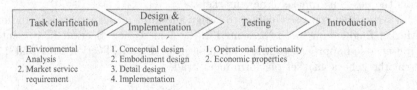

Figure 2.3: The Market Engineering process[Neumann, 2004]

Definition 2.2.2. Market Engineering process
The ME process consists of the four stages (1) Task Clarification, (2) Design and Implementation, (3) Testing, and (4) Introduction. These stages are subdivided into several phases.

(1) Task Clarification

At the very beginning of the ME process, it is important to conduct an environmental analysis and to elaborate the market service requirements.

- *Environmental analysis*
  The environmental analysis starts with (i) the market definition, including the determination of the trading objects, potential customers and their endowment, preferences of customers and other constraints. Once the market is defined (ii) a market segmentation (regarding e.g. customer or product groups) is examined. Finally, (iii) a market target is determined, meaning that it has to be decided which of the market segments to focus on for trading.

- *Market service requirements*
  The environmental analysis serves as starting point to identify basic requirements of the electronic market. It comprises the socio-economic environmental aspects such as the (potential) number of agents, their preferences (private or common values), and resources. Additional services to meet customers expectations are elaborated and also legal aspects are analysed. Important requirements regarding the business process (e.g. cost coverage), incentives for participation, or computational requirements are defined.

(2) Design and Implementation

The second stage is structured into four phases:

- *Conceptual design*
  At the beginning the market system is defined with abstract descriptions regarding the market rules, the infrastructural requirements and the business rules as identified in Stage 1.

- *Embodiment design*
  The abstract descriptions of the conceptual design phase are redefined into semi-formal description of the institutions such as trading protocols. Often there are diverse trading protocols (or descriptions) for one and the same trading mechanism. The descriptions of the embodiment design phase abstract from implementation details.

- *Detail design*
  Detail design starts with building the layout of the system, which is subsequently refined and which finally results in a complete and detailed system model, e.g. based on UML. This model also considers implementation details.

- *Implementation*
  The predefined and developed software model is implemented using a standard software development process.

(3) **Testing**

The developed system is tested regarding its operational functionality and its economic properties.

- *Operational functionality*
  It is important to assure that the implemented system works correct. Therefore, it has to be checked if the code maps to the specified requirements (verification). Common techniques such as unit testing can be applied. Additionally, it is necessary to verify if the requirements themselves are correct or if additional requirements exist (validation).

- *Economic Properties*
  Electronic markets can be analysed with respect to their economic performance either on an analytical basis, using experimental techniques or based on simulation. Theoretic analysis is not suitable for all markets and market environments. Especially the behaviour of human economic agents is not always obvious and hard to model. Therefore, game theoretic experiments can help to gain new insights. It is also possible to apply simulations for testing and evaluating electronic markets.

(4) **Introduction**

After comprehensive tests, the developed market service can be launched and operated. Market Engineering recommends to permanently observe and reassess the market. The gathered feedback helps to improve market services and facilitates the redesign of markets.

The explanations of ME have shown how a structured and theoretically well-founded approach can assist in the development of electronic markets. The electronic market institution is subject to different rule types that have to be carefully determined and implemented. Since electronic markets are services, they normally also contain business rules that impose fees to the users in order to cover at least the costs for service providing. ME helps the designer and/or operator to systematically work on the design of electronic markets and thus, survive the competition of market platforms.

As a next step the question arises if the Market Engineering approach can be systematically facilitated. It has been pointed out that markets are configured on basis of market microstructure parameters. Consequently, it is possible to develop a market platform that allows the configuration of markets on basis of such parameters. Such a generic market platform fastens and simplifies the development of electronic markets, and it can serve as a kernel for computer aided market engineering. There has been some effort put in the development of generic platforms – from auction systems to negotiation systems. The next section provides an overview on the work about generic market and negotiation platforms. The shortcomings of the discussed systems motivate the development of a generic market platform that builds the basis for a tool suite enabling computer aided market engineering. The generic market platform and the computer aided market engineering approach are discussed in Section 2.3.

2.2.2 Generic Design Approaches

Electronic marketplaces basically differ in the negotiation and auction protocols
being implemented as well as in the software prototypical implementation. During
the last years, some research was done on generic electronic market systems that
is capable to provide various protocols or even to allow an easy configuration of
various market mechanisms. In most of the examples discussed below, the key to
a generic as well as flexible and reusable platform (c.f. Mäkiö et al. [2004]) is the
standardization of the individual trading or negotiation process in one reusable
process.

In general, trading is understood as economic interaction for resource allocation. It has been pointed out earlier that besides hierarchical coordination markets
are another instrument for economic interaction and that negotiations can constitute a market since they are based on explicitly defined rules. These rules are the
basis of a well-structured process, defining the interaction of the involved parties
and the circumstances under which the interaction takes place. The identification
of the basic rules, parameters, and components is crucial for standardizing and
automating negotiations and auctions since all auctions are standardized negotiations [Kersten and Teich, 2000]. First steps toward the identification of the rules
and the criteria have been made by Ströbel and Weinhardt [2003] in the Montreal
Taxonomy, which allows a characterization of a number of electronic negotiation
designs and systems.

Anadalingnam et al. [2005] introduce four categories of auction design components: (i) a winner determination component, (ii) a payment determination
component, (iii) a component defining the information flow, and (iv) a component
defining the bidding language. Referring to the argumentation of Anadalingnam
et al. [2005] all auctions are precisely variations of these four auction components.
For each auction, the rules within the components have to be designed and specified.

Focusing this model of four components with its rules it offers a high degree
of flexibility and variety. Up to 18 different basic auction types or market settings,
e.g. auction formats, are comprised by this model, spanning an auction design
space with four dimensions.

The model suggested by Wurman et al. [1998, 2001] is based on characteristics or parameters that are common to many auction types such as single sided
or double sided auctions, as well as multi-commodity auctions, e.g. combinatorial
auctions. It identifies the three independent core activities (i) bidding rules, (ii)
clearing policy, and (iii) information revelation, various parameters that span a
multi-dimensional auction design space – most of the well known auction mechanisms can be mapped into this design space. The Michigan Internet AuctionBot
[Wurman et al., 1998] is a general platform for price based negotiation providing
the flexible approach of decomposition and parametrization of auction mecha-

nisms. The AuctionBot is an auction server allowing to run a large number of auctions simultaneously. Participants may not only submit bids in existing auction and use the platform for trading and exchanging goods; participants even may design markets (auctions) and initiate them within the core server. Additionally, an agent interface is supported, allowing agents to access all of the features of the AuctionBot presented in a web interface to human participants.

The Generic Negotiation Platform (GNP) is an auction-oriented platform supporting different types of auctions which are considered as a special case of negotiations. Benyoucef et al. [2000] present a concept to setup and implement a platform allowing an easy change of the negotiation protocol. Started with a Generic Experimentation Engine (GEE) a software prototype for game-oriented experimentation, the GNP is an extension of the GEE towards negotiation processes. The negotiation process is modelled as a finite state machine (FSM) – with the states of the auction and with the input and output alphabet as the input-messages and output-messages that can be possibly sent by participants and received by participants. The transitions of the states are caused by messages which describe the process flow. The FSM Model was introduced by Kumar and Feldman [July 1998] for describing the interaction of building blocks which are common to different business processes. The *deal object, inbound messages, out bound messages*, and the *product description* form the four building blocks. Benyoucef et al. [2000] extended the FSM not being sufficient for their use: auction rules concerning policy decisions on anonymity, restriction, rules for closing the auction, and services provided to the participants were added.

A market framework implementing common auction formats that can easily be adapted to new application domains and that allows a dynamic configuration is the *Global Electronic Market (GEM)* (c.f.Reich and Ben-Shaul [1998]). GEM supports various market mechanisms based on a generic structure or architecture. The genericity of the system is based on the decomposition into independent components, more precisely, parameters tailoring distinct aspects of market mechanisms. Core of the GEM is the Market Layer, one of three layers implemented in the system, being divided in *Front End, Trading Floor* and *Back End*. In particular the *Trading Floor* is the heart of the market consisting of a component called Order Verifier determining which orders to accept, the Market Maker component, solving the allocation problem and determining the price, and the Schedule component, managing the timing of the orders to be executed. Additionally, a dynamic configuration of the auction is facilitated by a meta-component called Builder for initializing and replacing components during run-time.

MARI, the *Multi-Attribute Resource Intermediary*, is yet another example for a generalized platform involving the buying and selling of goods and services where price is just one of a multitude of possible factors influencing the decision to trade [Tewari and Maes, 2000]. MARI relates not only to the auction systems presented above. Even more it can be related to negotiation systems such as *Invite* as presented by Kersten et al. [2004]. Buyers and sellers are asked about their preferences for the transaction partner as well as their preferences towards the attributes of the object to be traded. Each party is allowed to choose or associate weights from an underlying ontology; attributes can be chosen as being fix or flexible. The chosen weights determine the utility function, being selected automatically by the software as an element of a set of different preference or utility functions MARI offers. Based on the identified preference function and weights, the system matches possible sellers to buyers due to a certain request and determines the price to pay. In contrary to the auction based systems, the auction or negotiation mechanism is fixed and can not be changed. Therefore, the flexibility is given by MARIS's interaction with the user, decomposed in single steps.

The platform *Invite* is a system allowing to study various protocols and solutions in the field of negotiations. Many e-negotiation systems (ENS) have been conceptualized and deployed for specific applications or situations. Thus, most of them just implement one single negotiation protocol which is fix and can not be changed or easily configured. The invite system is mainly based on two components: (i) the negotiation process model and (ii) the negotiation protocol. The negotiation process is the framework providing the sequencing of phases in the negotiation. Phases can be revisited or can be ignored – not necessarily all phases have to be passed. The negotiation process of Invite consists of five phases: (i) planning, (ii) agenda setting, (iii) exchanging offers and arguments, (iv) reaching an agreement, and (v) concluding a negotiation. The negotiation protocol defines precisely the activities that are permissible in every state of the negotiation process. It is possible to flexibly adapt different protocols to the same underlying process. The activities, the sequence of activities and the states as a result of the activities define the protocol and thus, the type of negotiation. Note, activities are considered as the most concrete component of a negotiation. Based on the manifold negotiation situations and participants Invite is a flexible ENS supporting various protocols and supporting the design of new protocols.

The presented platform have in common the key idea of configuring a variety of electronic auctions. Nevertheless, the systems are restricted to some particular auction formats. In order to develop a tool suite for computer aided market engineering, it is necessary to provide a market server that is capable of designing and operating not only standard auction types, but also more complex formats like multi-attribute auctions, or combined formats like dynamic market models as explained earlier. When adding components that facilitate the evaluation of electronic markets set up and operated at the market server, a first step towards computer aided market engineering would be done. The following section introduces the idea of computer aided market engineering as it was suggested by Neumann [2004], and describes the generic market platform meet2trade that together with additional software components enables the evaluation of markets, e.g. through simulations or experiments.

2.3   Computer Aided Market Engineering

Neumann [2004] proposes *Computer Aided Market Engineering (CAME)* to computationally support the design, development, and implementation of electronic markets. Figure 2.4 illustrates the CAME process, comprising the four phases (i) design, (ii) configuration, (iii) test, (iv) operation. According to the ME process, CAME starts with the design of an electronic market. A knowledge database that

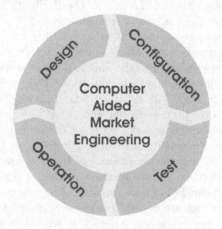

Figure 2.4: The Computer Aided Market Engineering (CAME) process

contains research results of electronic market institutions, assists in choosing the appropriate market structure within the design phase. The next step (ii) is to configure the electronic market considering the chosen design. This configuration phase (c.p. the design and implementation stage of ME) is supported by a generic market platform that is able to operate various electronic markets. In order to ensure that the designed electronic market is sufficient for the intended application, tests are needed (c.p. the testing stage in ME). This is step (iii) within CAME approach.

ME considers theoretic analysis as well as experimental and computational methods for evaluating electronic markets. These tests can be partially supported by software tools e.g. for conducting experiments or for running simulations. The test results are stored in a knowledge database, which can be used to solve future design issues. After sufficient tests, the electronic market is ready for operation (iv).

Ideally, the new defined markets run on a predefined and already existing market platform. This allows the electronic market designer to renounce general design issues of electronic market platforms (e.g. accessibility, message exchange issues, database access, graphical front end). Markets are permanently controlled in order to evaluate performance or anomalies. These operational information are stored in the same knowledge database to facilitate the design of new markets and to enhance the performance of existing markets.

As a central component in CAME, a generic market platform is necessary. For that reason, the market platform meet2trade was developed to provide a flexible configuration of electronic markets and to enable research on various electronic markets [Weinhardt et al., 2005]. The flexibility was developed regarding two aspects. Firstly, according to the idea of CAME, the objective was to facilitate a fast development and evaluation of electronic markets with different market structure due to the need for individual solutions. Secondly, the aim was to provide flexibility also for end users especially in the variety of configurable market structure for single sided auctions.

Flexibility can be achieved through (i) selection, (ii) configuration and (iii) combination. The least comprehensive step toward providing flexibility to end-users is maintaining a set of auctions the user can select from. The next step is allowing the user to submit ONE order to a combination of markets at once. This combination ranges from simple sequences of markets the orders passes through to a complex structure with parallel and sequential segments. The most advanced step is to allow the user complete control over the market structure giving him the possibility to design his own market. To facilitate this market configuration process, a description language, the Market Modelling Language (MML), was developed. This language makes it possible to configure an auction by setting the appropriate parameter values. Since it is possible to describe market rules with the setting of market parameters, it is – to some degree – also possible to combine auction parameters to create new auctions. meet2trade supports the combination of market structure parameters settings.

The design and the combination of market rules allows to study certain effects in both auction types, single sided and double sided auctions. Continuous Double Auctions (CDA) are well suited for liquid products whereas Call Markets are used in markets with less frequent trade. Of course, the liquidity of an market fluctuates (e.g. dependent on the time of the day or specific information). Hence, it appears helpful to choose the market rules dependent on external factors (such as volatility, amount of orders in the order book, etc.). It is also possible to combine a Call Market with a *hit&take-market* that allows to immediately match a selected order even though it is in the order book of a call market.

Apart from classic CDAs the introduction of products with multiple attributes for matching or the idea of bundle trading leads to a couple of interesting research areas. meet2trade realises both, bundle trading and multi attribute auctions, and was designed to facilitate research on such mechanisms.

In single sided auction it is quite common to combine certain market rules. It can be observed at on-line auction houses that ascending auctions are combined with options such as a fixed price at which the product can be immediately bought. In order to attract bidders, e.g. discounts are offered to the first bidder. Such rules have certain effects on the market participants behaviour. meet2trade provides many of the suggested parameters.

The next section presents the conceptual platform design. Section 2.3.2 describes additional features such as special order types and tools developed in order to facilitate the evaluation of auctions.

2.3.1   Conceptual Platform Design

The meet2trade software suite follows a client server architecture. There is need to process a large amount of data centrally, such as user data (user entries, depot data), product information, and the electronic markets themselves. On the other hand it is necessary to provide a high accessibility to the market system. A client server architecture accomplishes these requirements. The meet2trade server is written in Java using the Enterprise Java Beans (EJB) concept. EJB is a server side component architecture for distributed computing developed by SUN Microsystems. EJB run on an application server that enables scalability of client requests. Beans can be distributed and fulfil diverse tasks, such as database access processing the order entry. Figure 2.5 depicts the overall architecture with the core components running on the application server. meet2trade uses a JBoss application server and the SAP database.[18]

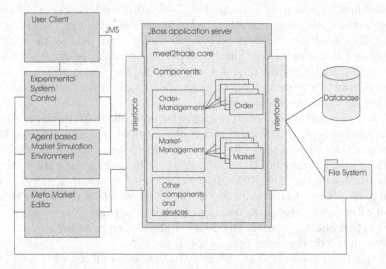

Figure 2.5: The architecture of meet2trade

The core functionality of the server is to deploy various auction mechanisms, manage the user accounts and depots, enable a configuration of electronic markets, and administrate the various users' orders of different types. Each user participating at meet2trade must be registered to log into the system. The users' endowment

---

[18]SAP   DB   has   become   MaxDB,   an   open   source   database   available   at
http://www.mysql.com/products/maxdb/

of money and goods is stored within the user depot. After a successful trade, the user depot is updated. Thus, the clearing and settlement takes place within the platform. Therefore, the users' data is actual and appropriate.

In order to participate at a certain electronic market, the user specifies her offer to buy (bid) or sell (ask) within an meet2trade order object. Such an order object is a generic component containing all relevant information, e.g the price and the volume the participant is willing to pay or asking to get and the market the order is sent to. The server processes the received orders within the order management component. Orders are autonomous objects that are able to enter and exit a market according to its specifications. This enhances the users' functionality.

Products are sorted in product categories. Attributes are assigned to products in order to characterize the product. Attributes can be used for matching in multi attribute cases. For the standard auctions the basic attributes are volume and price. Products can be dealt on several markets. Consequently, the market list within the meet2trade-client is ordered hierarchically by product category and products. Orders for one product that is dealt in more than one markets can be sent to several markets displayed in the market list as long as a bid withdrawal is allowed within these markets – otherwise the same order could be matched twice.[19]

The market management administrates all registered markets. A market has two different states, *open* or *closed*. Orders can only be sent to open markets and are stored within the order book of the market. The visibility of the order book is dependent on the market's specifications. Markets can be described and configured by the Market Modelling Language (MML). The configuration of markets is described in more depth in Section 2.3.2.

To achieve a high degree of platform independence, the meet2trade client was developed as Java application. For communication between client and server the standard Java Message Service (JMS) is used. This enables distributed reliable and asynchronous communication. The messages are encoded in XML schemata and therefore provide a high degree of readability and re-usability. In order to keep the client generic, it is necessary to adapt the components to the market's requirements. Consequently, the design of the Graphical User Interface is defined in XML messages according to the requirements of the specific market and the available orders. The GUI description messages are provided by the meet2trade core. For a comprehensive description of the meet2trade-system it is referred to Weinhardt et al. [2005].

Additionally, meet2trade provides services and components beside the market core such as an experimental system, a simulation environment or bundle trading. These components are described in more detail in the next subsection.

---

[19]The problem of orders in many markets has been addressed by Czernohous et al. [2003]

2.3.2   The meet2trade Software Suite

The platform provides functionality to support steps within the Computer Aided
Market Engineering (CAME). As described earlier, the aim of CAME is to provide
users a toolkit to simplify the development and evaluation of electronic markets.
The configuration of electronic markets is supported by the Market Modelling
Language (MML) that allows the easy configuration of electronic markets. For
evaluation, the platform provides the meet2trade Experimental System (MES)
to conduct game theoretic experiments and the Agent-based Market Simulation
Environment (AMASE) for simulation purposes. The generic meet2trade-client
enables the user to immediately use the configured market, since the client GUI
automatically adapts to the market input requirements.

Apart from meet2trade as a CAME-software, the system has realised two
additional features, *innovative order types* to facilitate trading and a *bundle trading
component* that allows to deal a basket of several interdependent products.

The special components of meet2trade are presented in more detail in the
next sections.

Market Modeling Language (MML)

Understanding markets as sets of rules and components enables a parametrized approach to market configuration. The *(MML)* was developed to describe electronic
markets' parameters (c.f. Mäkiö and Weber [2004a]) to facilitate the development
of electronic auctions. Auction components are managed within a Meta Market
object which also stores the superordinate rules of auction components such as
the start and stop time (c.f. Mäkiö and Weber [2004b]). In order to enable users
to simply define electronic auctions the Meta Market Editor (MM-Editor) was
developed. The editor permits users to select parameters and to assign parameter
values, and hence, configure an electronic auction.

A generic process is part of all meet2trade-markets. In order to configure
markets, additional parameters can be chosen. These parameters concern e.g. the
information revelation (how much information to provide to whom), restrictions
on the participation (who is allowed to participate, single-sided vs. double sided),
the definition of events, or additional parameters such as price discount for first
bidders. The combination of the generic process with the parametrization approach
makes meet2trade a powerful auction configuration platform.

meet2trade Experimental System (MES)

In order to apply economic experiments for the assessment of electronic markets the meet2trade-Experimental System (MES) was developed. So far, there are
some generic frameworks to setup and conduct economic experiments, but none
was specifically designed for experiments on electronic markets. The user interface
of electronic markets can be quite complex in order to display specific information.
Consequently, MES was designed to overcome these shortcomings. This approach

on the one hand facilitates experimental studies since the market has to be modelled only once within meet2trade, and on the other hand confronts subjects with the same look-and-feel of the meet2trade-client instead of a new and different GUI of some kind of experimental standard software as z-Tree.[20]

MES provides a graphical user interface to administrate experimental settings. The settings are stored in an XML-coded file. It is possible to determine experiment characteristics such as the allowed users, a questionnaire to examine the users understanding, the configuration of the trading screens, or duration of an experimental round.

Human-Computer experiments can be conducted through integration of software agents of the Agent-based Simulation Environment (AMASE). The application of human-computer experiments opens new ways in the analysis of electronic markets.

Agent-based Market Simulation Environment (AMASE)

Computational approaches are more and more used in economics to study complex systems. The ability to model individual strategies within software agents enables economists to study markets' outcome, bidders' behaviour, and market dynamics under certain institutional and environmental rules. Agents applied in simulations normally use simple decision rules, learning algorithms, or statistical analysis to adapt their strategies. The fundamentals of computational economics and agent-based simulation are presented in Section 3 in more detail.

AMASE was developed to enable discrete event market simulations. It is based on the Java Agent DEvelopment Framework (JADE) and supports the automated repetition of simulations and the definition of a sequence of settings. Auction can be defined on meet2trade as well as within AMASE. As such it provides a flexible testbed for many electronic auctions. A requirement analysis which has led to the development of AMASE is comprehensively presented in Chapter 5.

Innovative Order Types

Stock exchanges and other trading systems presently face increasing competition. Besides the trading costs, innovative features become more and more important. This concerns either the market rules or the capability of orders. These new features have to be evaluated before being introduced in real-life markets. Hence, meet2trade has implemented some new order types.

Kunzelmann and Mäkiö [2005] present two distinct order types, the *pegged* and the *bracket* order, which enhance the traders opportunities. Especially retail investors are inferior to better informed traders since they can not react on market movements as quick as professional traders.

---

[20]http://www.iew.unizh.ch/ztree/index.php

Thus, the *pegged* or *relative order*[21] offers traders the opportunity to always beat the best ask (or best bid respectively) by bidding with one increment difference within a defined limit. This means that a relative sell order is always one Cent below the current best ask as long as the price is equal to or higher than the specified limit. Accordingly, a relative buy order is one Cent higher than the current best bid as far as the price is equal or below the specified limit. This mechanism increase the trade probability and reduces the risk of being outbid by better informed traders.

The *bracket order* combines a limit and a stop order. A limit specifies the threshold below which a seller is not willing to sell and above a buyer is not willing to buy. Stop orders are used to avoid heavy losses or to take out profits. Consequently, bracket orders define both, an upper and lower bound for selling/buying. In case of buy orders, the lower bound is determined by the limit price and the upper bound by the stop price. For bracket sell orders, the upper bound is fixed by the limit price and the stop loss price determines the lower bound. This mechanism release the trader from permanently watching the price movements.

meet2trade has realised the described and several additional order types. This allows for comprehensive studies of the effects using such order types.

Bundle Trading

Investment returns can be optimized by diversification of a portfolio. Markowitz [1952] developed the Portfolio Selection theory to optimize portfolio returns at reduced risk. Changes in the portfolio often affects more than one stock. In cases of portfolio optimization the occurring trades are often dependent on each other, meaning that e.g. one stock is just sold if one or certain other stocks can be bought at a specific price. The trading of several dependent orders is known as bundle trading. Grunenberg et al. [2004] note that a great amount of daily trading is caused by program trading.[22] Unfortunately, the trading of bundles as a whole is not supported by the present trading systems of stock exchanges, but appears to provide additional support especially to professional traders.

Grunenberg et al. [2004] propose a mechanism to solve the linear optimization problem concerning bundle trading. This optimization was implemented with the mathematical programming optimizer *CPLEX*[23] and integrated in meet2trade. Thus, effects of bundle trading can be studied with meet2trade.

---

[21]Kunzelmann and Mäkiö [2005] introduce a pegged order which is better described as a relative order. For that reason we use the term *relative order* in the following.

[22]Grunenberg et al. [2004] refer to a weekly report of the New York Stock Exchange (NYSE) where more than 40% of daily trades are caused by programm trading.

[23]http://www.ilog.com/products/cplex/

2.4 Summary

This chapter introduced into underlying economic theory for the present work. The first subsection presented electronic markets, starting with the fundamental work of Smith [1982] on markets in general and the extension of Holtmann [2004], Neumann [2004] toward an electronic market framework. Definitions of markets, negotiations and auctions were provided, and strategic bidding under uncertainty was discussed. The literature review on bidding under uncertainty has bred out basic propositions that will be picked up in the simulative analysis of that problem in Chapter 6.

The founding work on electronic markets directly led over to Market Engineering, the structured approach for the development of electronic markets introduced by Weinhardt et al. [2003], Neumann [2004] and Holtmann [2004]. Markets are not only a collection of rules, but, a real or virtual, place for the exchange and allocation of goods (or property rights) supplied and demanded by (human or artificial) agents. These agents exhibit certain behaviour. It is the interaction of these individual agents within a particular environment that makes the analysis of electronic markets a difficult task. The outcome of electronic markets is not obvious and only in a few abstract cases analytical solvable. This is the reason why it is important to study electronic markets and to apply the lessons learned in the development process of markets. Market Engineering proposes a structured process for the electronic market development that includes the comprehensive market analysis.

The development of electronic markets can be facilitated by market platforms that allow users to individually configure their individual market model. Such a generic market platform is also useful for market engineers who not only want to develop new markets but also study the market outcome and the bidders' behaviour. With the development of the generic market platform meet2trade a first step was made towards computer aided market engineering. The platform meet2trade does not only provide a GUI and a market modelling language for market configuration, but also an experimental system for conducting economic experiments as well as a simulation environment for agent-based simulations. The CAME approach is supposed to not only assist a market engineer during configuration, but also to provide knowledge about the effects of certain market parameters. The next steps towards CAME are to further develop the existing toolsuite meet2trade and to attach a knowledge database to store the gathered results from simulations and experiments.

The main focus of this work is on analysing electronic market using agent-based simulation. The next Chapter introduces in the theory of software agents, multi-agent systems and the development of simulation models.

Chapter 3

Agent-based Computational Economics

Research in social science was for long affected by two commonly accepted approaches for gaining insight: induction and deduction. With induction one derives general principles from particular cases, e.g. through pattern discovery in empirical data or observation of certain rules. In the deductive approach a set of axioms is defined and the consequences deriving from these assumptions are proven [Axelrod, 2003]. This approach can also be described as inferring the particular from the general. These techniques are applied in many fields of economic research. Game Theory uses deduction to solve for equilibria, macro economics uses deduction to explain equilibria, e.g. on money or goods markets. Empirical surveys (inductive reasoning) are used for macro economic analysis or in econometric theory.

Most economic theories apply the method of induction and/or deduction in a static way. Game theory, for example, studies static equilibria. The model dynamics to establish the equilibrium are studied in extensive form games. It is not always possible to develop the extensive form of a game. This is the starting point for *Computational Economics* (CE). This fairly new branch of economic research is firstly interested in the system's dynamics and the processes leading to observed phenomena by conducting simulations. Secondly CE provides computational techniques to support e.g. the solution for equilibria.

Simulations are often understood as an alternative approach of doing research in social science. Ostrom [1988] argues that social science theory can be expressed either by mathematics using formalized expression, or by verbal explanation. Additionally, he puts simulations as a third opportunity of expressing theoretical propositions in computer models. This can be understood as using simulations as a third methodological approach apart from deduction and induction. In the context of evaluating electronic markets, Neumann [2004] determines simulation as a third research method beside axiomatic reasoning (cp. deduction) and experimental techniques (cp. induction). Conducting a simulation starts – comparable to deduction – with the determination of assumptions. In a deductive approach these assumptions are proven. Simulations are not applicable for theorem proving, but generate data that can be inductively analysed. Insofar, simulations use techniques from both, induction and deduction, though the data, the induction is based upon, is not observed within the real world but in a model based on assumptions. Hence, simulations can also be understood as doing thought experiments, where assumptions may be simple but the consequences may be not obvious (see e.g. Axelrod [2003]).

The use of computational theory in science started with the invention of computer machinery. In the beginning it was mainly used for numerical computations, especially in natural science or engineering science, e.g.in physics or mechanical engineering. When computing power became less expensive, computational methods became more popular, not only for numerical solutions of complex mathematical problems, but also for the study of complex (dynamic) system models. Nowadays, computational methods have found their way in many fields of economic research such as macroeconomic growth theory, evolutionary game theory, or mechanism design. Its popularity can be observed in the still growing amount of papers using computational theory. But CE is not yet perceived as an independent research area in social science, such as game theory, although computational economists are trying to establish it as such. Problems in that concern are the lack of a common agreed-upon definition for CE, the little agreement on how computational results are being presented, and the lack of a common pool of methods and language (see e.g. Judd [1997], Byde [2002], Axelrod [2003]). Amman [1997, p. 103 f.] provides a definition for CE:

"To me, Computational Economics is a new methodology for solving economic problems with the help of computing machinery. Hence, Computational Economics is not restricted to a specific branch of economics. Any line of economic research that uses this new methodology fits the definition of Computational Economics. The only restriction we have to make is that this new methodology has a value added in terms of (economic) problem solving [Lakatos, 1970]." The focus in this explanation is on the methodology as a value adding tool for problem solving. Often it is the case that all computational methods used in economic research are subsumed in CE (cp. Judd [1997]). But still, until now there is no explicit classification of computational methods and their fields of application known. The Society for Computational Economics[1] entertains special interest groups which may serve as a starting point for a classification of the research in CE. The interest groups can be subsumed into three areas: (i) certain fields of application, e.g. econometrics and statistics, finance, political economy or market theory, (ii) computational methods, such as numerical methods (e.g. numerical integration methods, functions approximation, or searching), agent-based approaches, or system dynamics, and (iii) teaching. This classification shows that the understanding

---

[1]http://wueconc.wustl.edu/~sce/

of CE only from a methodological point of view might be to narrow and that CE can also be seen as a separate research domain such as game theory which leads to the following definition:

Definition 3.0.1. Computational Economics
Computational economics is a branch of applied mathematics that studies economic systems by using computer based methods for both, descriptive and normative research.

The common objective in science is to gain cognition by observing a distinct part of reality. Therefore, reality or rather the system to be studied is reproduced in a model.

Definition 3.0.2. System
A system is a closed part of reality consisting of interacting components embedded in an environment. Systems have different states, which can be fully described by the state variables at any time. State variables include the input and output of the system.

Real world systems or system models can be scrutinised by experimental methods, or by building formal mathematical models for analytic evaluation and deductive reasoning. This approach is feasible for analysis of simple models. Adding more detail to refine simple models increases the complexity, and thus, renders more difficulty in finding analytic solutions. This is where computational techniques can support researchers to better find solutions and explanations in the study of complex systems. In that sense, *"Computational Economics can help to study qualitative effects quantitatively "*[Judd, 1997].

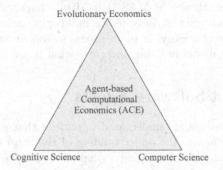

Figure 3.1: ACE at the interface of Cognitive Science, Computer Science and Evolutionary Economics, source: T. Eymann at http://www.econ.iastate.edu/tesfatsi/ace.htm

Agent-based Computational Economics (ACE) is one specific branch within CE. It describes the *"computational study of economies modelled as evolving systems of autonomous interacting agents"* [Tesfatsion, 2002]. This research approach

builds upon the understanding of economy not from the macro level perspective of
a system of aggregated demand and supply, but from a micro level as the result of
the interaction of numerous independent individuals. Krugman [1996] notes in a
talk[2] that economics can be understood as the study of those phenomena emerging
from the interactions among intelligent, self-interested individuals. ACE conducts
interdisciplinary work on the interface of Cognitive Science, Computer Science,
and Evolutionary Economics (see also Figure 3.1). Hence, ACE can be defined:

Definition 3.0.3. Agent-based Computational Economics
*Agent-based Computational Economics is a methodological approach to study dy-
namic economic systems of numerous independent components. The system behaviour results from the interaction of these components. It is one branch of Computational Economics.*

First work in this area was done by von Neumann [1966] with the theory
on self-reproducing automata. Schelling [1969] was one of the first social scientists
who conducted studies of macro behaviour from a micro behavioural view. In
his models of segregation he observes the phenomenon of cultural segregation in
American residential districts into areas of white and coloured citizens. In these
times computational power was limited. During the last decade, computational
progress made large scale agent populations possible. That is also why most of the
work on ACE was done in the last ten to fifteen years.

The present work introduces ACE for evaluating electronic markets. The next
subsection introduces agent theory and provides explanations and definitions for
software agents in order to build a common understanding for software agents.
These definitions provide the basis for Section 3.2 that introduces Multi Agent
Systems (MAS). The theory of MAS is used in Chapter 5 to build an agent-
based simulation environment. In order to build appropriate simulation models
that correctly represent reality, it is necessary to follow an accepted approach.
Therefore, theory on model building and simulation is presented in Section 3.3.

3.1   Intelligent Software Agents

Intelligent software agents are understood as entities that perform tasks autonomous. From the beginning, the understanding of the term *agent* offered a spectrum from software objects performing a small task (e.g. control of a thermostat)
to pieces of software representing humans and carrying out complex tasks. Today,
there still exist various definitions of software agents depending on the research
area and its focus. In general the *intelligent agent* concept characterizes independently acting and interacting software entities. The terms *software agent* and
intelligent agent are often used synonymously. Brenner et al. [1998] differentiate
non-intelligent agents and intelligent agents whereas in fact non-intelligent agents

---

[2]The talk was given to the European Association for Evolutionary Political Economy and is
published as an essay.

work independently, but not flexible by obeying determined rules. An agent waiting for a certain market price to buy a specified amount of stocks without considering other factors as actual information and trends is one example for a non-intelligent agent. In fact, there are many examples where the term (software) agent is applied to objects that are even not a single software entity, but a particular mechanism or method. Often the outcome of such objects appear to be the result of interacting agents. The proxy-bidding mechanism on eBay is such an example, which frequently is denominated "agent". In the following, the term *software agent* is used synonymously for *intelligent software agent*.

One common characteristic of software agents is their ability of independently solving appointed problems. Weiss [1999, p. 1] characterizes an intelligent software agent as *"computational entity [. . .] that can be viewed as perceiving and acting upon its environment and that is autonomous in that its behaviour at least partially depends on its own experience."*

The concept of agents was picked up by economists and also industry researchers for different reasons. Economists use agents in complex models of economies to represent human behaviour or to conduct game theoretic experiments with simple automata. Industry researchers identified a high potential for agents in business applications, e.g. for optimization (classical Operation Research problems) or in the internet economy to assist humans or even to perform tasks on the behalf of humans. Since the fast success of agents in business applications was not achieved, agent technology lost attention in both public and scientific communities. Nevertheless, agent technology has made huge progress in science as well as in business applications. For better understanding a definition for software agents is provided in the next section.

3.1.1 Characteristics of Software Agents

Computer scientists have the most precise understanding of agents that is not always considered among economists or IS researchers. Still there is an ongoing debate on what piece of software can be called agent. The present work will not contribute to that debate, since the focus is on the idea of *simulating* evolving system while using agents as a tool. Thus, the following gives a relatively general definition of software agents:

Definition 3.1.1. Software Agent
An intelligent software agent is a software entity that individually pursues a specified goal. It is characterized by not less than characteristics (1)-(4) and the three optional characteristics (5)-(7): (1) the ability to interact with its environment, (2) autonomy, (3) reactivity, (4) proactivity, (5) social capabilities and communication capabilities, (6) adaptivity, (7) rationality.

Additionally, agents might be able to move within an electronic network, or agents possess a human like character. Software agents are not economic agents in the narrow sense, but they act on behalf of economic agents[3] (see 2.1.2 for the definition of economic agents). or are used to simulate the behaviour of economic agents. The definition names seven characteristics that are presented in more detail in the following.

(1) Interacting with the environment

One of the fundamental characteristic of agents is their ability to interact with their environment. The environment is defined as the totality of all software or human agents, their characteristics, environmental rules of other system related components, endowment, system rules and other objects such as goods or sensors. Agents do not necessarily possess total information about the environment. Interaction enables the agent to coordinate tasks and subtasks in cooperative and competitive environments to reach specified objectives. In a cooperative environment, agents work toward a certain (possibly common) goal together with other agents, whereas in competitive environments agents work independently from others and might have contradictory objectives (see Weiss [1999, p. 1 ff]).

Agents can interact directly, e.g. using a common language, or agents interact indirectly perceiving changes in the environment. Agents must not always act truthfully, so they might also try to confuse other agents. Figure 3.2 depicts an agent in its environment. An agents receives input from the environment that builds his perception of the environment. Agent's actions influence and change the environment.

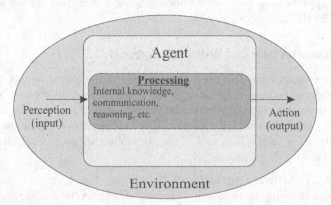

Figure 3.2: Agent embedded in its environment

---

[3]For instance, eBay provides a so called *proxy agent* that on behalf of an economic agent automatically increases the bid price in an ascending internet auction to a specified bid ceiling. The proxy agent's description do not match the strict software-agent definition that requires all above listed seven characteristics to be fulfilled. However, this work also considers a proxy agents as intelligent software agents.

(2) Autonomy

A fundamental characteristic of intelligent agents is the ability to act autonomously. Agents possess all necessary capabilities to decide on which action to take. Consequently, agents need certain capabilities and knowledge of rules to understand the environment. Hence, agents can own or develop different behaviours to determine their action in specific environments during environmental changes. Communication rules are an example for specific *social knowledge*. The agent's decision depends on its perception and understanding of the environment and the agent's internal state. The internal state is private information to the agent and not known to any other agent.

The arbitrative characteristic for agents is not only their autonomy, but the degree of autonomy. Castelfranchi [1995] describes autonomy as agents' capability of acting independently from third party intervention (e.g. humans). Alternatively, Jennings and Wooldridge [1998] point out that the capability of *flexible autonomous acting* in different environments constitutes the intelligence of software agents.

(3) Reactivity

Agents interact with their environment. The environment can be described by certain parameters and rules. It can be totally virtual (e.g. in a model), real or a combination of real and virtual. Other agents or humans can also be part of the environment. For successful interaction, agents must be capable to react on environmental changes in adequate time. In many (complex) systems, one agent might only have partial knowledge of the environment which leads to uncertainty. In systems with dynamic environments, agents must be able to adapt to and react on new situations. That is, a simple rule-based behaviour (precondition-action-postcondition) is not sufficient in such environments. Consequently, agents must be reactive on (ex ante) unknown situations to independently reach the specified goals (see also Wooldridge and Ciancarini [2001]).

(4) Proactivity

To assure goal-directed actions, agents must not only exhibit reactive behaviour, but need to perform objective driven proactive behaviour. Therefore, in addition to react on environmental changes agents act opportunistic to reach their individual goal. It might appear that individual goals can no longer be achieved or are not reasonable. In that case, agents should be able to either adapt their goals or try to provoke environmental changes to make the goals achievable. Wooldridge and Ciancarini [2001] point out that it is difficult to find a good balance between reactive and proactive behaviour.

(5) Social ability and communication

To understand the environment agents need social ability and must be able to communicate with other agents and where applicable with humans (see also Genesereth and Ketchpel [1994]). This calls for particular (formalized) knowledge and a common language, a so called *Agent Communication Language (ACL)*. An ACL enables agents to coordinate their actions, to solve problems cooperatively or competitively, or to negotiate (cp.Weinhardt and Gomber [1999], Brenner et al. [1998], Wooldridge and Jennings [1995]). Agent-based negotiations and auctions can, for example, be used for automated resource allocation. Communication is discussed in more detail in Section 3.2.

(6) Adaptivity

An additional attribute for agents' intelligence is the ability to learn. For learning agents collect information and gain experience by assessing past actions and collected information. Consequently, agents need to distinguish useful and useless information collected by observing environmental changes and must be able to reason about the own past actions and the perceived changes. As a result agents learn to adapt to the dynamic environment, and thus, exhibit adaptive behaviour (cp. Brenner et al. [1998]).

(7) Rationality

Agents are supposed to act rational. Rationality in this context is defined as actions taken exclusively to achieve or at least get closer to a certain goal or subtask. Agents will not take action if they know that it will be useless or impedimental in respect to achieve the agent's goal. It is assumed that one agent does not have contradictory goals (cp. Rosenschein and Genesereth [1985], Galliers [1988]).

Agents might also have optional characteristics such as mobility or human-like characters. Especially in peer to peer (P2P) networks and other networks mobility is helpful. Human-like characters are more common in computer game industry or for assistance in standard software or on web sites. Although not relevant for this work these aspects are presented in the following for completeness reasons:

- Mobility

  Mobile agents are able to move in electronic networks. This allows to build or instruct agents on a local machine and send them to other hosts to fulfil the desired tasks. E.g. a "shopping assistant" agent is developed locally, endowed with private information, and autonomously moves in the network to find a specified product. The agent gains more flexibility if it is not bound on one distinct resource and helps to reduce data load by shortening the communication distance between agent and the counterpart. To increase performance in huge agent populations it is useful to distribute agents on computing resources.

  In some applications it is useful to put an agent on a mobile device such as a mobile phone, a mobile computer, or a small smart item[4] as it is used in logistic networks. Such mobile agents can monitor processes or perform location dependent tasks.

---

[4]A smart item is a micro sensor system with small computational capabilities.

An other application for mobile agents are simulations of virtual landscape where agents are able to move on in order to fulfil tasks (e.g. see Epstein and Axtell [1996]). Mobility as well as communication in general pose questions on security of networks and computing resources that are not part of the present work.

- Character
  In certain applications it is important that agents show human characteristics. Especially in cases with intensive human-agent interaction the depiction of emotions can facilitate communication (cp. Brenner et al. [1998]). Emotional state can be expressed through text interfaces or virtual human-like graphical bodies, so called avatars. At the moment there is not much use of avatars for simulations, especially for market simulation. Therefore, avatars are not subject of the present work.

Computational economists do not strictly stick to these definitions. From the economic perspective it is important that software output (e.g. bids) can be interpreted as decisions of autonomous entities or humans. ACE apply computer science techniques. Especially agents' proactive and reactive capability is characteristic in computational economics research. The ability to learn strategies in order to compete in a certain environment is often used for economic simulations. The following section gives an introduction to agent learning that is often used in agent-based simulations to learn optimal strategies and to identify evolutionary stable states.

3.1.2 Agent Learning

Agents assess environmental changes after having performed a certain action (ex post analysis). If the gained information is used for future decisions, one speaks of agent learning. The collection of information and knowledge as well as the integration into decision making are performed independently by the agents. This results in a better performance and can be applied to different internal processes such as decision making or planning.

Some algorithms have been developed to transfer natural learning processes into computer science. Widely used are *genetic algorithms (GA)* which were firstly introduced by Holland [1992a]. GA combine certain coded strategies (often bitstrings are used) following rules known from inheritance in biology. Other common algorithms are action-based reinforcement learning, Q-learning and classification systems (cp. Tesfatsion [2002]).

Agent learning is also in the focus of ACE. The level of learning can be distinguished in *central (isolated)* learning and *distributed (interactive or social)* learning (cp. Sen and Weiss [1999]). Centralized learning is an internal process within one single agent, whereas decentralized learning is conducted by a group of agents cooperatively. In a Multi Agent System (MAS) it is possible that one agent takes part in many decentralized learning processes at the same time. Certainly, it is also possible that several agents follow a central learning strategy synchronously. Vriend [2000] presents a study for genetic algorithms learning in a standard Cournot oligopoly on a social and on an isolated basis. The economic output differs in respect to the applied learning level. This study can also serve as an important example for how careful simulation models and agents have to be set up since small changes in the model result in substantial changes in the simulation output.

Besides the learning level, Sen and Weiss [1999, p. 262ff] distinguish six characteristics of learning processes, namely *(i) degree of decentralization, (ii) characteristics of interaction, (iii) involvement, (iv) goal specific characteristics, (v) learning method*, and *(vi) existence of feedback*.

The degree of decentralization refers to the before mentioned isolated and distributed learning. Frequency of interaction or distinct patterns of interaction are examples for characterising an interaction. The degree of involvement depends on the relevance of involvement (how much did the agent contribute to reaching the learning goal) and the role played during involvement (generalist that performs all learning activities versus specialist that contributes to specific activities). Goal specific characteristics refer to the way of improvement to reach the goal. Learning methods differ *(i) in the way, the learning is applied*, e.g. learning from examples, by analogy, or by supervision, and *(ii) in the amount of necessary repetitions*. The feedback is an indicator for the achieved level of performance and can be distinguished in *supervised* learning, *reinforcement* learning and *unsupervised* learning. Agents in supervised learning should reach a goal in the most accurate way. The feedback specifies the performed action of the learning agent and can be understood as a kind of teacher. This kind of learning is not so much used in simulations so far. Reinforcement learning rates the utility of the present action and tries to maximize utility. Unsupervised learning works without direct feedback on a trial-and-error basis. In general, feedback can be received indirectly through other agents or by observing changes in the environment. The application of learning for ACE is further discussed in Chapter 4. Specific learning methods are also presented in that chapter.

Learning mechanisms are one important component of agents' internal decision making processes. Generally, the question arises, how an agent is built and organized. The next section introduces one common agent architecture.

3.1.3 Agent Architecture

This section describes the organization of an agent according to Wooldridge [1999]. The agent architecture describes the conceptual design of agents. Agents are embedded in an environment that is characterized by its state at a distinct point in time. Consequently, the environment can be described by a set of states $S = \{s_1, s_2, \ldots\}$. Agents influence the environment's state through their actions. Each agent can choose an action out of a set of alternative actions $A = \{a_1, a_2, \ldots\}$ dependent on the environmental state. Thus, an agent is characterized by mapping sequences of environmental states S^* to actions A as function $action : S^* \rightarrow A$.

The sets S, A and the function *action* describe a standard agent.

The changes in the environmental states are dependent on the agents' action and can be characterized by a function $env : S \times A \to \varphi(S)$ that maps the possible state transitions from state s_i choosing action a_i:

$$(s_i, a_i) \to env(s_i, a_i) \qquad (3.1)$$

In a deterministic environment a certain action results in a distinct environmental state. The function $env(s_i, a_i)$ of state action pairs are sets consisting of single elements.

Reactive agents are described by functions *action* : $S \to A$. Each reactive agent can be transformed into a corresponding standard agent, but not vice versa.

Agents do not know environmental states, instead they have a perception P of environmental states S. The function *see* : $S \to P$ maps environmental states S to the set of perception P. Therefore, agents can have the same perception of different environmental states, leading to: $s_1 \neq s_2$, but $see(s_1) = see(s_2)$ and $s_1 \equiv s_2$. The equivalence relation $\equiv$ divides the set of environmental states S into distinguishable and non-distinguishable sets. An agent has perfect perception if the number of distinguishable perceptions equals the number of environmental states: $|\equiv| = |S|$. On the other hand if there is no distinguishable perception, the set of distinguishable perception has size one: ($|\equiv| = 1$).

The last section presented work on intelligent agents. Normally, for simulation purposes many agents are used. A system with more than one agent is called Multi Agent System. The following subsection gives an introduction to Multi Agent Systems.

3.2 Multi Agent Systems

Two or more software agents acting in one system constitute a *Multi Agent System (MAS)* (cp. Huhns and Stephens [1999]). At present MASs are part of numerous research projects. In the mid 1970s the research area *Distributed Artificial Intelligence (DAI)* evolved with the subareas *MAS* and *Distributed Problem Solving Systems (DPSS)*. Agents in MAS coordinate knowledge and activities and reason about the coordination process. DPSS subdivide certain problems and distribute the subtasks to various nodes (agents) sharing the knowledge about the problem. The modern concept of MAS includes both described components. Thus, nowadays MAS is used as a synonym for DAI.

Agents exist and act in a physical (real) or computer based (virtual) environment which can be characterized by certain attributes. The environment together with the agents comprise a MAS. If agents can join or leave the system at any time, the system is called *open*. In closed systems the maximum number of agents is fix from the beginning. Weiss [1999, p. 4] gives an overview of possible attributes characterizing MAS in Table 3.1. These attributes are helpful for the model classification in ACE.

	attribute	range
	number	≥ 2
	uniformity	homogeneous ... heterogeneous
agents	goals	contradicting ... complementary
	architecture	reactive ... deliberative
	abilities (sensors, effectors, cognition)	simple ... advanced
	frequency	low ... high
	persistence	short-term ... long-term
interaction	level	signal-passing ... knowledge-intensive
	pattern (flow of data and control)	decentralized ... hierarchical
	variability	fixed ... changeable
	purpose	competitive ... cooperative
	predictability	foreseeable ... unforeseeable
	accessibility	unlimited ... limited
environment	dynamics	fixed ... variable
	diversity	poor ... rich
	availability of resources	restricted ... ample

Table 3.1: Characteristic attributes of Multi-Agent Systems (MAS), source: Weiss [1999, p. 4]

Basic characteristics for the intelligence of agents are their ability of proactive and reactive behaviour within the environment. A single agent cannot develop intelligent behaviour from scratch. It is the interaction with the environment that enables agents to learn and adapt. On the one hand, the intelligent behaviour of *single agents*, and on the other hand, the development of intelligence *within the population* is of interest. In market based simulation, it is also the group behaviour, which is in the focus of the research. But for interaction and common problem solving agents need to communicate and to coordinate their actions. Hereby, in the process of information exchange, it is to differentiate between *interaction* and *communication*. Huhns and Stephens [1999] understand communication as the simple information exchange and internal processing, whereas interaction structures the communication process and therefore, enables a conversation through communication. Consequently, a conversation consists of a sequence of message exchange processes (communication). This sequence is specified by a *Conversation Policy (CP)* that can be expressed through Petri-Nets. The following sections explain the aspects of communication and interaction, coordination, cooperation and negotiation in MAS.

3.2.1   Communication and Interaction in Multi-Agent Systems

Interaction enables agents to influence each other, to coordinate tasks, to simple exchange information, or to negotiate. Communication is one of the fundamental problems in the development of MAS. In principle, there are two possibilities of influencing each other. Firstly, agents can gather information from sensors or by observing other agents' actions. They can draw conclusions from these observations and can influence others indirectly by their own actions. Secondly, the more obvious possibility of influencing each other is by direct communication. *Agent Communication Languages (ACL)* have been developed to facilitate agent interaction. These ACLs lie one logical layer above the transport protocols TCP/IP and serve for communication on social and intentional level. Therefore, particular parameters are defined that specify the message content or determine parameters for interpretation such as the ontology (cp. Dignum and Greaves [2000]). Ontologies taxonomically describe objects, concepts and relations and thus, provide the basis for understanding. This enables knowledge and information exchange between agents (cp. Huhns and Stephens [1999, p. 94]). An explicit and precise description of the syntax, semantic and practical use is essential for open systems and for the understanding of third parties. Unique and general languages constructed with consistent and logic semantics are, on the one hand, very expressive, and on the other hand need comprehensive deductive mechanisms. Such ACLs are particularly important for heterogeneous MAS (cp. Dignum and Greaves [2000]). The use of a standard ACL in ACE facilitates the extensibility and ease of understanding for other researchers.

The *Knowledge Query and Manipulation Language (KQML)* was developed by the *DARPA*[5] *Knowledge Sharing Effort (KSE)* as the first ACL. It was used for information exchange between knowledge based systems and for communication between agents. KQML is a widely used ACL. *FIPA-ACL* was developed by the *Foundation for Intelligent Physical Agents (FIPA)* and replaces the variety of KQML dialects. The FIPA-ACL includes a precise semantic model.

Agent theory describes the agent's available action alternatives, its concluding behaviour, and its planning and goal oriented strategies in a formal model. An ACL is supposed to provide a relationship between this agent theory model and the semantic model. Both, KQML and FIPA-ACL, provide a simplified model of natural language and therefore close this gap.

The most problematic assumption for semantic models of ACLs is that agents do not communicate any fact which they do not believe themselves. This assumption is not always true. Agents might communicate wrong information to mislead opponents and to draw advantage of that situation. It is also possible that there are situations, where the used ACL is not powerful enough to express a statement or where communication difficulties arise due to defective communication, e.g. messages arriving in wrong order.

Communication is the fundament for interaction of agents. But to achieve common goals, agents also need to coordinate their actions. The following section describes the coordination issue in more detail.

---

[5] The Defense Advanced Research Projects Agency (DARPA) is an organization of the United States Department of Defense managing and directing selected research and development activities. More information is found on: http://www.darpa.mil/

3.2.2   Coordination in Multi Agent Systems

Agents need to coordinate their actions for smooth operation of a MAS. Markets are known as coordination mechanism. For simulation and agent-based application of markets, agents need to understand this coordination mechanism. Thus, agents need to consider not only their own action alternatives but also the anticipated actions of other agents (cp. Jennings [1996]).

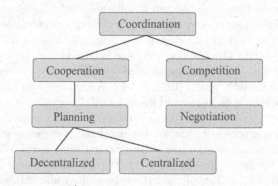

Figure 3.3: Taxonomy for Coordination, source: Huhns and Stephens [1999, p. 83]

There are various reasons for coordination, e.g. dependence on particular actions, common frameworks or lack of information as well as different knowledge. The coordination process turns out to be different dependent on the environment and the will for participation and integration of the agents. Negotiations are one adequate mean for coordination in a competitive environment where agents have rival goals. In contrast, agents use cooperation in an environment where they follow common goals. Figure 3.3 shows different coordination mechanisms. It is to be noticed that these alternatives are not compulsory, since coordination can also take place without (direct) communication, e.g. if agents know the behavioural model of other agents and thus, are able to interpret actions (cp. Nwana et al. [1996], Huhns and Singh [1994]).

Besides cooperation and negotiation models, various approaches for agent coordination exist. One example is *Organizational structuring* where the structure of the organization is analysed in advance and a *Master Agent* breaks down the task into small jobs carried out by *slaves*. Alternatively, the master agent serves as information exchange platform.

Cooperation

If two or more agents are working together to reach a common goal or to achieve advantage for all participants, this is defined as cooperation [Doran et al., 1997]. Agents build a road map for cooperation and need to harmonize this plan with other agents. Principally, cooperation is possible through centralized or decentralized organization. In centralized planning, a coordination agent collects all individual plans of the other agents, reviews these plans and checks for inconsistencies or conflicts. In the next step the central agent modifies and adapts the plans and put the plans together to an overall cooperation plan. In decentralized planning, each agent possess a model of the other agents' plan. Agents work together to improve the individual plans [Nwana et al., 1996]. In both cases, centralized and decentralized planning, agents need to exchange messages to coordinate the individual plans. The content meaning of these messages must be unambiguous. Consequently, coordination primitives are introduced according to the *Speech Act Theory* [Haugeneder and Steiner, 1998, Searle, 1969]. These coordination primitives consist of types and objects where types specify the nature of the message (e.g. inform, request, query, deny). The message object specifies the goal, the plan or the task to be performed. The definition of these primitives is determined within the ACL.

The information processing is a problem in both approaches, decentralised and centralised. A problem in a decentralized approach is the amount of shared information through message exchange. These messages must be processed and result in increasing information traffic. Central approaches are less complex than decentralized approaches, but since all information flows to the central agent, the information processing at the central agent might become a bottleneck.

Competition

In competitive MAS, agents pursue different goals that are either dependent on each other, or concurrent. To reach the individual goal, coordination is necessary. Buyers and sellers in a market have different interests, since sellers want to gain high profits and buyers want to spend as little money as possible. Therefore, agents need to negotiate to reach an agreement. Auctions are one way of negotiations. For reasonable negotiations, agents need to be capable of considering both, their own beliefs and desires as well as intentions about others. Nwana et al. [1996] discuss three negotiation models: (1) game theoretical negotiation, (2) plan-based negotiation, and (3) negotiation approaches according to human negotiations using certain artificial intelligence techniques.

The game theoretical approach dates back to Rosenschein [1985]. Agents are allowed to submit proposals and counter-proposals to maximize their utility. This process is organized by a negotiation protocol. Each action has a certain utility which is determined by a reward function known by both negotiation partners. This is also the central point of criticism, since the rewards and utilities of rivals are often unknown in reality. Rosenschein even analyses games with two agents that posses the same internal model. He was able to contribute results about false information and its positive influence on the negotiation result.

In plan-based negotiations, agents firstly develop separate plans and coordinate them in a second step. The coordination proceeds in the same way as the centralized and decentralized cooperation described earlier in section 3.2.2. Consequently, it has the same advantages and disadvantages as in the described approach.

Additional approaches were developed according to human negotiation processes which usually consist of many stages. Nwana et al. [1996] refer to an approach developed by Bussmann and Müller [1992] which is based on a simple but common cyclic negotiation model. The process starts with proposals of one or more agents. These proposals are reviewed by the participants in the next step and matched with the own preferences. Subsequently, agents inform the other participants about agreed points and not matched criteria. Each agent updates his knowledge about the others preferences. The process repeats with new proposals considering the received information. Conflicts are solved separately.

Having introduced the basic agent concepts, the following sections briefly introduce in the methodology of simulations.

3.3 Building Multi Agent-based Simulation Models

In general, simulation in economics does not differ from simulation in other fields. It is understood as a particular type of modelling the real world or other systems [Gilbert and Troitzsch, 2005]. Simulations are an intuition of real world processes over time [Banks, 1998] and support the study of these systems. Therefore, simulation models represent real world systems in a less detailed and less complex way, described by input and output variables and certain system states. An artificial history of the system is generated during the course of the simulation. This artificial history is used for observation and to draw inferences concerning the objective of the study. Gilbert and Troitzsch [2005] understand simulations as a method for theory development, since a specific theory can be studied within a simulation and the results are used to refine theory. This process is also depicted in Figure 3.4.

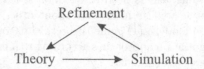

Figure 3.4: Simulation for theory development

1. **Benefits of simulation**

   The advantage of simulations compared to other research methods is primarily the fact that the simulation designer is in control of any parameter to adapt to problem specific circumstances. This allows for both, normative and descriptive studies. A well designed simulation system can help to understand and explain real world systems and to describe certain observed phenomena by comparing different simulation settings. Descriptive application of simulation can especially be used for teaching and training. Additionally, normative studies can be conducted by changing a particular parameter and studying the consequences for the system's development and its output. This helps to diagnose systems. The simulation speed can be varied (in fact this allows to compress/expand time) which enables the study of slow motion activities as well as the study of long periods of time. In comparison to other research methods such as experiments or surveys, simulations are less expensive, because no expenses for resource acquisition or for the reward payments in experiments are necessary.

Agent-based simulations in particular provide some additional advantages. Axtell [2000] remarks that agents allow for modelling heterogeneous behaviour and to limit rationality. This is not possible in mathematical theorizing.

2. **Difficulties of simulation**
   On the other hand, simulation face divers problems. It is difficult to build appropriate models which accurately represent the real systems. Therefore, it is essential to prove the correctness of the simulation model. In some cases it is difficult to identify mistakes in a simulation model. Wrong conclusions are drawn (from incorrect simulation models) and are taken for granted. Thus, the quality and the correctness of simulation results is a sensitive issue. The development of good models is often not only difficult but also time consuming. It may also be difficult to interpret the collected data.

Concluding can be stated that simulations are helpful for certain problems but are not the one-size-fits-all solution. In the following, a classification of simulation models is presented as well as a methodological overview.

3.3.1 Characteristics of Simulations

Simulations can be classified by different characteristics. Law and Kelton [2000] differentiate simulation models along three dimensions: *(1) discrete versus continuous, (2) static versus dynamic*, and *(3) deterministic versus stochastic*.

The state variables change either discrete or continuous in respect to time. In economic systems markets with a continuous order flow can be seen as continuous systems, whereas markets with matching at certain points of time are discrete systems.

Static simulation models represent systems at a particular time or compute solution for systems where time plays no role (e.g. the computation of complex utility functions/optima). These are often statistical models in which the magnitude of parameters is estimated through simulation. In contrast, dynamic systems evolve over time such as the simulation of stock markets.

Deterministic systems contain no stochastic data or process. The most simulation models are discrete, dynamic, and stochastic models. These type of models are called *discrete-event simulation models*.

Gilbert and Troitzsch [2005] give a good explanation for the logic of simulation that is also depicted in Figure 3.5. Gilbert and Troitzsch distinguish *statistical* and *simulation* models, which are both abstraction of the real system. Statistical

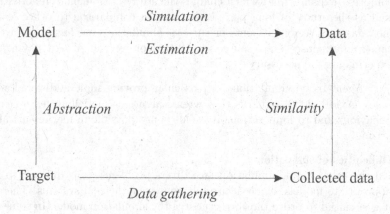

Figure 3.5: The logic and use of (statistical) models, estimation and simulation; source: Gilbert and Troitzsch [2005, p. 16f]

models often consist of a set of equations, whereas simulation models are either implemented as software or as physical systems. It is assumed that data of the real system can be collected at least partly and then compared to the estimated data in a statistical model to find similarities, or to calibrate the simulation model to data of the real system. Statistical models are used to find predictors for the parameters, to measure their magnitude and to explain correlations between parameters and thus, provide a static view on the model. Complementary, simulation models are implemented to understand, explain and/or predict processes, and thus, deliver a dynamic view on the system.

3.3.2 Developing and Applying Simulations

Building simulation models and conducting simulations follows an intuitive structured approach (see e.g. Banks [1998], Gilbert and Troitzsch [2005]) that is also applicable to agent-based models. In the following the steps toward an agent-based simulation are explained in more detail.

(1) **Problem definition**
    The first step is to define the problem and to determine the *target* system of the study. In order to prepare for building the model, it is necessary to consider if simulation is a reasonable approach for the defined problem and

to assess to which extend the simulation is able to contribute to the problem's solution? Hence, the target system is observed and analysed to identify characteristic parameters and initial conditions and states. If possible, it is useful to gather data from the real system which can be used later in the simulation development for calibration of the model.

(2) **Model conceptualization**

The developed problem and system description help to construct a conceptual model. Gilbert and Troitzsch [2005] suggest to start with the decision on the underlying theory of the simulation approach. This serves as a starting point for literature review and the formalization of the simulation model. Thus, it is necessary to make assumption and to determine the system's states. For agent-based simulations it is necessary to determine *(i) agents and their behaviour, (ii) the environment,* and *(iii) dynamic components* such as the agents' actions and environmental changes.

Regarding the agents, it has to be defined which internal states an agent consists of and how the agent perceives its environment. These states together with the agent's set of possible actions determine the agent's type.

The environmental states are to be defined (e.g. time steps, rounds, amount of agents, open vs. closed, geographic details, communication constraints). An overview on environmental characteristics was provided in Section 3.2.

Having defined agents and environment, the factors are identified that influence changes in the model's states. This includes agents' actions, the agents' interaction amongst each other (agent-agent) and with the environment (both, agent-environment and environment-agent), or external factors affecting the environment.

These identified components build the model that might be very detailed. Axelrod [2003, p. 4] argues to consider the complexity of the model. The simpler the model the easier it is to understand and explain its output. Therefore, most simulations follow the KISS principle (Keep It Simple Stupid) or as Einstein formulated: *"Keep the model as simple as possible, but not simpler."* But the consideration of simplicity versus accuracy depends on the purpose of the simulation. In order to explain and understand certain effects, it is helpful to keep the model simple, whereas for prediction or training it is necessary to build an accurate model. Figure 3.6 depicts this issue. The model should be easy to understand and to interpret, which facilitates the understanding and the comparison to other models.

(3) **Simulation model implementation**

Having developed the conceptual model, it has to be translated into a system model. The simulation model design itself is a four step process consisting of *(i) implementation, (ii) verification, (iii) validation,* and *(iv) sensitivity analysis.*

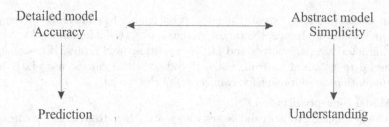

Figure 3.6: The level of abstraction/simplicity vs. level of detail/accuracy in a simulation model

For the implementation, one has to decide either to use an existing simulation tool or to implement the model using a common programming language. This depends on the models requirements. Gilbert and Troitzsch [2005] determine some requirements for the programming language or the simulation tool respectively: There is need for well-structured implementation and incremental refinement, as well as easy and rapid debugging. Most simulation need to handle huge amounts of data while running as efficiently as possible. Some of these requirements are contradictory, thus, the trade-off is simulation dependent.

Once a model is implemented it needs to be verified. This means testing the model if it works in the way as it was conceptually formalized. Unit tests are an appropriate approach for verification of single software components. Therefore, test programs are written that use specific input that produces a known output. Input/output analysis can also be applied to the simulation model as a whole. The output of the simulation can be compared to the expected output for verification.

In the next step, the verified model is validated against real world data, to prove that the computer model is eligible to represent the real world system. The validation has to be carefully applied, since there are some pitfalls to consider (cp.Gilbert and Troitzsch [2005]): The real system and the model might be subject to some stochastic process, which makes it difficult to produce the same results. It is also possible that the simulation is path-dependent, meaning that the outcome depends on the precise initial condition. Sometimes the simulation results match the real data just occasionally, although the model is not appropriate or vice versa (the model is appropriate but the real data is incorrect). If the model is too simple the simulation results cannot be mapped to the real system data. Figure 3.7 illustrates the steps of the model implementation.

After comparing the model to the real system behaviour, sensitivity tests can be performed. This is an important step in order to calibrate the

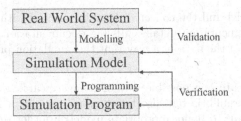

Figure 3.7: The development of simulation models; source: Vincent [1998, p. 56]

model and to understand the model's behaviour. Sensitivity analysis measures the impact of changes in parameter values on the model's output.

(4) **Conduct simulation and evaluate results**
If the model is set up appropriately, the simulation settings are defined and one can start to run the simulation. In many simulations, stochastic processes have an impact on the simulation results. Stochastic processes are introduced either to represent real world random processes, or to integrate processes that are not being modelled explicitly.[6] In that cases it is necessary to repeat the simulations to generate an appropriate data basis for the evaluation and in order to observe the model's behaviour under several conditions [Gilbert and Troitzsch, 2005]. The simulation data of one simulation run is biased, since the parameters depend on each other. The data from a replicated simulation run with different initial values is independent from the first simulation run. These independent replications are the basis for further evaluation using statistical methods that assume independent and identically distributed data (iid).

The generated simulation data is evaluated applying statistical and mathematical software packages. The standard methods also applied in experimental research can be used. This includes both, descriptive statistics and inductive methods, such as variance, regression analysis and hypothesis tests.

(5) **Making results public**
Axelrod [2003] points out that the publication of the results is often neglected. There is no common agreed upon standard for the publication of simulation results. Simulations and their results are only useful for scientific research if the work is published assiduously, meaning that the reader must be able to reproduce the simulation. This is an important issue, since there are often ambiguities or lacks in the description, which make the replication of the simulation impossible. Therefore, a comprehensive documentation of

---

[6]Gilbert and Troitzsch [2005] note that stochastic processes are used for guessing/estimating parameter values in absence of more accurate information.

both, the model and the collected data, is essential without going to much
into the implementation details. Missing documentation opens the door to
manipulation of the data in a way that the simulation produces the desired
outcome.

Simulation models are one possible way of doing research that allow scientists
to study not only equilibria but also the dynamic process of interacting components. It is important to build appropriate models in order to obtain interesting
and meaningful results. The robustness of the model play an important role for
the quality of the results. Single simulation runs do not contribute to assess the
robustness of a model. The presented approach supports the building of simulation models. Nevertheless, it is important to carefully develop a simulation model.
Multi Agent-based Simulation (MABS) enables the modelling of rationality and
bounded rationality. In economics it is often assumed that economic agents act
completely rational. In reality it is observed that this is not the case, since humans
are also influenced by social and cultural norms, wrong or missing information.
The interaction of different behaviours can be studied with the help of MABS.

3.4   Summary

In this chapter, the theory of Agent-based Computational Economics was introduced. In contrast to classic approaches like General Equilibrium Theory that analyse aggregated supply and demand, agent-based approaches build models from the
bottom up. Thereby, characteristic market participants are modelled as software
agents that interact with each other. Individual and bounded rational behaviour
can be integrated in the model. The study of markets as evolving and dynamic
systems of agents gives insight into market research from a new perspective.

Section 3 not only presented basic work on software agents and Multi Agent
Systems, but also provided an introduction to simulation theory. In order to conduct research using simulation, it is necessary to build appropriate models and to
consider some basic rules. A guide for model building and fundamental rules for
simulations were described.

Part II

Agent-based Simulation
Approaches and Tools

Chapter 4

Methodological Approaches of MABS in Economics

One of the most difficult problems in the development of simulation models is to decide which methodological approach to follow. There is a variety of methods available such as system dynamics, queuing models, agent-based simulation, or stochastic models. Just a few of these will produce appropriate results applied on a specific problem. The use of simulations in economics has rapidly grown in the last years and some work was done on the question of how to apply certain methods (e.g. Gilbert and Troitzsch [2005]). Agent-based simulation is one of these approaches that itself provides several mechanisms such as genetic algorithms, stochastic components, or other evolutionary techniques. Thus, the decision on which method to apply has to be posed on this level.

In the last years more and more effort has been made to link agent-based simulation approaches to economic research. Economist are still suspicious of agent-based simulation approaches, since the simulation model's underlying theory is often not linked to existing economic theory. Agent-based economics researchers have started to close this gap, although there are still open issues.

To the authors knowledge, there is no summary on possible agent-based simulation techniques and the existing link to economic theory. Since such an overview on the one hand facilitates the work of agent-based economics researchers, and on the other hand makes ACE more credible among economists, this chapter presents the main agent-based modelling techniques and summarises literature on bridging the gap to economic theory. Axtell [2000] presented a valuable analysis of the use of agent-based simulation in respect to the solvability of the underlying theoretic model. He argues that there are three distinct alternatives for the usage of agent-based techniques:

(i) *fully solvable models,*

(ii) *partially solvable models,* and

(iii) *insolvable models.*

In the first class of models (i), agent-based simulations are applied to models that are completely solvable. In this case simulations serve for model validation, exemplification of the solution, or for application of stochastic simulations. For example, it is often the case that solutions to mathematical models are only found in numerical form. If there are numerical samples available, an agent-based model can be applied to validate the results.

In those cases in which there are not only a numerical but a solution in closed form,[1] simulations can be applied to better present the solution or to study the dynamics of the model.

Many models are based on stochastic functions, e.g. the output of the model is dependent on stochastic input. The functional relation between input and output may be determinable. In such cases stochastic sampling on basis of agent-based simulations can be applied that randomly draws input values in order to determine the output. Stochastic sampling in general is known as "*Monte Carlo simulation*" and a common approach in science.

In many cases it is only possible to partially solve a mathematical model (ii), e.g. if the solution is only possible under restrict assumptions that make the results ambiguous, or if the model can not be solved. In such cases agent-based simulation can be applied complementary to mathematical theorizing. Axtell [2000] remarks that it has to be distinguished between simulation as instantiation of a mathematical model and simulation as supplement to mathematical models. The former case is equivalent to (i). In order to simplify such complex models, assumptions are necessary. Agent-based models allow to relax such assumptions since heterogeneous agents can be implemented. This makes it possible, firstly to apply agents in simple models that are restricted by many assumptions and validate the outcome with the partly available solutions, or numerical results. In a second stage, the assumptions can be relaxed and the (same) agents can act in the more complex environment. This facilitates a structured analysis of the model.

Insolvable models (iii) are rarely analysed in scientific papers since they do not bear new insights in a given problem. Nevertheless, agent-based simulation might be a starting point in order to better understand models that are not mathematical solvable.

The described classification has a problem-oriented character, giving more insight to the question *which* problem/model is handled in agent-approaches. As

---

[1]The term *closed form* denominates mathematical solutions of functions or equations in a general and explicit form with a finite amount of operations. That is, e.g. the integral of a function such as $F(x) = \int f(x) = x^2 + cx + 1 dx$ can be generally solved. Sometimes it is only possible to provide an approximation for an integral and compute numerical examples. Such solutions are not considered "closed form".

argued earlier, there is also need for a method-oriented view on agent-based simulation, answering the question *how* to apply agent-based simulation and *which* techniques to use. There are different techniques applied in agent-based simulation. The four most popular approaches that are found in literature are *pure agent-based simulation, Monte Carlo techniques, evolutionary (genetic) approaches*, and *reinforcement learning techniques*. The first approach builds agent societies on basis of simple rules. Monte Carlo simulations are used either to sample complex models or to model stochastic processes, e.g. not deterministic behaviour. The main criticism agent-based simulation is exposed to, is the insufficient theoretic basis. In recent years, it was started to link agent-based approaches to well founded theory. Evolutionary mechanisms according to biological studies have been widely used to model evolving systems. Today, evolutionary techniques are applied according to well founded game theoretic approaches as evolutionary game theory. Besides evolutionary mechanisms, it is popular to apply reinforcement learning methods that are related to Markov theory and stochastic games.

Certainly, it is not possible to provide an unambiguous classification, since the discussed approaches can also be combined. Nevertheless, it is essential to present the four mainly applied techniques and related theory. Therefore, the following sections summarize these four methods. Since the economic analysis conducted in Part III of this work applies a reinforcement approach, reinforcement learning and Markov games are presented in more detail in Section 4.4.

4.1   Pure Agent-based Simulation: The Bottom-up Approach

The basic idea of agent-based simulation approaches is to build simple models of a real world system in which agents interact on basis of social rules. It was the 2005 Nobel prize laureate Thomas Schelling who introduced one of the first agent models in order to explain cultural segregation in American housing areas [Schelling, 1969]. He studies spatial arrangements where agents of different characteristics prefer to live in a neighbourhood of a certain characteristic, e.g. the colour of the neighbours. Agents have preferences that at least a particular fraction of the neighbourhood has their own colour. Changing these preferences certainly leads to different compositions of the neighbourhood.

In what is denominated the pure agent-based approach, the model consists of several agents, the environment the agents act in, and interaction rules. These interaction rules are fixed for the agent, meaning that the agents' action sets are not changed, as it is the case if using learning mechanisms such as reinforcement learning or genetic algorithms. Bonabeau [2002, p. 7280] presents a very simple but striking example that explains the model dynamics by changing fixed interaction rules:

In a group of 10-40 agents each agent is assigned a protector and an opponent randomly and secretly. Each agent tries to hide from the opponent behind the protector. This simple rule will result in a highly dynamic system of agents moving around in a seemingly random fashion. Changing the rule in such a way that the agents have to place themselves between opponent and protector, the system will end up in everyone clustering in a tight knot.

This example shows how simple rules result in complex dynamic systems. Epstein and Axtell [1996] incrementally developed Sugarscape, a model of a growing artificial society that received much attention in the agent-based research community. Agents are born into a spatial distribution, the Sugarscape. Agents have to eat sugar in order to survive and thus, move around on the landscape to find sugar. Starting with simple movement rules, more and more social rules like sexual reproduction, death, conflicts, history, diseases, and finally trade are introduced. This results in a quite complex society that allows to study several social and economic aspects.

As a last example may serve the computational market model of Steiglitz et al. [1996] that builds a small society of agents that can either produce food or gold. Each agent needs food for survival and is equipped with a certain skill level of producing gold or food. Food can be traded for gold. In such a simple model, agents switch from producing food to gold or vice versa if the exchange rate passes their individual level from which on it is more lucrative for them to produce the other product. This results in a cyclic trade behaviour with large amplitudes of volume and price. When adding speculators, agents that have the capabilities of storing gold and food, the price stabilises significantly.

The described examples give an introduction of how to use agent models in their simplest form. It is difficult to analyse the described models analytically. These models use the normative effect of agent simulation by controlling and adding particular rules and their impact on the model's behaviour. Often, economists are interested not only in the dynamics of model, but also in stability. Economists want to discover equilibria states and optimal strategies that lead to equilibrium. Pure agent models are not well suited for finding new strategies. This is why, learning techniques or stochastic components have to be used. Such approaches are introduced in the next sections.

4.2 Monte Carlo Simulation

In general, the term *Monte Carlo (MC)* denotes methods for mathematical experiments using random numbers. Monte Carlo methods became known explicitly in the *Manhatten Project* developing the nuclear bomb during the second world war. The research group around John von Neumann namely the researchers Ulam, Metropolis and Fermi developed this method and applied random number experiments. The name *Monte Carlo* is ascribed to Metropolis who alludes to Ulam's passion for poker by referring to the famous casino of Monte Carlo. A first article to stochastic experiments and the title *The Monte Carlo Method* was published by Metropolis and Ulam in 1949 [Metropolis and Ulam, 1949]. In fact, stochastic processes for experiments are known from earlier years,[2] but the method was systematically developed primary in the late fourties of the 20th century by Ulam, Fermi, von Neumann and Metropolis, and thus, was available for application in manifold scientific fields since then.

The problems studied by Monte Carlo methods can be distinguished in *probabilistic* and *deterministic* problems [Hammersley and Handscomb, 1964]. Probabilistic problems determine cases where random variables are used to model real stochastic processes, e.g. in queuing theory. One speaks of deterministic Monte Carlo cases if formal theoretical models exist that are not possible or hard to solve numerically. In these cases, the Monte Carlo method helps to find solutions applying random numbers, e.g. in computing the number π.[3] In the social science, the Monte Carlo method is applied to different problem structures. In *Operations Research (OR)* probability distributions are used within models, e.g. in queuing theory. In other fields, e.g. in finance, stochastic processes are used to simulate order flows in stock markets.

In agent-based simulation, Monte Carlo methods are used for both, probabilistic and deterministic, models. In most of the agent-based simulation models, probabilistic MC-methods are applied, e.g. to assign valuations to agents, or to simulate noise. A well known example is the contribution of Gode and Sunder [1993] in which a double auction market is simulated by agents with zero intelligence. Instead of implementing fixed strategies, agents in this market draw their bid value from uniform distributions regardless of true valuation. This strategy is used to represent bounded rational agents.

Cai and Wurman [2005] apply a deterministic MC approach to sequential, (possibly) multi-unit, sealed-bid auctions. The agents sample the valuation space of the opponents and solves the incomplete information game that results of the sample. The results of the samples are aggregated in a policy. This approach is used since the "straightforward expansion of the game is intractable even for very small problems and it is beyond the capability of the current algorithms to solve for the Bayes-Nash equilibria" [Cai and Wurman, 2005, p. 154]. As explained earlier, it is an appropriate approach to use stochastic sampling if the problem is hard, or not possible to solve.

The next section introduces into evolutionary approaches for agent-based simulation.

---

[2]Hammersley and Handscomb [1964] refer to work by Hall [1873] that describes the computation of π by means of random processes.

[3]A needle of length l can be dropped on a board with parallel lines of distance l. Then the number of trials N and the number of areas R in which the needle has dropped are counted. Hence, π can be computed as $\pi = 2l^2 N/R$

4.3   Evolutionary Approach

Starting in 1975, John Holland was the first who transferred the idea of biological genetic evolution to artificial adaptive systems [Holland, 1992a]. In biology, the genotype is stored on chromosomes that are combined during reproduction. The biological improvement mechanisms are used in computer science as search technique. Genetic algorithms (GA) have become popular for economic simulations in order to model learning of economic agents.

Basically, actions or a sequence of actions are assigned values, e.g. performance, utility, payoff, etc. The actions are genetically encoded as strategies, e.g. in string or binary representation. This chromosome representations builds the genetic strategy set. A subset of the strategy set forms a *population*, also called *generation*. Each strategy of a population is assigned a value, also called fitness, representing how good the strategy performed in the past. At each time playing one strategy out of the pool of one generation the strategy earns a reward that serves as feedback for the performance of this particular strategy. The fitness is adapted according to the reward. Some strategies will perform better than others. After a sufficient amount of repetitions, the population starts reproduction by replication (selection), recombination (crossover) and mutation to produce a new generation of strategies.

As such, GA builds beliefs for rules in response to experience. The frequency of representation in a population and the fitness of a given strategy indicate the performance of that strategy. In order to determine optimal strategies, it is necessary to search the strategy set. This is done by manipulating the population with the three basic genetic modification mechanisms: selection, crossover, and mutation. Selection simply means that the strongest strategies of a population in terms of fitness are identically reproduced into the next generation. During crossover, two chromosomes are drawn out of the population and split at a randomly drawn position. Than the chromosome parts are recombined with the ones of the other chromosome. The crossover operator is also understood as an innovation mechanism. Mutation is an operator that randomly manipulates a single bit or character of the chromosome. This is also understood as an operator for experimentation.

GA have been widely used for simulating adaptive and bounded rational agents in economics. An early application was described in Miller [1986], and Axelrod [1987] who applied GA to the prisoner's dilemma, and Andreoni and Miller [1990] simulated auctions under human like behaviour. Holland and Miller [1991] give a brief overview on artificial adaptive agents in economic theory. Arifovic [1994] remarks that one of the basic questions in applying GA to economic problems is how well suited GA are to discover Nash equilibria and to model individual and social learning.

Game theory studies strategic situations of agents assuming fully rational agents. The analysis of such models is often difficult or impossible. Agent-based simulation using GA models the economy as bounded rational agents that try to adapt to their environment. Bringing together both views is an important step towards a better understanding of the economy. Kirman [2004] argues for a middle way of pure agent theory and game theory. Advances in this direction have been made, e.g. by Marimon [1993] who compares evolutionary processes with learning models, or by Riechmann [2002] who compares evolutionary game theory and GA learning. The latter author is able to show links between GA and evolutionary game theory, i.e. GA can be understood as "a specific form of a repeated evolutionary game" Riechmann [2002, p. 58]. The game theoretic concepts of evolutionary stable states and Nash equilibria are applied to GA. Although the analysis is mainly valid for single population GA, the findings are an important step in bridging theoretically well founded game theory approaches to computational evolutionary techniques.

The next chapter introduces in reinforcement learning theory which is also applied in the economic model of this work in Chapter 6.

4.4 Reinforcement Learning

Reinforcement learning (RL) is a goal directed, trial and error learning procedure. According to Kaelbling et al. [1996], RL has relations to cybernetics, statistics, psychology, neuroscience, and computer science. Sutton and Barto [2002, p. 16] allude to the origin from two threads that developed independently. The first thread derives from learning by trial and error inspired by research in psychology. This approach was already pursuit in the early work of artificial intelligence. The second main thread concentrates on the problem of optimal control and its solution through value functions and dynamic programming. The merge of both research branches turns RL into an important research approach that is theoretical well founded from a (human) behavioural point of view as well as on basis of economic theory.

The "Law of Effect" states that it is more likely to choose out of a set of possible actions that action which results in the largest satisfaction [Thorndike, 1898, 1911].[4] Thereby, the largest satisfaction is determined by trial and error and in the course of time the action with the best outcome in the past is chosen. This effect combines the two characteristic and important aspects, search (selection) and memory (association). RL is selectional since it tries alternatives and selects the best one by comparing consequences. It is also associative because the action selection depends on particular states. Erev and Roth [1998] additionally consider the "Power Law of Practice" that was introduced by Blackburn [1936]. The law states that learning at the beginning of the process is more intensive and reduces during the course of time.

---

[4]It was Edward L. Thorndike who studied this effect in animal experiments during the years 1898 to 1911. Catania [1999] remarks that Thorndike has published a couple of articles (Thorndike [1898, 1901, 1907, 1909, 1911]) where he implicitly refers to the law of effect without explicitly defining it. It is the 1907 monograph in which the term is used the first time. This makes it difficult to determine the date of origin for correct citation.

The optimal control branch was initiated among others by Bellman [1957a] for designing a controller that minimizes a measure of a dynamic system's behaviour over time. His approach implements an optimal return function and uses (dynamic) system states. These two factors define the *dynamic programming equation* that is also known as *Bellman equation*[5] for discrete values. The discrete stochastic version of the dynamic control problem became known as Markov Decision Process (MDP) [Bellman, 1957b] that specifies a course of state transitions that are independent from state transitions in the past. Howard [1960] contributed the policy iteration method that was modified by Puterman and Shin [1978], and Puterman [1994]. These contributions are the basis for the RL theory. The idea of MDP links the computer science theory of RL to economic theory of stochastic games as it is shown in Section 4.4.2.

The development of RL from psychology at the one hand, and mathematics on the other hand, turns RL into a qualified foundation for agent-based simulation. It is possible to model human behaviour as e.g. Erev and Roth [1998] have shown. Additionally, the models have a mathematical foundation that can be linked to economic theory. The next section describes the RL mechanism. Section 4.4.2 introduces the link to stochastic game theory.

4.4.1   The Learning Model

Reinforcement learning focuses on goal directed learning of agents in an uncertain and possibly dynamic environment. Agents seek to achieve goals by performing actions that result in (delayed) rewards. The agents can learn from rewards received in the past by assigning the rewards to actions that were performed in a particular state. At the beginning of the learning process, agents do not have preferences for certain actions. Thus, agents proceed by trial and error in order to explore the best action.

The model is characterised by the environment and agents that interact with the environment in order to achieve a particular goal. Agents are not certain about their environment since they do not possess all information. Instead, agents have a perception of the environment that gives an indication about the actual state that consists of environmental and (optionally) agent internal state parameters. Agents face the problem of deciding which action to take in a particular state.

This decision problem is often described as the n-armed bandit problem. A n-armed bandit is also understood as n one-armed bandits.[6] Since the reward is not deterministic it is difficult for the agent to determine an optimal policy. The agent faces the problem of either exploiting the action space by choosing action with high values, or exploring the action space by trying actions with low values. The

---

[5]Bellman's work is based on work of the Irish scientist William Rowan Hamilton (1805-1865) and the German mathematician Carl Gustav Jakob Jacobi (1805-1851). The Hamilton-Jacobi equation is a non-linear differential equation for the description of a system's behaviour.

[6]A one-armed bandit denominates a gambling machine with one arm that can be pulled at specific costs. The one-armed bandit stochastically pays a reward greater or equal to zero.

probability of making a win is equal for all actions regardless of their performance in the past. The decision problem of exploration versus exploitation applies to all reinforcement learning problems.

Reinforcement learning is well-suited to determine an appropriate action-selection mechanism by optimizing the direct feedback from the environment. The agent identifies certain environmental states and maps its perception of these states into particular actions. The tuple (S, A, P, r) describes a set of environmental states S, a set of possible actions A, a probability $P : S \times S \times A \rightarrow [0, 1]$ for the transition from state s_1 to state s_2 by choosing action a, and a scalar reward function (reinforcement) $r : S \times A \rightarrow \mathbb{R}$. The reinforcement is non-deterministic in the most cases, i.e. taking action a in the same state at two different points of time might not result in the same reward and transition.

Each agent holds a policy π that maps the actual state s to the action to be performed. The optimal policy maximises the sum of the expected rewards. The present value of a state is determined as the discounted sum of future rewards received by following some fixed policy π in state s, i.e. $V_\gamma^\pi = E(\sum_{t=0}^{\infty} \gamma^t r_{s,t}^\pi)$. Thereby, $r_{s,t}^\pi$ is the stochastic parameter for the reward r at t time steps after the realization of policy π in state s, using the discount rate γ ($0 \leq \gamma < 1$) (cp. Sen and Weiss [1999, p. 266]).

The value function maps states to state values. It can be approximated by any kind of function approximator such as a look-up table or a multi-layered perceptron. The problem of finding the optimal agent's behaviour is equivalent to finding the optimal value function.

Different methods for models of optimal behaviour have been proposed in literature. Kaelbling et al. [1996] distinguish model-based and model-free approaches that are summarized in Table 4.1. Here, the term "model" consists of knowledge about the probability of the state transitions $P : S \times S \times A \rightarrow [0, 1]$ and about the reinforcement function $r : S \times A \rightarrow \mathbb{R}$. In most economic models the state transition is not known to the agents. One speaks of model-based approach if estimates for the model (P and r) are learned and used to find an optimal policy. In model-free approaches, the optimal policies are learned without building a model. Since Q-learning is the mainly used method for economic models it is explained

Model-based	Model-free
Value Iteration	Adaptive Heuristic Critic (AHC)
Policy Iteration	Q-learning
Modified Policy Iteration	Averaged values

Table 4.1: Reinforcement learning approaches for model-based and model-free settings.

in more detail in the remainder of this section. It was proposed by Watkins [1989] and is an asynchronous dynamic programming approach.

In general, dynamic programming provides algorithms to compute optimal policies in Markov Decision Processes (MDP). Howard [1960] defines MDP by a set of states, a set of actions, and a transition function. A MDP satisfies the Markov property that states that transitions in the actual state are independent from previous states. That is, the history of how a particular state was reached has no impact on the transition probabilities of further states. Reinforcement learning models that satisfy the Markov property are Markov Decision Processes [Sutton and Barto, 2002]. Note that MDP theory assumes a stationary environment, i.e. the probabilities of state transitions or of receiving a specific reward do not change over time.

Q-learning is often used in ACE, since the approach can be linked to Markov games as one branch of game theory. This is the reason for explaining Q-learning in the following in more detail. Markov games are presented in more detail in Section 4.4.2.

Q-learning can be understood as controlled Markov process. Agents control the state transitions by performing actions. For each policy π, an action-value Q is defined that determines the "*expected discounted reward for executing action a at state x and following policy π thereafter*" [Watkins and Dayan, 1992, p. 280]:

$$Q^*(x, a) = R_x(a) + \gamma \sum_y P_{xy}(\pi(x))V^*(y) \qquad (4.1)$$

where γ is the discount factor of future rewards, V^* is the optimal value in state y, P_{xy} is the probability function for the transition from state x to y. Since $V^*(y) = \max_a Q^*(y, a)$, the Q-learning rule can be recursively defined:

$$Q(x, a) = Q(x, a) + \alpha(r + \gamma \max_{a'} Q(x', a') - Q(x, a)) \qquad (4.2)$$

The tuple $\langle x, a, r, x' \rangle$ determines the experienced transition from state x to x' while performing action a and receiving reward r. It can be shown for bounded rewards and learning rates $0 \leq \alpha < 1$ that $Q(x, a) \to Q^*(x, a)$ with probability 1 for an infinite number of repetitions of playing action a in state x [Watkins and Dayan, 1992, p. 282]. Having converged to optimal Q^*, it is optimal for agents to act greedily, i.e. in state s to choose the action with the highest Q-value.

Improvement to this algorithm have been proposed. An important contribution was done by Erev and Roth [1998], who developed a descriptive model for human-like learning behaviour in strategic environments. The reinforcement learning algorithms presented by Erev and Roth can be used for stateless learning. The performance of the Erev-Roth algorithm was tested for models of experimental economics and the result of the simulation was compared to the experimental results of human subjects. It was shown that the computational results were similar to the experimental results.

The basic difference to Q-learning is in the action selection. The Q-learning algorithms applies an exploration rate in order to assure the exploration of certain actions. Therefore, the agents decides arbitrarily whether to explore or to exploit. During exploitation the action with maximum Q-value is chosen. The Erev-Roth algorithm introduces propensities in action selection. A propensity q_{nk} to choose a particular action k is assigned to each possible action k of agent n. This propensity is adjusted in respect to the achieved result (reward). The probability $p_{nk}(t)$ for choosing a certain action at time t results from $p_{nk}(t) = q_{nk}(t) \sum_j q_{nj}(t)$.

Since this algorithm on the one hand simulates human behaviour and on the other hand builds upon the fundamental work of reinforcement learning with good characteristics to converge to stable states, it is used in many social studies, e.g. in market simulations in Nicolaisen et al. [2001].

The next section introduces the theory of stochastic games and links reinforcement learning techniques to game theoretic approaches.

4.4.2 Markov Games

Markov games (MG) are a subfield of game theory. Since the seminal work of Shapley [1953] MG are widely studied and also known as *stochastic games (SG)* [Owen, 1982]. MG can be described as a tuple $\langle n, S, A_{1,...,n}, T, R_{1,...,n} \rangle$ where n describes the number of players, S is a set of states, $A_{1,...,n}$ are the action sets of each player, T is a transition function $S \times A_1 \times ... \times A_n \times S \rightarrow [0,1]$ that is controlled by the current state and the performed actions, and R_i is agent i's reward function $S \times A_1 \times ... \times A_n \rightarrow \mathbb{R}$.

Each player i wants to maximise the expected sum of discounted rewards $E(\sum_{j=0}^{\infty} \gamma^j r_{i,t+j})$. A policy π maps states to actions $S \rightarrow A$, thus, the goal is to find an optimal policy for each state. A policy is said to be optimal if there is no other policy that achieves a better result at any state. Comparing stochastic games and classical game theory, it can be remarked that stochastic games are an extension of matrix games to multiple states [Bowling and Veloso, 2000] i.e. each state can be described as a matrix game. Matrix games are determined by the tuple $\langle n, A_{1,...,n}, R_{1,...,n} \rangle$ where n is the number of players, $A : A_1 \times ... \times A_n$ is the joint action set and A_i is the action set available to player i, and player's i payoff function R_i.

Alternatively, MG can be understood as the extension of a Markov decision problem (MDP) to multiple players. MDPs have at least one optimal policy [Littman, 1994]. In Markov games the performance depends on the opponents' actions. Thus, it is not simple to determine optimal policies. A common approach is to evaluate each policy assuming the opponents best choice , i.e. to maximize the reward in the worst case. Littman [1994, p. 158] states that each Markov game has a non-empty set of optimal policies that might be probabilistic.

In order to solve stochastic games for optimal policies, several algorithms were proposed. For the analysis, it has to be distinguished between zero-sum (also called purely competitive) and general-sum games. In zero sum games, the agent's payoff sum up to zero, whereas in general-sum games the sum of payoffs can be different from zero. Almost all algorithms developed are applied to zero-sum games. Shapley

[1953] has shown that there are equilibria solutions for zero-sum games, and Filar
and Vrieze [1997] were able to demonstrate the same for general-sum games.

Both, reinforcement learning theory and game theory, have developed algorithms in order to find optimal policies. Nash-equilibrium solutions are one solution
concept in game theory. In Nash equilibrium, each agent's strategy is a best response on the other agents' strategy. Each finite bimatrix game has at least one
Nash equilibrium in mixed strategies. The fundamental difference between game
theory solution concepts and reinforcement learning is that game theory assumes
that the model of the game is known to the players. Reinforcement learning is
basically applied to unknown models. Nevertheless, the approaches are very similar. Shapley [1953] proposes to compute the quality of each action a of state s:
$Q(s,a) \leftarrow R(s,a) + \gamma \sum_{s'} T(s,a,s')V(s')$, and the value $V(s)$ of a state as the
value of the matrix game at state s. The value operator is given by the minimax
value of the game. The difference of this algorithm to MDP's value iteration is
that the *max* operator was replaced by the *value* operator.

According to this approach, Littman [1994] proposes the minimax-Q algorithm. It replaces the max operator in Q-learning with the *value* operator:

$$Q(s,a) \leftarrow (1 - \alpha)Q(s,a) + \alpha(r + \gamma V(s')) \tag{4.3}$$

and

$$V(s) = \max_{\pi(s,\cdot) \in \Pi(A_1)} \min_{a_2 \in A_2} \sum_{a_1 \in A_1} \pi(s,a_1)Q(s,a_1,a_2) \tag{4.4}$$

It can be shown that in the zero-sum case this algorithm converges to the true
values V^*. Consequently, it is straightforward to use Q-learning mechanisms for
learning in stochastic games. This is possible for a single-agent learning environment. Hu and Wellman [1998] have introduced an algorithm for multi-agent
learning in two player games. It is assumed that agents not only observe their
own actions and payoff but also the competing agents immediate payoffs. Under
these assumptions the algorithm converges to Nash equilibrium strategies. Unfortunately, the assumption of observing the competitors immediate payoffs is not
applicable in many cases.

This section has presented theoretical work in both fields, game theory and
computer science that builds the foundation for solving Markov games. Nevertheless, there is still much theoretical work needed in order to proof convergence of
Q-learning algorithms in multi-agent learning environments.

4.5 Summary

This chapter has introduced the main techniques used in agent-based simulation,
starting with the fundamental pure-agent approach that implements agents, the
environment and sets of simple (mostly) static interaction rules of which the agents
are allowed to choose. It is not intended to use evolutionary techniques in order
to find new strategies.

Another approach is the Monte Carlo technique that can be used either probabilistically to model real world processes, or deterministically in order to find solutions by sampling the solution space. Often Monte Carlo techniques are combined with other simulation approaches.

Evolutionary methods are applied to search for stable states and to identify optimal strategies. Early work was done in order to link computational methods such as genetic algorithms to economic approaches such as evolutionary game theory. A better theoretical base is essential for economist to gain more confidence in agent-based techniques.

Reinforcement learning was presented in more depth since this method is used in the model presented in Section 6 of this work. The theoretical foundation is developed by bridging game theory and computer science theory on basis of Markov decision problems and Markov games. Some work was found for proving the convergence of RL-methods to equilibrium of economic games. Still, the assumptions in the mathematical foundations are strong, so that the link is only well-founded for zero-sum Markov games. It is still necessary to prove the convergence to optimal behaviour in the more common case of general-sum games. Nevertheless, the progress and the results made in this area are promising. Reinforcement learning is also applied in Part III of this work which contributes interesting results to both areas, economics and computer science.

The presented classification of agent-based approaches can not be claimed comprehensive. Of course, there are a couple of other techniques known in computer science such as neural networks or classifier systems. It is difficult to find a strict classification, since many simulation models combine the presented techniques. Nevertheless, it is adjuvant to distinguish the most popular approaches and to map them to economic theory.

In the next chapter, existing tools for agent-based simulation are analysed in respect to some previously analysed requirements. Additionally, the agent-based simulation environment AMASE is introduced that is used for the simulation in Part III.

Chapter 5

Agent-based Simulation Software

Software agents are used for simulations, for business applications or to ease the work of humans. It is quite common for human agents to delegate the bidding in auctions to software agents. The internet auction house eBay, for instance, offers proxy agents that automatically rise the user's bid to a user defined bid ceiling as far as competing bids are submitted to the auction. Although prohibited by eBay, sniping agents are used by bidders to automatically submit a bid at the latest possible time before the auction closes.

Agents can also perform more complex tasks. The Trading Agent Competition (TAC)[1] regularly conducts a tournament to find the most efficient trading agent. In the classic TAC scenario the TAC-agents are travel agents with eight customers. The travel agent has to arrange a weekend trip dependent on the customers' preferences including a flight, accommodation arrangements, and entertainment events.

On the other hand, software agents are used in various simulation models in social science. These models often reflect reality quite good. It is also possible to apply the simulation to a real system and not only to a model of reality. If we think of electronic markets, it is absolutely possible to conduct agent-based simulations on real electronic markets. This approach offers some advantage such as the possibility to test and analyse that market instance which is later on operated in real business, or to conduct experiments with human and software agents. Therefore, agents must be able to cope with simulations and real markets. Additionally, this requires an agent-based environment that allows agents to enter and leave the simulation framework, e.g. to train separately and later on enter the (controlled) simulation environment.

---

[1]http://www.sics.se/tac/page.php?id=1

In fact, there do exist a lot of agent simulation frameworks in social sciences. Many of them are implemented for special purposes and only some of them have been built to support research in different domains. It is one objective to identify market simulation specific requirements. The link from real-world application to simulation frameworks is just one example for such requirements.

Therefore, this chapter starts with a requirement analysis for an agent-based *market* simulation framework and discusses the features and functionality of agent-based simulation software in the social sciences in respect to the presented requirements. The analysis identifies the agent framework JADE as suitable to build an agent-based simulation environment (AMASE) which is also connected to the meet2trade-platform, and thus, allows to study markets running on meet2trade. This interplay of the simulation environment and the generic auction platform is an important step towards CAME. Before presenting the market simulation environment in Section 5.3, its underlying agent framework JADE is presented in more detail in Section 5.2.

5.1   Design Objectives for Agent-based Simulation Software

The basic concepts of software agents were introduced in Section 3.1, including architectural, communication and coordination aspects. This knowledge is used for the development of an agent-based simulation environment in this section that starts with the functional and technical requirements for such framework in the present subsection and continues with a comparison of presently existing simulation software.

It is surprising that there is not much literature, neither on the evaluation of existing simulations software, nor on the discussion of general requirements for it. Gilbert and Bankes [2002] provide a very brief comparison of agent-based simulation software and Tobias and Hofmann [2004] compare the four agent-based simulation platforms RePast, Swarm, Quicksilver, and VSEit. It are Marietto et al. [2003] who refer to this lack of evaluation and present basic requirements for agent-based simulation. The following requirement analysis considers the work of Marietto et al. [2003], but generally, it is guided by three basic aspects:

1. In a first step, the software must be able to conduct market simulations in a timely efficient manner. The architecture should be kept modular, and as such, flexible and extendible so that market instances can easily be exchanged.

2. The simulation software has a generic interface that makes it possible to interconnect agents with external tools and market platforms as meet2trade. This interconnectivity of agent-based simulation software and external mar-

ket platforms is one basic requirement for computer aided market engineering and the test of real world markets.

3. The agent simulation environment is kept flexible so that future extensions are possible to use agents not only for simulation but e.g. also for market services such as bidding in real world auctions on behalf of humans.

Generally, the simulation software should enable users to set up agent-based simulations for electronic markets. Time and effort in programming and generating such simulations should be acceptable. Therefore, requirements are discussed comprehensively in the following section.

5.1.1 Functional and Technical Requirements

This section aims to specify the functional and technical requirements of the agent-based simulation environment. The functional requirements describe what the system is capable to do, whereas the technical requirements concern (software) technical restrictions, interfaces to other systems or the programming language.

Generally, the agent-based simulation environment is constructed to assist market designers and researchers to evaluate an electronic market. Agent technology enables researchers to produce populations of agents of certain types. The electronic market to be evaluated can be operated in manifold ways, since the simulation environment's architecture handles markets as exchangeable objects. In a first step, the market instance can be implemented as one object of the simulation environment, i.e. it is build as a model of a "real" electronic market. Additionally, an interface is provided to allow for interconnection to external market instances, e.g. running on a market platform. In Chapter 2.3 the generic market platform meet2trade was introduced. It has been pointed out that such a generic market platform is a necessary component for computer aided market engineering, since it allows to design a variety electronic markets, and thus, to study the impact of different market parameters. A connection to meet2trade enables software agents to participate in markets operated on the platform. Thus, the simulation environment must be adaptable and extendible to meet these needs.

In the following, some general requirements of agent simulations and some specific requirements with respect to the meet2trade-platform are identified. The requirements concern both, functional and technical aspects for the agent-based market simulation environment. These requirements are used for a comparative analysis of agent-based simulation software in Section 5.1.3.

(1) Functional Requirements

(1.1) *Overall Requirements*
The software should be easy to use and support the basic simulation features such as

- defining a simulation via a graphical user interface (GUI),
- easily changing simulation settings,
- saving/loading simulation settings,
- specifying a sequence of simulations (either repeating the same, or running a new simulation),
- defining the duration of the simulation run,
- loading populations of predefined agents,
- adding, launching, and removing agents.

Since many simulations just differ in a few parameters changes of agents, the simulation software should support the easy parametrization of agents' characteristics. In order to observe the simulation during runtime, the visualisation of parameters is necessary that strictly depends on the parameters' characteristics. Hence, the parameter visualisation should be configurable.

(1.2) *Simulation Control*
An agent-based simulation consists of distributed processes (agents) performing individual tasks. The objective for a control entity is to coordinate these decentralized processes. A simulation flow protocol is to be defined to coordinate the sequence of processes and to allow specific adaptation of each process (of the control entity and agents) as well as subordinate tasks in simulations. This keeps the simulation environment flexible, adaptable and extendible.

Marietto et al. [2003] discuss the need for the integration of controlled and non-controlled environments. In controlled environments, the simulator is in control of each event or action. In non-controlled environments the simulator has no or only partial control of the environmental parameters and events. The authors present two scenarios. In the first scenario, an agent might act in both, the simulation environment and the real world, at the same time (this case might occur in human-computer experiments where agents conduct a simulation and also play against humans). In the second scenario, an agent firstly acts in the controlled environment (e.g. a training phase). Afterwards, the agent shifts to the real world to perform tasks, and finally, returns into the controlled environment. Therefore, it appears reasonable to separate the simulation design pattern from the agent-domain dependent behaviour.

(1.3) *Analysis and evaluation*

In order to analyse the simulation the researcher observes changes of state variables that describe the state of the system. Such changes occur due to different events. Marietto et al. [2003] distinguish two kind of events: (i) behavioural events, and (ii) cognitive events. The first subsume events that can be observed by *external* observers (e.g. sending messages, changes in amount and type of agents, or external communication). The latter describe events within the agents' internal architecture. The simulation environment should support the logging of both types of data.

In general, the gathered simulation data must be stored in an appropriate format. This format depends on the statistical tools used for the evaluation, the amount of generated data and the access efficiency. The data-sets can be logged either in a database or in a generic format on a single file system. A common standard for simulation data are comma separated values (csv). For the evaluation of the simulation data statistical packages can be used for ex-post analysis. The integration of statistical standard packages into the simulation environment can be considered integrated to better support graphical and statistical analysis at runtime.

(1.4) *Connectivity to meet2trade*

The simulation software should be mainly used to evaluate electronic markets. The generic trading platform meet2trade enables users to configure electronic markets. Hence, an expedient requirement is to equip simulation agents with meet2trade communication capabilities. Agents can be used to conduct performance tests of new markets as well as for simulative analysis of bidders' behaviour and market outcome. It is also possible to run experiments with humans and software agents, since the market platform provides a graphical user interface for experiments. As further extensions, agents can be implemented to provide market services (e.g. to trade on behalf of humans).

(1.5) *Availability of Software*

Two basic requirement to the software are (i) its cost-free availability and (ii) open source code. Costs are often a problem in academia due to budget constraints. Additionally, commercial software is often not available open source. An open source code facilitates the understanding of the system and makes the system flexible for specific extensions. If errors occur during the simulation, it has to be checked whether the model produces errors or the used simulation package contains programming errors.

(1.6) *Organizational abstractions and multiple societies*

Relations of agents can be defined in organizational abstraction such as *groups* and *roles*. Zambonelli et al. [2001] point out that agent societies can be understood as a computational organisation. Thus, organisational abstractions are important for the analysis of such systems. The ability of agents to not only identify different organizational entities but also to reason about them enables the analysis of social aspects.

This requirement is of minor interest in the present work and thus, is neglected in the following. Nevertheless, it is to be considered for further development of the platform.

Having defined the functional demand, the next paragraphs presents the technical requirements.

(2) Technical Requirements

(2.1) *Use of programming language Java*
Sun's programming language Java has developed to currently one of the most important programming languages and it is widely used, especially for network applications. This is also due to the fact that Java software can be developed machine independently and the applications can be operated on various operation systems as Microsoft Windows, Unix, Linux, or Apple OS X. It's widespread use and the platform independence guarantee that the simulation software can be widely applied and further developed.

(2.2) *Manage Scheduling Techniques*
An important advantage of simulations is to be conducted in a controlled environment. This allows not only to control many state variables, but also to reproduce simulation results. The simulation environment controls state transitions. Common simulation schedules are, for example, discrete event or discrete time simulation. The simulation environment should provide libraries to support such management techniques.

(2.3) *Extensibility*
Extensibility is a basic factor for successful applications. Many simulations differ in their specific requirements and the software used (e.g. additional software packages). This makes individual solutions necessary.

Beside the already explained integration of meet2trade-communication functionality, it might be useful to integrate other trading systems, e.g. for multi-attribute trading. The simulation software should be designed that further extensions are possible. An object oriented approach facilitates later extensions.

(2.4) *Distributable Agent Platform*
The distribution of agents over several computers is important to realise large agent populations (scalability). The resources of one single computer are restricted to a certain amount of agents (dependent on the agent capabilities and their size respectively). A distributable agent platform inhibits a resource bottleneck by distributing the agents on many computers.

(2.5) *Standardized communication*
Section 3.2 gave an overview on agent communication standards. Communication is an essential task in MAS. Standards are necessary to enable the

communication amongst agents and to facilitate the understanding of the communication by other humans. Agent Communication Languages (ACL) specify the message structure and a semantic model. Conversation protocols structure the communication process. Thus, it is essential to endow agents with communicative functionality. The basic communication standards, e.g. KQML, FIPA-ACL as introduced in Section 3.2 should be supported. Additionally, the integration of ontologies can be considered to enhance the agents communication capabilities. Ontologies can ease the interactions of software agents and humans.

(2.6) *Agent development*
Agent templates facilitate the development of simulation specific agents.

(2.7) *Java Message Service integration*
The generic meet2trade-client uses Java Message Services (JMS) to ensure distributed reliable and asynchronous communication. The messages are encoded in XML schemata, and therefore, provide a high degree of readability and re-usability. In order to enable communication to meet2trade, it is necessary to integrate JMS into the simulation environment.

(2.8) *Compatibility with JBoss*
The meet2trade-platform is deployed on the application server JBoss. As described earlier, the simulation environment is to be designed to facilitate later extensions, e.g. for additional market services. Thus, the MAS should be compatible with the JBoss technology and if applicable integrated into the application server. This requirement is not obligatory, since it is not relevant for the simulation tasks itself. From a software tool-suite development point of view, this requirement builds the basis for innovative value adding features (e.g. agents that assist humans or act on their behalf).

The critical question in assessing the presented requirements is whether *to use one of the existing and commonly used simulation tools*, or *to build a problem specific solution*. Many simulation software tools have grown from specific problem related software implementations and have been developed to more flexible software that is more widely used. Nevertheless, there is no standard tool available satisfying all needs. For that reason it is necessary to discuss some of the standard tools concerning the present requirements in the next section.

5.1.2 Agent-based Simulation Software – An Overview

The scientific community has developed a variety of simulation software. Some simulation tools are more widely used, others are not longer supported. This section gives an overview on known simulation tools for agent-based simulation.

Most of the simulation software was developed for studies in the social science that are concerned with group behaviour in agent societies. *Sugarscape* presented by Epstein and Axtell [1996] is probably the most famous simulation model of artificial societies that describes an artificial 2-D landscape endowed with sugar. Agents populate the sugarscape, eat sugar, move, combat and reproduce. Many simulation models refer to the basic idea of sugarscape and implement a 2-D landscape. Leigh Tesfatsion maintains a comprehensive list of tools for agent development on her web sites.[2]

Serenko and Detlor [2002] and Tobias and Hofmann [2004] evaluate software for agent-based simulation and present a list of software tools. Table 5.1 summarizes 36 software package for agent development and/or simulation. Since Serenko and Detlor [2002] report about 60 mobile agent tools on the list administrated by Fritz Hohl,[3] and about the same amount on the list provided by AgentBuilder.[4] It is to be remarked that Table 5.1 can just give an overview on selected popular agent-development tools in the community, and certainly, cannot be comprehensive.

---

[2]General Software and Toolkits: http://www.econ.iastate.edu/tesfatsi/acecode.htm

[3]see http://reinsburgstrasse.dyndns.org/mal/mal.html This list is no longer maintained and represents the status of 2004.

[4]see http://agentbuilder.com/AgentTools/index.html This list is under construction.

Table 5.1: Agent-based simulation tools and agent frameworks

No.	Simulation tool and application	Language	Origin	Licence
1	**ABLE: Agent Building and Learning Environment** `http://www.alphaworks.ibm.com/tech/able` Framework, component library, and productivity tool kit for building intelligent agents using machine learning and reasoning using Java Beans (AbleBeans).	Java	[Bigus and Bigus, 2001] IBM T. J. Watson Research Center	IBM registered users, commercial licence available
2	**AgentSheets** `http://www.agentsheets.com/` An agent-based authoring tool to build simulation models and publish them as Java applets on the web. It defines the programming language VisualAgentTalk (VAT) which is used to create simulations.	Java	[Repenning, 2000] AgentSheets Inc., Boulder	commercial
3	**Ascape** `http://www.brookings.edu/es/dynamics/models/ascape/main.htm` Agent modelling environment to support the design, analysis and distribution of agent-based models. The framework supports complex model design.	Java	[Parker, 2000] The Brookings Institution, Washington D.C.	free
4	**Aspen** `http://www.cs.sandia.gov/tech.reports/rjpryor/ index.html` Aspen is a simulation model for the U.S. economy using time-dependent Monte Carlo methods.	for parallel computers	[Pryor et al., 1996] Sandia National Laboratories	available for general use
5	**Breve** `http://www.spiderland.org/breve/` Environment for the simulation of decentralized systems and artificial life suited for 3D-world simulations with continuous time and continuous agent states.	steve	[Klein, 2002] Hampshire College, Amherst	open source, GNU General Public License
6	**Cormas** `http://cormas.cirad.fr/` Natural resource management, interaction between resources and societies.	VisualWorks (SmallTalk)	[Bousquet et al., 1998, Proceedings Volume II] Centre de coopration internationale en recherche agronomique pour le dveloppement, France	open source, free licence
7	**Cougaar: Cognitive Agent Architecture** `http://www.cougaar.org/` Architecture for the construction of large-scale distributed agent-based applications such as logistics planning. It is applied in chaotic environments.	Java	[Helsinger et al., 2003] BBN Technologies, Cambridge, MA	open source, Cougaar Open Source License

continued on next page

continued from previous page

No.	Simulation tool and application	Language	Origin	Licence
8	**ECHO** http://www.santafe.edu/projects/echo/ Developed for ecological research and interaction of agent populations and environment.	C for UNIX/Linux	[Holland, 1992b, Jones and Forrest, 1993] Santa Fe Institute, NM	open source
9	**JADE: Java Agent DEvelopment Framework** http://jade.tilab.com/ Java based framework to develop agent applications according to the FIPA specifications. It is an agent middle-ware implementing an Agent Platform and a development framework. It is not a simulation tool but it can be used for simulations.	Java	[Bellifemine et al., 1999] Universit di Parma	open source, GNU public licence
10	**JAS: Java Agent-based Simulation library** http://jaslibrary.sourceforge.net/ Java toolkit for creating agent-based simulations. JAS is a clone of the Swarm library.	Java	[Sonnessa, 2003] Universit di Torino, Italy	open source, GNU Lesser General Public License
11	**JASA: Java Auction Simulator API** http://www.csc.liv.ac.uk/~sphelps/jasa/ JASA is a Java library containing classes for the development of auctions and trading agents. It provides reference implementations for distinct learning algorithms and auctions. An integration of RePast for visualizing and controlling simulations is possible.	Java	[Phelps et al., 2002] Agent Applications, Research and Technology group of Liverpool University	open source, GNU General Public License
12	**jES: Java Enterprise Simulator** http://web.econ.unito.it/terna/jes/ SWARM-based simulator for the construction of simulation models for enterprises to analyse the behaviour and network interaction.	Java	[Terna, 2004] Universit di Torino	open source, free
13	**LS/TS Living Systems Technology Suite** http://www.whitestein.com/pages/downloads/docs.html Multi Agent System for professional development and operation of industry solutions.	Java	[Whitestein Technologies, 2005] Whitestein Technologies, Switzerland	commercial
14	**Lsd: Laboratory for Simulation Development** http://www.business.aau.dk/~mv/Lsd/lsd.html Framework for evolution simulation modelling, as exemplified by the Nelson-Winter Model [Nelson and Winter, 1982] of Schumpeterian competition in a market economy.	C++	[Valente, 1999] International Institute for Applied Systems Analysis (IIASA), Austria	open source, GNU General Public License
15	**MadKit: Multi Agent Development Kit** http://www.madkit.org/ Platform built upon the AGR (Agent/Group/Role) organizational model: agents are situated in groups and play roles. Used for ecological systems.	Java, Python, Scheme, BeanShell, Jess	[Gutknecht and Ferber, 2000], Laboratoire d'Informatique, de Robotique et de Microlectronique de Montpellier (LIRMM)	GPL/LGPL license

continued on next page

continued from previous page

No.	Simulation tool and application	Language	Origin	Licence
16	**MAGSY** http://www.dfki.uni-sb.de/~kuf/magsy.html Development platform for MAS based on OPS5.	OPS5 (based on BLISS)	[Fischer and Windisch, 1992] German Research Centre for Artificial Intelligence, Saarbrücken	free
17	**MAML: Multi-Agent Modelling Language** http://www.maml.hu/ MAML is a language to write models for the simulation platform SWARM. It was implemented to facilitate the usage of SWARM especially for non-programmers. The language is planned to be developed to a complex modelling environment.	Objective-C	[Gulyás et al., 1999] Complex Adaptive Systems Laboratory, Central European University, Budapest, Hungary	open source, GNU public licence
18	**MASON: Multi-Agent Simulator Of Neighborhoods** http://cs.gmu.edu/~eclab/projects/mason/ Multi-Agent Simulator Of Neighborhoods for social science and, artificial intelligence and robotics.	Java	[Luke et al., 2003] Evolutionary Computation Laboratory (ECLab) and Center for Social Complexity, George Mason University, VA	open source, free
19	**MIMOSE: Mikro- und Mehrebenenmodellierungs-Software** http://www.uni-koblenz.de/~moeh/projekte/mimose.html Model description language and experimental frame for the simulation of populations with non-linear, quantitative and qualitative relations, stochastic influences, birth and death processes.	Modeling language itself, Kernel is written in C for UNIX, Solaris	[Möhring and Ostermann, 1996] Computer Applications in the Social Science, Universität Koblenz, Germany	free
20	**Moduleco** http://perso.univ-rennes1.fr/denis.phan/moduleco/ The modular multi-agent platform is designed to simulate markets, organisations, social phenomena and population dynamics. Available as plug-in for Madkit.	Java	[Phan and Beugnard, 2001] Universit Bretagne Occidentale	open source, GNU General Public License (GPL)
21	**NetLogo** http://ccl.northwestern.edu/netlogo/ As the next generation of StarLogo it is a multi-agent programming language and modelling environment for simulating natural and social phenomena.	Java	[Wilensky, 1999; Tisue and Wilensky, 2004] Center for Connected Learning and Computer-Based Modeling, Northwestern University, Evanston, IL	open source, free
22	**Ps-i** http://ps-i.sourceforge.net/ Computational Modeling Platform for Problems of Ethnic Conflict, Globalization, State Stability, and Terrorism.	C, Tcl	[Lustick, 2002] University of Pennsylvania	GNU General Public Licence

continued on next page

continued from previous page

No.	Simulation tool and application	Language	Origin	Licence
23	**RePast: Recursive Porous Agent Simulation Toolkit** http://repast.sourceforge.net/index.html Agent-based simulation toolkit designed for use in the social science. It is borrowing many concepts from SWARM. It supports the development of flexible models of living social agents including a variety of agent templates.	Java, C++, C, Visual Basic	[Collier et al., 2003] University of Chicago	open source, free
24	**SDML: a Strictly Declarative Modeling Language** http://cfpm.org/sdml/ Declarative language that represents agents and their environments as collections of rulebases and databases. Each agent has its own set of databases and rulesbases.	Smalltalk	[Edmonds et al., 1996] Centre for Policy Modeling, Manchester Metropolitan University	open source, GNU General Public License
25	**SeSAm: Shell for Simulated Agent Systems** http://www.simsesam.de/ Generic environment for modeling and experimenting with agent-based simulation.	Java	[Klügel et al., 2003] Chair of Computer Science VI, Artificial Intelligence and Applied Computer Science, Universität Würzburg, Germany	open source, LGPL-Licence
26	**SimAgent** http://www.cs.bham.ac.uk/~axs/cog_affect/sim_agent.html A toolkit developed to support exploratory research on human-like intelligent agents that are not limited to a specific agent architecture.	Pop-11, Poplog	[Sloman and Poli, 1996] School of Computer Science, University of Birmingham	open source, free
27	**SimBioSys** http://www.kumo.com/~david/SimBioSys/ Framework to facilitate the construction of evolutionary simulations in biology and the social science.	C++	[McFadzean, 1994] University of Calgary	open source, Artistic License
28	**Sim2Web** No URL available General Framework for web-enabling economic and financial simulations based on the JAS libraries.	Java, Python, XML-RPC	[Margarita and Sonnessa, 2003] Universit di Torino, Italy	open source, free
29	**SimPack** http://www.cise.ufl.edu/~fishwick/simpack.html Collection of C++ routines and program for computer simulation.	C++, Java	[Fishwick, 1992] Computer and Information Science and Engineering, University of Florida, FL	GNU Public License (GPL)
30	**SimPy: Simulation in Python** http://simpy.sourceforge.net/ Discrete event simulation language for process-based simulations providing components of a simulation model.	Python	[Miller, 2005]	open source, GNU Lesser GPL (LGPL)

continued on next page

continued from previous page

No.	Simulation tool and application	Language	Origin	Licence
31	**StarLogo** http://education.mit.edu/starlogo/ Programmable modeling environment to simulate real life phenomena such as bird flocks, traffic jams, ant colonies, market economies.	Logo, Java	[Epstein et al., 2000] MIT Media Lab	open source, free
32	**Sugarscape** http://www.brook.edu/es/dynamics/sugarscape/default.htm Simulation platform to study social phenomena of populations of agents living on a spatial environment called sugarscape. The study include birth, death, disease, cultural process like trade, combat or social networks.	Object Pascal, Java	[Epstein and Axtell, 1996] The Brookings Institution, Washington D.C.	available with the book
33	**Swarm** http://www.swarm.org/wiki/Main_Page Software package for multi-agent simulation of complex systems consisting of code libraries. It is used for simulations involving a large number of agents behaving and interacting within a dynamic environment.	Objective-C, Java	[Hiebeler, 1994] University of Michigan originally developed at Santa Fe Institute	open source, general public under GNU licensing
34	**TeamBots** http://www.teambots.org/ Simulation environment for robot hardware. The control system for the robots can be applied in both, the simulation and on the hardware.	Java, C	Tucker Balch Carnegie Mellon University	open source, free
35	**Quicksilver** http://quicksilver.tigris.org/ Environment for quick development and testing of agent models. The models can be run as applets or MIDlets.	Java, PL/SQL, Prolog	[Burse, 2000]	GNU Lesser Public License
36	**VSEit: Versatile Simulation Environment for the internet** http://www.vseit.de/VSEit09/VSEitDoc/About.html Modeling and simulation framework for flexible creation of simulation models that allows the integration and smooth refinement of different types of models.	Java	[Brassel, 2001] Department of Sociology, Technical Universität Darmstadt (TUD)	open source, free

It has been pointed out that the simulation software should be implemented in Java for technical reasons and to make the software usable on different operating systems. Thirteen of the presented software packages are written in other languages than Java, six combine other languages and Java, and seventeen are written entirely in Java. Many of the presented tools were not fully available open source and free (1,2,13,32), not available at all at the beginning of the present research project (7,10,11,12,18,25), are not longer maintained or only marginally supported (28,35,36), or have been developed for other purposes (15), e.g. robotics or simulation of ecological systems. The NetLogo/StarLogo family is a programming language itself that belongs to the *Lisp* language. It is derived from the programming language Logo developed for educational use in schools and was realised in Java. Thus, NetLogo/StarLogo are not appropriate for the purpose in this work. Moduleco was developed for cognitive science simulation. The documentation is low and there are only a few articles available, so this toolkit is not considered in this evaluation. This leaves Ascape, JADE, MadKit, RePast and Swarm for more accurate evaluation.

ASCAPE

Ascape is a free[5] and open source Java library for agent-based modelling developed at *The Brookings Institution*.[6] The idea for Ascape stems from Sugarscape [Epstein and Axtell, 1996] and follows some ideas of Swarm [Dugdale, 2005]. It is reported to be simpler to use than Swarm and excellent for simulations of agents on a rectilinear grid [Gilbert and Bankes, 2002, Dugdale, 2005, Foucart, 2001]. It is intended to be an *expressive* (ability to define a complete model in smallest possible description), *generalized* (apply and test the same basic modelling idea in many different environments), *powerful* (provide high level use-oriented tools for model interaction without programming) and *abstract* (highest possible abstraction level for modelling ideas and methodologies) modelling toolkit [Parker, 2001].

Ascape implements two fundamental concepts: *agents* and *scapes*. In Sugarscape the term *scape* expresses a territory on which agents live. In the Ascape framework scapes are essentially collections of agents, meaning scapes represent behaviour of collections of agents [Inchiosa and Parker, 2002]. Since a scape is considered an (first-class) agent itself, it allows for building hierarchies of scapes and thus, composing models of models respectively. Agents are allowed to be member of more than one scape.

The framework focus on simulation especially of agents on a 2D-grid which is of minor importance for the simulation of electronic markets. From an agent application development perspective, Ascape appears neither to be well suited for experiments with software agents and humans, nor for enabling agents to act on external platforms such as meet2trade.

---

[5]For non-commercial use.
[6]http://www.brook.edu/

JADE

JADE is a software framework for agent development written in Java. It is an agent-middleware for run-time execution of P2P applications developed at TILAB (Telecom Italia Lab).[7] It conforms to the FIPA specifications for multi agents systems, thus, specifying key agents for management, enabling interoperability with other systems due to standardized communication using various ACL standards, and specifying ontologies for interaction between systems [Bellifemine et al., 2001]. It is based on four principles: *(i) interoperability* (JADE agents can interoperate with agents of the same (FIPA) standard on other platforms), *(ii) uniformity and portability* (the API (Application Program Interface) is independent from underlying Java version and network and thus, applicable to J2EE[8], J2SE[9], J2ME[10]). *(iii) ease of use* (the middleware hides its complexity and provides simple APIs for development), and *(iv) pay-as-you-go philosophy* (features not used are not relevant to the programmer and produce any computational overhead) [Bellifemine et al., 2003].

The framework follows the FIPA specifications for MAS and provides an Agent Management System (AMS), an Agent Communication Channel (ACC) for agent communication inside and outside the platform, a Directory Facilitator (DF) to provide a yellow page service, and a GUI to manage agents and the agent platform. JADE agents can be executed in web-browsers and mobile devices. Since the platform is distributable on a network, agents can move from one node on the platform to another. The communication is asynchronous and is understood as one possible action.

JADE was not developed for simulations, but to build MAS and MAS applications. Nevertheless, many agent-based simulations and applications were build on a JADE basis and the user community is growing. However, there is no simulation environment so far. Since JADE is fully compliant with FIPA, provides many features, and is executable on various devices and operating systems, it shows a high potential for the development of simulations on the edge of research and business applications (e.g. agents not only participating in simulations but also providing services in real world applications). It provides full API documentation and a user mailing list is entertained by the development group.

---

[7]http://www.telecomitalialab.com/ITA/index.htm

[8]J2EE: Java 2 Platform, Enterprise Edition defines a standard for the development of component-based multitier enterprise applications. See http://java.sun.com/j2ee/ for detailed description.

[9]J2SE: Java 2 Platform, Standard Edition defines a standard for the development of applications on desktops and application in embedded environments. See http://java.sun.com/j2se/ for further explanations.

[10]J2ME: Java 2 Platform, Micro Edition provides an application environment for small systems such as mobile devices. See http://java.sun.com/j2me/ for more detail.

MadKit

The multi agent platform MadKit is based on the Aalaadin or AGR (Agent Group Role) generic meta model [Ferber and Gutknecht, 1998, Gutknecht and Ferber, 2000]. The Aalaadin (meta) model follows an organizational perspective on MAS based on the three main concepts (i) agents, (ii) groups, and (iii) roles. Principally, agents play roles within one or more groups. Roles are understood as *"the abstract representation of an agent function, service or identification within a group"* [Gutknecht and Ferber, 2001]. Ferber and Gutknecht [1998] argue to use an *organizational* rather than an *agent-based* approach to better reflect social structures. In the agent-based view social structure emerge from patterns of actions arising through interaction. In contrast, the organizational view understands an organization as a framework for activity and interaction defined by a groups-roles relationship. Thus, an organization is a structural relationships between a collection of agents. The inner agent architecture is not defined within the model.

MadKit realises this organizational view in a generic, highly customizable and scalable multi agent platform. This is achieved by implementing the three design principles: *(i) micro-kernel architecture, (ii) agentification of services,* and *(iii) graphic component model.* The micro-kernel is defined as *"a minimal set of facilities allowing deployment of agents services"* [Ferber and Gutknecht, 1998] such as control of local groups and roles, agent life-cycle management, and local message passing. Platform services such as distributed message passing or migration control are provided by agents (e.g. communicator agent, group synchronizer agent) and summarized as agentification of services. Each agent is on default member of the *local* group on the local micro-kernel, whereas the *system* group is restricted to agents that not only can access the micro-kernel but also potentially have control over life-cycles of other agents. Agents can be distributed on different computers. The graphic component model delegates responsibility for the GUI to each agent and can be run in three different modes: development environment (G-Box), console-only mode, and applets.

MadKit was developed as a different approach building MAS focusing on the organizational perspective. In the meanwhile many applications have been developed for MadKit and some simulation environments such as Moduleco are available as plug-in for the platform. The handling of divers communication languages makes the platform interoperable. However, as outlined earlier a role based model is of no interest for the present approach.

RePast

The simulation framework RePast was developed at the Social Science Research Computing of the University of Chicago[11] to create agent-based simulations and is based on the computer language Java [Collier et al., 2003]. Its overall goal is to enable social simulations of agents as social actors with cascading and recombinant goals and to allow *"situated histories to be replayed with altered assumptions"* [Collier et al., 2003]. It aims to support the modelling of belief systems and agents, organizations and institutions as recursive social constructions. The libraries include objects for creating, running, displaying (charts), and collecting data from agent-based simulations. RePast shares some ideas with Swarm and is sometimes described to be the Java version of Swarm [Foucart, 2001]. Additionally, it provides an interface for interoperability with Geographical Information Systems (GIS). The Simbuilder RePast add-on permit users to rapidly set up models for simulation by using the computer language *Not Quite Python* of the Python programming language family.

According to Swarm, RePast implements a schedule object that manages all occurring events and changes to the states of infrastructural components, and thus, the simulation flow. Therefore, RePast allows to build simulations as state machines enabling discrete event simulations. It consists of two basic components, the *infrastructure* and the *representation*. The infrastructure contains all mechanisms that run the simulation, and display and collect data. The state of the data display and data collection objects constitute the infrastructure state. The representation comprise the simulation itself that is constructed by the modeller. Its state is described by the current values of all agents' variables, the current values of the space/spaces in which the agents operate, and the state of any other representational object. The history of representational states is the simulation history.

The described features and structure of the platform show the primary intention of RePast to simulate agents embedded in an geographical environment (rectilinear grid or imported landscape information from GIS). As Ascape and Swarm it provides rich simulation features but lack the ability to distribute agents on different computers and use ACL for communication. Since RePast is continuously improved, it was announced that a next version will also provide a distributable platform.

---

[11] http://sscs.uchicago.edu/

Swarm

The Swarm framework was developed at the Santa Fe institute[12] to manage agents and the environment for interactive experimentation in the scientific research of different disciplines. The framework was originally developed in Objective C, but in the latest version a Java add-on is available. Its overall goal is to provide a tool that facilitates the use of agents and space and that can be used interactively and via batch jobs. As mentioned earlier, Swarm uses a discrete step function for scheduling of events, and thus, enables agent-based discrete event simulations. Over the years it has become an efficient, reliable and reusable software for experimentation [Minar et al., 1996].

The basic object of Swarm is an agent interacting with other agents via discrete events. Additional concepts are space objects to store environmental states, analysis objects to observe other objects and the object list manager containing lists about all objects in the system. Each object in Swarm is characterized by a *name* (unique ID), *data* (the local data defining the state of an object), and *rules* (set of functions to handle any message received including the step function) [Hiebeler, 1994]. Agents can be subsumed in collections, the so called *swarm*. A swarm can itself be an agent and can own another swarm as well. This concept is quite similar to the concept of *scapes* in Ascape. Agents are put together in a swarm by defining a schedule of events. For the analysis of results, each object implements the *probe* facility that allows to measure data from running simulation. The probe interface can be used for displaying data or to test the software. Swarm does not require any particular type of environment.

Swarm is one of the most famous simulation platforms and widely used in research. According to the simulation frameworks Ascape and RePast, it is especially applicable to simulations within a specific environment. Due to its hierarchical structure it is also useful for the simulation of populations of agents. It lacks the possibility to distribute agents on various computers and does not support ACL. Also, it appears not to be extendible for services or agent (business) applications.

5.1.3 Requirements Analysis of Agent Platforms

Having presented the main agent simulation frameworks, in the following it is discussed to what extend these software tools match the established requirements and if so, which of these frameworks is best suited for the development of a market simulation environment. The comparison is also summarized in Table 5.2.

(1.1) *Overall Requirements*

Among the five software frameworks introduced above, Ascape, RePast and Swarm are explicitly designed for simulations. These three frameworks are strongly related and borrow features from each other. They provide rich simulation features, charts for data visualization and statistical libraries as

---

[12]http://www.santafe.edu/

well as data export. JADE and MadKit are primarily used for the development of MAS and were not explicitly designed for simulations. Nevertheless, both frameworks are used for simulations and Moduleco provides a simulation plug-in for MadKit. Both frameworks do provide an agent management GUI. It is also possible to implement particular agent GUI.

(1.2) *Simulation control*

The simulation control is dynamic in RePast and Swarm whereas Ascape offers a sequential rule based execution. JADE and MadKit do not offer simulation control. None of the platforms integrates controlled and non-controlled environments, but both, JADE and MadKit, are well suited to enable such an integration, since they are also applicable for real world requirements.

(1.3) *Analysis and evaluation*

All frameworks offer graphical functionality, Ascape, RePast and Swarm offer additional statistical libraries. JADE and MadKit provide a GUI for agent management and JADE has rich functions for debugging e.g. by sniffing agents.[13] Neither JADE nor MadKit provide statistical libraries, but support agent specific GUI implementations. Data export is supported in Ascape, RePast, Swarm and in the latest version of JADE.

(1.4) *meet2trade connectivity*

Since all frameworks are implemented in Java or provide Java-libraries, the precondition for establishing communication to meet2trade is fulfilled.

(1.5) *Availability of software*

All frameworks are available free of charge under free, GNU or GPL licenses. JADE is also allowed for commercial application under GNU.

(1.6) *Organizational abstraction and multiple societies*

Just MadKit implements a groups/roles model but Ascape, RePast and Swarm allow agent aggregation in one object which implicitly provides abstractions. Relations have to be explicitly defined and implemented in JADE, since agents are defined as self-sufficient entities. Aggregation of agents is prohibited under JADE.

(2.1) *Use of programming language Java*

It was required that all of the analysed frameworks use Java for implementation. RePast and Swarm additionally provide implementations in other computer languages and script languages for the definition of simulations.

(2.2) *Manage scheduling technique*

Simulations in Ascape, RePast and Swarm are event-based. MadKit manage personalized scheduling techniques and JADE uses a round robin schedule for internal behaviour. It also implements events but no parametrization for scheduling techniques.

---

[13] A *sniffing* agent eavesdrop all incoming and outgoing messages of one agent for debugging.

(2.3) *Extensibility*

All platforms claim to be extendible due to clarity in coding and open source availability. JADE appears to be the most flexible platform, since it is even executable on small and mobile devices and provides agent mobility services.

(2.4) *Distributable agent platform*

JADE is fully distributable on different computers even small/mobile devices and agents can move around. MadKit is also distributable but agents can't change their location. None of the other frameworks is distributable, but it is announced for next versions of RePast.

(2.5) *Standardized communication*

Ascape, RePast and Swarm do not support standard ACL or ontologies, but implement their own standard. MadKit offers synchronous and asynchronous communication. It is planed to integrate standard ACL in MadKit. Since JADE is FIPA-compliant the communication is standardized and different ACLs are usable. It also supports ontologies.

(2.6) *Agent development*

None of the frameworks has any restriction on the agents' internal architecture. Agents are implemented as objects an can run as threads. JADE and MadKit also allow agents to run as Java applets.

(2.7) *JMS integration*

Since all frameworks are implemented in Java, the use of JMS for communication to meet2trade is principally possible as far as there are no framework specific restrictions that are presently not known.

(2.8) *Compatibility with JBoss*

Neither Ascape, RePast nor Swarm appear to be integratable into JBoss application server. MadKit uses JavaBeans, thus, an integration into JBoss might be possible. There is an integration solution for JADE called Blue-JADE. This enables JADE to be operated as an application on JBoss and opens the door to use JADE e.g. for additional services or other (non-simulation specific) applications.

Ascape, RePast and Swarm are widely developed agent simulation platforms that facilitate the work of researchers in many disciplines. They provide rich functionality for simulation and evaluation purposes. This includes overall simulation requirements, simulation control and a GUI for simulation management and control. Additionally, these simulation environments provide packages for statistical functions and data export.

MadKit is also used for simulations and follows the AGR model. This makes it a valuable tool for simulating group dynamics and organizational approaches. As the three other tools, it provides overall simulation features, simulation control

Requirements	Ascape	JADE	MadKit	RePast	Swarm
Overall require-ments	rich simulation features avail-able, GUI	simulation features not available, agent mana-gement and GUI	plug-ins for simulations available, agent mana-gement and GUI	rich simula-tion library, Simbuilder (GUI)	rich simulation library, GUI
Simulation control	sequential rule based execution	not available	plugins for simulation control avail-able	dynamic control	dynamic con-trol, change parameters dependent on simulation series
	integration of (non-) controlled environments not available	(non-) con-trolled en-vironment realizable	integration of (non-) controlled environments not available	integration of (non-) controlled environments not available	integration of (non-) controlled environments not available
Analysis and eval-uation	graphical and statistical functions, data export	GUI for ver-ification, data logging available, statistical and chart function not available	graphic com-ponent model, statistical and chart function not available	graphical and statistical functions, data export	graphical and statistical functions, data export
meet2trade inter-operability	implementable	implementable	implementable	implementable	implementable
Availability of software	free	open source, GNU	open source, GPL	open source, free	open source, GNU
Organizational ab-straction and mul-tiple societies	no groups/roles model, scapes as abstraction	no groups/roles model, rela-tions have to be explicitly established	groups/roles model (n:m relation), inner group characteristics	no groups/roles model, agent aggregation possible	no groups/roles model, agent aggregation in swarm class
Computer lan-guage	Java	Java	Java, Python, Scheme	Java, C++, C, Visual Basic, Not Quite Python	Objective C, Java
Manage schedul-ing technique	event-based simulation, no explicit schedule that could be parametrized at runtime	sequential scheduling, no parametriza-tion, events	manage per-sonalized scheduling techniques	event-based simulation	event-based simulation
Extensibility	possible due to model encap-sulation and open source	possible due to open source, mobile de-vices, FIPA compliant	possible due to open source, plug-in concept	state machine provides exten-sibility	extendible, support for other lan-guages
Distributable agent platform	not available	fully dis-tributable, even on mobile devices	distributable	not available (planed)	not available
Standardized com-munication	own standard, no open stan-dard supported	asynchronous communica-tion, ACL messages avail-able, support for codecs and ontolo-gies, FIPA compliant	synchronous/ asynchronous message ex-change, no support for ontologies and standard ACL	own standard, no ontology or standard ACL support	own standard, no ontology or standard ACL support
Agent develop-ment	scapes (collec-tion of agents), objects, threads	threads, runnable as applet	objects, threads, applets	agents as ob-jects, threads	object, thread
	no predefined architecture	no predefined architecture	no predefined architecture	no predefined architecture	no predefined architecture
JMS integration	implementable	implementable	implementable	implementable	implementable
Compatibility with JBoss	not available	integration available (BlueJADE)	possible	not available	not available

Table 5.2: Requirements analysis of agent platforms

and GUI for agent management. In contrast, MadKit does not support statistical functions for evaluation.

JADE is no simulation tool, but a powerful multi agent development framework. In fact, it provides templates for GUI development, but it lacks overall simulation features and simulation control. The newest release provides functionality for data logging. Statistical functions are not available. On the other hand if simulation control classes are added, JADE enables not only controlled environments but also non-controlled environments, which non of the other tools is capable to. Additionally, it implements the standard communication which complies with the FIPA standards and also includes ontology support. These communication capabilities make it a flexible and highly interoperable agent framework. This is probably the reason why it has been used for many agent-based simulations although it misses a standardised simulation control. Besides the advantages in communication and non-controlled environments, JADE is fully distributable which is advantageous for large scale agent applications. In contrast to the other agent frameworks, it can be executed on the JBoss application server which is of interest if agents are supposed to provide additional market services.

Ascape, MadKit, RePast, and Swarm lack standardised communication, the capability to distribute agents over several computers, and the support for non-controlled environments. It is not possible or difficult to add such functionality. Especially simulations in non-controlled environments are important in order to study effects if agents trade with humans. On the other hand, simulation control functions and a simulation control GUI can be embedded into JADE. Therefore, to benefit from these advantages, it was decided to implement the agent-based market simulation environment (AMASE) on basis of the JADE libraries by adding simulation control functions and an interface to meet2trade.

AMASE provides an easy-to-use GUI for setting up simulations, a flexible technique for management scheduling and an modular approach to enable agents to participate in simulations. This makes it possible to have agents participating in simulation and also acting in other (real world) environments. This is a valuable step toward the requirement of integrating controlled and non-controlled environments. Before presenting AMASE in Section 5.3 the JADE middleware is introduced in Section 5.2.

5.2 The Java Agent Development Framework

The JADE platform was briefly discussed in the last section. Since the simulation environment AMASE is based on the JADE middleware the basic concepts of JADE are presented in the following subsections. JADE is compliant to the FIPA standards and thus, implements the FIPA platform architecture including standards for agent communication, agent management, and agent message transport. These core concepts are briefly explained in Section 5.2.1. JADE provides an agent model which implements an agent life cycle and introduces an agent behaviour concept that allows to manage different tasks in separate threads. The JADE agent model is presented in Section 5.2.2. The platform offers additional tools to facilitate agents development such as a *Remote Management Agent*, a *Sniffer Agent* to eavesdrop agent messages, and an *Introspector Agent* to log agents internal behaviours. These tools are described in Section 5.2.3.

5.2.1   Agent Platform Architecture

The main goal of the FIPA abstract agent platform architecture is to enable agent-interoperability and reusability of the platform [Fou, 2002]. The core component for interoperability is the agent communication that enables agents to pass semantically meaningful messages. Additionally, services for agent registration, service directories, and agent life-cycle management have to be provided. The JADE agent platform implements these specification. The JADE architecture is depicted in Figure 5.1. It consists of the *Agent Management System (AMS)*, the *Directory*

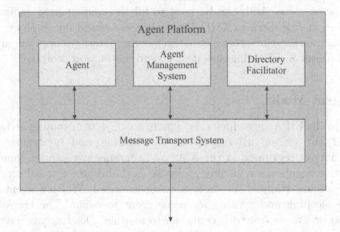

Figure 5.1: The architecture of JADE, source: Bellifemine et al. [2004]

Facilitator (DF), the *Message Transport System (MTS)*, and the *Agents*.

The AMS is itself an agent that exists in each Agent Platform exactly once. It is the management component that has supervisory control over all agents' access to and use of the Agent Platform [Bellifemine et al., 2004]. All agents are registered at the AMS and receive a unique Agent Identifier (AID). The AMS administrates an AID-directory and a directory for the agents' current states and provides Agent Life Cycle services.

The DF agent provides yellow page services to all agents. Each agents can register services and search the DF for service providers.

The platform can be distributed on different Java Virtual Machines (VM) that may either run on the same computer,[14] or on different machines as long as Remote Method Invocation (RMI) is possible within the network. A container is represented by an instance of a RMI server object and *contains* a set of agents. The set of all containers build the JADE platform. Each container manages message transport and agent life cycles locally. The AMS runs on the main container, other agents can run on both, the main container and remote containers. Agents are able to move between containers over the network by serialization. Special light weight container have been implemented to run on Java applets or on mobile devices.

The MTS determine the message transfer and the message representation. Messages are transported using RMI and are build of the content area and the header including necessary control information such as sender-AID, receiver(s)-AID, (mandatory) performative, encoding specification, ontology specification. Different Message Transport Protocols (MTP) are supported (e.g. HTTP MTP, IIOP MTP) and new MTP can be implemented and added easily. For interaction, agents not only need to exchange messages but also to understand their content. Therefore, an ACL can be used to fill the content area using a certain encoding format (e.g. String, XML, Bit) called *codec* and an ontology. It is possible to structure the conversations by exchanging messages applying a specified interaction protocol. FIPA has specified several interaction protocols.

5.2.2   Agent Model

According to the FIPA agent life cycle, agents are objects obtaining certain states: (i) initiated, (ii) active, (iii) suspended, (iv) waiting, and (v) transit. Initiated agents are not yet registered at the AMS and consequently cannot communicate, whereas active agents are registered, have an AID and access to all services. Suspended agents are stopped, no task is being executed. Waiting agents' threads instead are sleeping and waiting for some event to occur. The transit state is reached if agents move from one container to another. Dead agents have no state and are removed from the platform. The agent life cycle is also illustrated in Figure 5.2.

JADE implements a `Behaviour` Java class in order to model agents' tasks. Each `Behaviour` is a single thread and implements a specific capability of the agents. Different `Behaviour` instances can be added to the agent. As such, the set of tasks implemented as a `Behaviour` class build the agent's social and perceivable behaviour. JADE provides various `Behaviour` class implementations, e.g `OneShotBehaviour` or `CyclicBehaviour`. This modularization of tasks does not only facilitate the implementation of agents' capabilities but also increase efficiency during execution since inactive behaviours can be blocked until a certain event occurs, and do not consume computer resources in the meanwhile.

---

[14]This is possible since more than one VM can be executed on the same host, but results in an increase in overhead and thus, is not recommended.

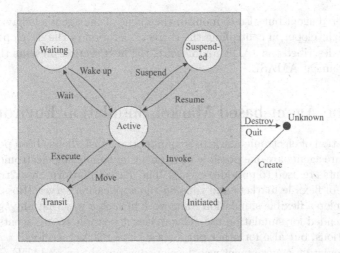

Figure 5.2: FIPA Agent Life Cycle, source: Bellifemine et al. [2004]

It is possible to add an individual GUI to each agent. JADE provides a `GUIAgent` class to implement agent specific user interfaces that fit with the Swing concurrency model.

5.2.3 Development Tools

JADE provides four agents to facilitate the development, debugging of agents and the control of the platform: *Remote Monitoring Agent (RMI), Dummy Agent (DA), Sniffer Agent,* and *Introspector Agent.*

The RMI is able to control the life cycle of the agent platform and registered agents. It is allowed to have several RMI agents (with different names) active on the same platform but just one RMI per container. The RMI provides operations for shutting down the agent platform, starting, killing, suspending, resuming and cloning agents. Agents can also be moved from one container to another as long as they support object serialization. Additionally, it offers methods for remote platform operations such as adding and removing remote platform (also non-JADE platforms are allowed). It is possible to launch a GUI for the DF to view description, register or deregister agents.

The DA enables the user to easily interact with other agents via a GUI. It is possible to compose, send and receive ACL messages.

The sniffer agent can track and display all messages sent to or from an agent or a group of agents. This supports the developer in monitoring the messages exchange process, e.g. according to a specified interaction protocol.

It is possible to monitor and control the agent life cycle of a running agent with the introspector agent that is not only able to track the exchanged messages of the monitored agent but also to monitor the queue of the agent's behaviours. This assists the developer in controlling the correct operation of the developed agents.

Having described the JADE middleware, the next section presents the simulation environment AMASE.

5.3   The Agent-based Market Simulation Environment

The evaluation of electronic markets is an important task. It has been pointed out that software agents are one possible instrument for simulating electronic markets. Often, agents are used to provide services. The market platform meet2trade offers the design of flexible markets and runs on the application server JBoss. The aim was to develop a flexible simulation framework in such a way that any `Agent` class can be extended for simulation use. This makes it possible to use agents not only for simulations, but also for other purposes such as market services.

The simulation environment was developed as an add-on to JADE. The architecture is described in the next subsection. The `SimulationControlAgent` (SCA) is the core of the simulation that manages the simulation and is described in Section 5.3.2. All agents participating in the simulation are equipped with the `AgentSimulationControlBehaviour` class that is described in Section 5.3.3. An example for using the environment is given in Section 5.3.4.

5.3.1   Architecture

AMASE uses the JADE Agent libraries that realise the *FIPA* specifications providing an agent platform (AP) with Agent Management System (AMS), Message Transport System (MTS), agents and additional services. Figure 5.3 displays the FIPA AP, the AMASE extensions and the communication to the meet2trade platform. The central agent of the JADE AP is the AMS keeping supervisory control over AP access and AP use. The AMS consists only once even on a distributed platform. The Domain Facilitator provides information (yellow pages) service within the platform. All JADE agents implement an agent life cycle and inherit functionality to add and remove certain `Behaviour` classes. Agents are capable to exchange messages over the MTS. JADE allows to distribute the AP on several computers, enabling agents to move between the computers. It does not provide any simulation specific functionality.

AMASE builds upon the JADE architecture. It uses JADE-MTS for message exchange among agents. All agents are full JADE agents. Figure 5.4 exhibits the basic components of the AMASE architecture. The SCA controls a simulation project by providing simulation management functions such as launching or removing agents, determining primary endowment, or managing the duration of the simulation. The project settings can be stored on the local file system. The `DataLog` component serves for logging the simulation data on the local file system. A GUI enables users to specify simulation project settings. The SCA owns

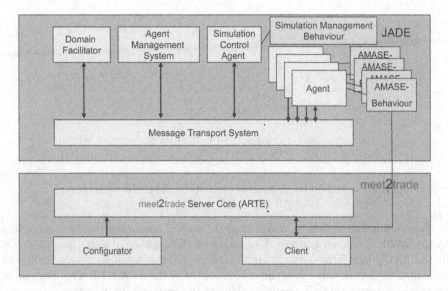

Figure 5.3: AMASE extensions to the JADE platform

the `SimulationManagementBehaviour` (SMB) which controls the simulation and provides communication capabilities to exchange control messages with the participating agents using standard ACL to advise the *start*, *stop* or *interruption* of a simulation. The communication is based on a specific defined interaction protocol. The SMB uses the `meet2tradeService` component to access the meet2trade-platform. The `AgentManagement` component stores information about the participating agents and their status. The communication is managed by a message control behaviour.

Simulation agents are enabled to participate in a simulation by implementing the `SimulationAgentControlBehaviour` (SACB) class. This behaviour manages the interaction with the SCA. A message control behaviour manages the message exchange with the SCA. Optionally, the `meet2tradeService` class provides connectivity to the meet2trade-system. The `LogManagement` component facilitates to store simulation data on the local file system. Apart from the communication between the SCA and the agents, the ability to communicate with other agents can be given to the simulation agents. This also enables simulation agents to communicate with any kind of agent, and thus, makes it possible to conduct simulation in controlled and uncontrolled environments. It is even possible to combine AMASE agents in experiments with human subjects. This is in particular important to enrich the research process in Market Engineering. The Simulation Behaviour component implements the simulation specific behaviour either as a particular behaviour class or by implementing the component's core functions. The AMASE specific behaviours are explained in Section 5.3.3.

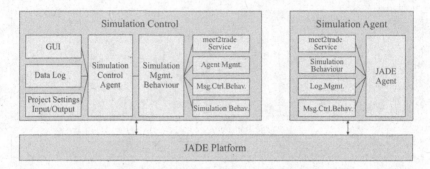

Figure 5.4: The basic components of the AMASE architecture

Simulation agents can be distributed on several computers (nodes) according to the JADE container concept. Regardless of the number of participating nodes in the JADE platform network, just a single SCA is needed. Functionality to distribute agents on other containers is provided in the SCA GUI. This is possible under the premise that all agents implement the serialization interface.

5.3.2   Simulation Control Agent (SCA)

The SCA is the core agent and serves as the central management entity. It enables discrete event simulation. AMASE Agents are coordinated by the SCA through control messages to synchronize agent activity. Control messages are exchanged using the JADE MTS and a specified interaction protocol. This protocol is defined in the `SimulationManagementBehaviour` (SMB) class. Users can either use the default SMB with certain control message sequence, or can adapt the SMB to partly change the interaction protocol.

Basically, AMASE distinguishes three types of simulations. Firstly, it supports uncontrolled environments, where only the start and the end of a simulation is signalized by the SCA. Secondly, round based simulations are enabled by defining the round through discrete events that are reported by the participating agents. Thereto, agents send control messages after having finished their task. According to the interaction protocol the next round starts after receiving all or a specified number of control messages. The third way is to discretise rounds by defining a fixed length in seconds. New rounds are announced by the SCA through control messages.

The simulation model has to be conceptually designed and than implemented. Models following one of the presented three types of simulation protocols can easily be created. A simulation model in AMASE consists of *one explicit SMB*, the *agents* (and their capabilities defined in the SACB), a *definition of the communication abilities/rules*, and the *initial endowment* of the agents. The simulation settings store the used SMB, the composition of the agent population, and the initial endowment of the agent. The simulations settings can be locally stored on the hard disc in XML-coded format. It is possible to run a series of predefined simulation settings.

For each simulation it is necessary to implement a SMB (and to implicitly define the interaction protocol) or to use the default SMB. The *behaviour* concept is explained in Section 5.3.3.

All agents used in a simulation must own the SACB that handles the interaction with the SCA and defines what action to perform in specific situations. It is possible to attach additional agent `Behaviour` classes to the SACB. The use and the functionality of the SACB is also described in Section 5.3.3. Implemented agents can be combined within different simulations as long as they use the same interaction protocol.

To facilitate the definition of simulation settings a GUI for the SCA was developed. It supports the user in specifying the agent population, their endowment, the SMB, and other parameter values. The GUI is presented in Section 5.3.2.

Simulation data can be stored in text files. The SCA provides functionality to write agent specific data in a text file using *comma separated values (CSV)*. This format can be read by many standard software for statistical analysis. AMASE was developed for both, simulations on the meet2trade-platform and pure AMASE simulations on a stand alone basis. This makes the platform usable not only for market simulations on meet2tràde, but also for various other kinds of simulation such as MAS for testing in software development. In some cases it might even be advantageous to set up small market simulation on an AMASE stand alone basis instead of using meet2trade due to performance reasons.[15] The data log functionality and the implementation of the interface towards meet2trade is presented in more detail in Section 5.3.2.

Graphical User Interface (GUI)

The SCA is equipped with a *Graphical User Interface (GUI)* that enables users to easily define simulation settings such as duration, types of agents or parameter settings. The GUI is divided in three main areas that are *(i) project tree, (ii) simulation settings*, and *(iii) simulation data display*. The GUI also provides a menu bar to handle basic functions and a status bar to display the progress of the simulation and e.g. elapsed time or rounds.

In the project tree area (i), simulation agents are displayed using two views, simulation based and JADE platform based. The simulation based view shows the simulation project name as the main node of the tree, all agent type names as children of the main node, and the names of the agents of one specific type as leaves of the tree. The JADE based view displays how the agents are distributed in existing containers of the platform. This view also allows users to drag and drop

---

[15] The exchange of messages by passing these messages to meet2trade is costly in terms of computational resources and thus, a pure AMASE simulation might save computing capacity and execution time.

agents from one container to another as long as the particular agent implements the serialization interface.

The simulation settings area (ii) is organized as a tabbed pane. It consists of six tabs: (a) general settings, (b) treatment, (c) communication, (d) agents, (e) products, and (f) endowment.

The general settings (a) define the settings name, an optional description, and the duration of the simulation – either specifying the number of rounds or the time period. The type of simulation (as described at the beginning of this section) is selected by specifying the type of rounds.

The treatment panel (b) facilitates to run series of different simulation settings. The settings have to be defined and saved. It is possible to define a sequence of simulation settings to be conducted and to specify the number of repetitions.

AMASE enables agents not only to use JADE communication but also to establish a communication to meet2trade. The communication type can be chosen on the communication tab (c). It is necessary to determine the connection information to meet2trade, e.g. IP-address, port number and database information. This connection information is sent to all agents before starting a simulation. As described earlier, the simulation protocol is defined within the SMB. A file chooser enables the user to specify and load the simulation specific SMB in the communication tab.

The agent tab (d) serves to load predefined `Agent` classes to the simulation. Therefore, an `Agent` class is selected within a file chooser, the number of instances of this class is specified and the SCA generates these instances. As soon as the agents are born, they are shown in the Project Tree panel. A list of loaded agents is also displayed in a table on the agent panel. It is also possible to remove agents from the simulation and platform consequently.

The product tab (e) was basically developed to facilitate simulations on meet2-trade that uses a database to manage user, product and depot entries. These entries can be created automatically by AMASE. The product tab serves to manage product entries in the meet2trade-database. The products are structured in product categories. Hence, it is necessary to first select and if necessary define a product category e.g. *stocks* or *bonds* for financial issues or books, DVD or CD for certain retail issues. Then, products of a particular category can be defined such as a certain company share or a certain book title. These newly defined categories and products can be automatically inserted into the database.

The endowment tab (f) facilitates the specification of the initial endowment of agents. It is possible to select a certain agent type and product and assign agents the initial endowment of the selected product. Therefore, a particular distribution can be chosen, e.g. by assigning equal values to all agents of one type, or draw values from one of the provided distributions. The determined values can be inserted into the database automatically.

The simulation data display (iii) is a panel for individual configuration. It can be accessed from the SMB. Data to be displayed can be sent to the SCA, processed by the SMB and displayed on the data display panel. There are excellent and free available Java libraries available for statistical data processing on the Internet such as *jfreechart*.[16] Hence, the data can be displayed dependent on the simulation specific data and purposes. Figure 5.5 shows a screenshot of the SCA GUI.

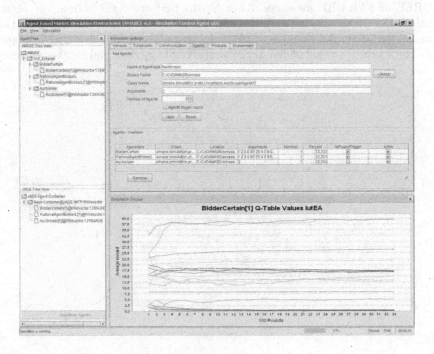

Figure 5.5: SCA GUI Screenshot

Data logging, communication and meet2trade interface

For the evaluation of simulations it is necessary to store the specific data. This includes input variables, output variables and variables determining the system's state. While running the simulation the change of system states builds an artificial history. In order to analyse this history the relevant data is stored by a logging service. Each agent that wants to log values instantiates the class **LogManagement**. This class provides log-methods that pass the variable value of any primitive type and the variable name to the SCA. The data is stored on the local file system on the computer that hosts the SCA.

SCA and simulation agents use the JADE-MTS for message exchange. The messages are defined according to the ACL message format. The sequence of messages is explained in the following example:

---

[16]http://www.jfree.org/jfreechart/index.php

The SCA announces changes in the simulation status by sending REQUEST message that include one of the action schemes (i) initialize, (ii) set communication, (iii) start, (iv) interrupt, and (v) stop. The agents answer either with AGREE or FAILURE messages. After having performed the action, the agents send an INFORM message with the action scheme *Done* and the related action scheme, e.g. start. An example of this interaction protocol is depicted in Figure 5.6. The schemes are embedded in the `amaseOntology` class and can be processed

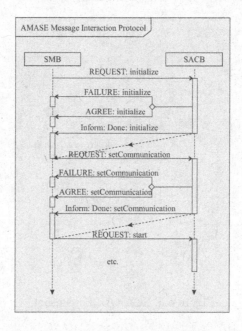

Figure 5.6: Sequence diagram of the AMASE control message interaction protocol.

by using the FIPA ACL codex. JADE provides ontology processing mechanisms. It was observed during simulations that the application of the ontology mechanism consume computing power. Thus, an alternative mechanism – a simple string parsing – was implemented to parse the action schemes. This increased the speed of message exchange tremendously.

Note that the communication between simulation agents is not affected by these design issues. The communication characteristics (interaction protocol, ACL, encoding, ontology, etc.) are defined by the user and implemented as a separate behaviour of the simulation agents.

The communication to the meet2trade-platform uses the platform's standard JMS interface and classes. These meet2trade-communication classes were modified in order to fit the agent requirements. An instance of the `Meet2TradeService` class is owned by the `SimulationAgentControlBehaviour` class and provides methods to easily send orders, receive order books, etc. Each agent can access these services via the SACB. The communication to meet2trade is technically based on the Java Message Service (JMS) that process message strings within a message queue. In the current implementation one queue is used for the communication between agents and the platform meet2trade. The messages are XML-encoded. The meet2trade-communication is provided as a simple service. For further information on implementation of the meet2trade-communication see also Weinhardt et al. [2005].

5.3.3 Simulation Agents and Behaviours

All agents in JADE are an extension of the `jade.core.Agent` class. Agent specific behaviour is added by extending the JADE `Behaviour` classes in the package `jade.core.behaviours`. In order to make the agent participating in a simulation it must implement the `SimulationAgentsControlBehaviour` from the package `amase.behaviours`. Simulation agents exhibit different states: (i) New, (ii) Initialized, (iii) Idle, (iv) Active, and (v) Stop. The transitions from one state to another provoked by the SACB. The sequence of states and transitions is fixed and visualized in a Petri Net in Figure 5.7.

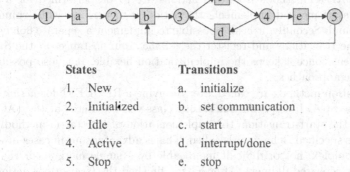

States	Transitions
1. New	a. initialize
2. Initialized	b. set communication
3. Idle	c. start
4. Active	d. interrupt/done
5. Stop	e. stop

Figure 5.7: Petri Net determining the sequence of agent states and transitions.

Having created an agent instance it holds the state *New* (i). It is registered at the SCA and waiting for initialization. Before being able to participate in a simulation the agent needs to run the initialize methods and hence, obtains the state *Initialized* (ii). Then, it needs to set up the communication – to log into meet2trade or to perform other communication tasks such as registering services at the DF. In the *Idle* state (iii), simulation agents wait for start requests to change into the *Active* state (iv). The Active state can either terminate regularly and change to idle, an interruption can be forced to change to Idle, or it can change to *Stop* (v). In the Stop state agents are logged out of meet2trade and reset themselves to a state similar to the Initialized state. Consequently, agents can again participate in a simulation by resetting the communication and thus, obtaining the Idle state.

Figure 5.8 exhibits an extract of the UML diagram for the AMASE behaviour classes. The diagram depicts the relation of the SMB to the SCA as well as to other important components such as the meet2trade service class. The simulation specific actions are either implemented in the SACB or in separate `Behaviour` classes. As such the SACB determines the agent type. The implementation of the SACB is presented in the next section. The SMB controls the simulation flow and is described in more detail in Section 5.3.3.

Simulation Agents Control Behaviour

The `SimulationAgentsControlBehaviour` (SACB) class enables the agent to participate in a simulation. It manages the communication of control messages with the SCA and implements the simulation specific behaviour of the agent. It also provides the `Meet2TradeService` class for communication with the meet2trade platform. There are two ways of implementing the simulation specific behaviour. Firstly, the SACB class contains transition methods to change the agent's internal state: *initialize*, setCommunication, *start*, *interrupt*, and *stop*. It is sufficient to implement these methods if certain actions are to be performed for a state change. The start-method implements the action(s) to perform while running a simulation round. Secondly, it is also possible to implement a separate `Behaviour` for each of the transitions and register these `Behaviour` instances at the SACB. This component concept keeps the implementation flexible. It is also possible to combine these approaches.

The transition methods are called after receiving a REQUEST for *action* messages from the SCA. If a specific `Behaviour` class was registered at the SACB to perform, e.g. the start-transition, the implementation of the start()-method is ignored and the specified Behaviour is called. This is advantageous in cases in which the task is complex, not or difficult handleable by a single method, or the task is periodically repeated (Timer). After having finished the (transition) action the corresponding *actionEnd*-method (e.g. initializeEnd) is called to notify the SCA if the action was completed successfully or not.

Having completed an action, the SACB changes its state and waits for control messages of the SMB that works similar. The SMB is further explained in the next section.

Simulation Management Behaviour

The `SimulationManagementBehaviour` (SMB) class controls the simulation flow. Each simulation must use the standard class or implement a specific SMB. This class manages *when* to call *which transition* of *which agent*. For that purpose the SMB follows a similar approach as the SACB by providing methods that can be

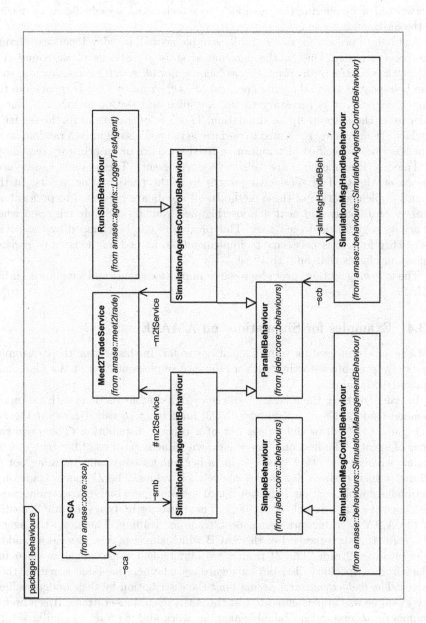

Figure 5.8: UML class diagram of the AMASE behaviour packages and corresponding components.

overwritten or by offering the possibility to attach a task specific `Behaviour` class to the SMB.

A standard process for method calls is implemented, but developers can change this process partly. Due to the determined state transitions of the simulation agents, the skeleton of the process is as follows: *initialize, setCommunication, start* (can be repeated after all agents are finished), *interrupt* or *stop*. If agents join the simulation later, it is necessary to call initialize and setCommunication first in order to set these agents up for simulation. The developer can control the sequence in which the agents are requested to perform actions. This might be a random order dependent on a specified distribution, a fixed sequence or an arbitrary sequence.

The described methods are called by system events. These events can be user actions on the GUI or received messages from the participating agents. In the default implementation of these methods, all agents are requested to perform actions synchronously and next actions (like new rounds) are only triggered when all agents have finished their task. This procedure can be changed by the developer. Therefore, it is necessary to implement the named methods or to register Behaviour classes that fulfil this task.

The following sections provides some examples for agents and simulations using AMASE.

5.3.4   Examples for Simulations on AMASE

AMASE has been used for some simulations so far. In this section three examples are briefly presented starting with a reference implementation of the Gode and Sunder [1993] paper.

In order to study the allocative efficiency of a double auctions with rationally bounded traders, Gode and Sunder [1993] implement so called *zero intelligence* (ZI) traders that draw bid values out of a certain distribution. There are two types of agents. The first one bids the drawn value regardless of her budget constraint, whereas the other type considers her budget constraint meaning not to sell under their costs or not to buy above their values. The ZI agents trade on a continuous double auction. It is shown that introducing a budget constraint raises the allocative efficiency close to 100%. These two agent types are implemented for the AMASE framework using meet2trade for trading. Therefore, the agents implement the *start*-method of the SACB which single task is to send a random order into meet2trade. The ZI traders without budget constraint draw their bid values from a specified distribution regardless whether the value is within their budget. The *budget contraint agents* limit the distribution by their budget values. This example was implemented to test the AMASE and meet2trade. It is a usefull example to understand how double auctions work and it produces similar results as found by Gode and Sunder [1993] and explained above.

An other example uses AMASE for a simulation of ascending single sided auctions with fixed and soft ends combined with a BuyPrice feature [Weber et al., 2004]. A BuyPrice is a posted price offer that allows traders to immediately buy the offered item and thus, stopping the running auction. Ünver [2003] develops a model for studying auctions with soft and fixed end. This model is adapted to the described problem and used for implementation in AMASE. Agents draw valuations for the offered item from a specified distribution and use a genetic algorithm to choose their bidding strategy. Since the agents perform a more complex task compared to the previous example, a specific BidBehaviour was implemented and registered instead of the default behaviour running the start-method. The auctions are operated on meet2trade. Since the auction was repeated several thousand times communication to meet2trade became a bottleneck. Consequently, the auction was also implemented as a JADE agent which increased performance tremendously.

A third example is a study conducted by Weber [2005]. The goal of this work is to study the impact of a bidding discount offered to the first bidder in an ascending single sided internet auction. In most ascending single sided auction the winner pays either the price of the highest bid or of the second highest bid. In order to encourage early bidding a discount is offered to the first bidder if at the end she is also the winner of the auction. An experimental approach was chosen for this study that uses AMASE agents for a preliminary experiment. In this experiment, humans play against AMASE agents that bid after a predefined bidding scheme. The experiment was conducted on the meet2trade-platform and shows the potential for human-computer experiments.

5.4 Summary

In the first part of this chapter design objectives for an agent-based environment are presented that is suited for market simulations in general and for simulations on the meet2trade-platform in particular. These basic functional and technical requirements derived from general specification for agent-based simulations and from trading platform specific needs. Common agent frameworks were presented and preliminary assessed regarding fundamental design issues. The most relevant software frameworks were analysed in more detail regarding the discussed requirements.

The agent middleware JADE was presented in the second section of this chapter, since it is used as the basic framework for the development of the Agent-based Market Simulation Environment (AMASE). JADE provides libraries for a highly developed FIPA compliant MAS that facilitates the administration and application of huge agent populations that are also distributable on different computers on a network.

AMASE was developed to add simulation functionality to the existing JADE environment. The main components and functionality are presented. The main component is realised as an agent instance that is capable to administer a simulation by message exchange with the participating agents. It makes use of the standard FIPA communication patterns and implements a straight forward interaction protocol to manage the simulation flow. The architecture uses the JADE behaviour concept, and thus, is flexible and easily extendible.

In the next part, the impact of valuation uncertainty on the bidder behaviour and the auction's outcome is studied. Section 6 poses research questions, describes the simulation model, and develops theoretic solutions as far as possible. The model is implemented using the AMASE environment. In Section 7, the results of the simulation are presented and discussed in depth.

Part III

Examination of Bidding under Uncertainty

Chapter 6

Simulation Design

In Part II, agent-based approaches and their link to economic theory have been discussed. The JADE-based simulation environment AMASE was developed which can be used for market simulations. In this part, reinforcement learning is applied to simulate bidder behaviour in electronic auctions using the AMASE environment. The economic problem is described in the following.

The bidding behaviour of (economic) agents in auctions is based on their valuations. The determination of these valuations is dependent on both, the characteristics of the item and the individual preferences of the agent. Economic theory assumes that agents behave in auctions rationally, which implies that the agents have determined their valuations of the item before they enter the bidding process. In private values settings, agents base their assessment of an item's value on information available to them such product features, age or other characteristics. This information together with the individual preferences build one's own valuation. Theory assumes that the information is available at zero cost. It has been outlined in Section 2.1.4 that situations exist in which information is not fully available at zero cost. As a result, agents might not be able to determine a distinct valuation, i.e. they are uncertain about their true valuation. Agents being certain on their valuation are called *certain agents* in the following, whereas agents that are uncertain on their valuations are called *uncertain agents*.

The costs of gathering information are often neglected by individuals. People may be aware of search costs such as internet service provider fees, travel costs, or telephone charges. Apart from these factors the information search is costly in time (opportunity cost). It is possible to determine the opportunity costs as a monetary value for searching (working) time.

The lack of information – regardless of the reason for the missing information[1] – leads to uncertainty about one's own private valuation. Let us assume that agents can spend an amount c on the acquisition of additional information.

---

[1]The lack of information might have different reasons, e.g. information is not available or unknown (natural resources), or there was no information search conducted.

This informations enables them to determine their true valuation. This raises the question if and at what time to acquire information. The decision whether or not to acquire information might be influenced by the behaviour of the competitors. Consider the following example:

Example 6.0.1. Paula wants to go skiing this winter and needs a roof rack for her car. She is not sure how long she wants to keep her car. This is why she is not willing to buy a new roof rack for 300 Euros. Consequently, she searches one of the known internet auction platforms to buy a used roof rack. How much is she willing to pay for this good? She determines her maximum willingness to pay at a level of 40 Euros without being sure if this is a reasonable decision and places a proxy bid at that level in the ascending proxy auction.[2] She outbids the actual highest bid at a price of 28 Euros. Then, Peter enters the auction three minutes before the displayed end and places a bid at 38 Euros. Thus, Paula is still the highest bidder at a price of 39 Euros. Anxious about not having determined her true valuation she starts searching for additional information about roof racks and finds that she can use the rack not only in winter but also in summer, e.g. for bicycles. Peter places a bid at 43 Euros while Paula finds the additional information about the alternative use of the item which makes her adjusting the valuation to 45 Euros. But she submits the bid too late; the auction has already closed and Peter wins the auction at a price of 41 Euros.

Example 6.0.1 illustrates that economic agents might be uncertain about their own valuations. The occurrence of competing bids can influence agents to search for additional information triggered by the time of occurrence or by the value of the bid. The information search is costly and thus can be interpreted as information acquisition. As long as the competing bid has no influence on ones own valuation, it is still a private value setting. A mixed case of private and common value components arise if the competing bids' valuations influence one's own valuation.

The described problem is known in literature as strategic bidding under uncertainty in ascending auctions and was discussed in Section 2.1.4. It is usually applied for explaining effects of takeover bidding or for analysing the case of a firm going public. Some authors discuss a two-person scenario and develop theoretical models under several assumptions. In fact, it is not easy to find a closed form solution for the problem. Rather comparative statics can be applied. The central propositions found in literature have been summarized in Section 2.1.4.

In general, it is investigated how uncertainty on the participants' own valuations impact their bidding behaviour, their payoffs, the auctioneer's revenue as well as the social welfare. This raises research questions on the strategic implications for bidding and the auction outcome which are related to the propositions P1-P7 (cp. p. 29) and are stated in the following:

---

[2] The ascending proxy auction in this examples implements a bid increment of 1 Euro. That means, if player A submits a bid of 10 Euros to the proxy and player B submits a bid of 20 Euros to the proxy, then bidder B outbids bidder A by 10+1=11 Euros.

(Q1) *Is it beneficial for the uncertain bidder to acquire information late?*
P1: It is advantageous for uncertain bidders to wait for competing bids conveying information about the competitors valuation before deciding on information acquisition [Compte and Jehiel, 2000].

(Q2) *Is there an incentive for the certain bidder to bid early?*
P2: The certain bidder profits from uncertain bidders that acquire information early in an auction [Rasmusen, 2005].
P4: Early bidding is likely to stimulate value discovery [Rasmusen, 2005].

(Q3) *How does uncertainty influence revenues of bidders and the auctioneer?*
P3: The auctioneer profits from bidders being uncertain [Rasmusen, 2005].

(Q4) *Is there an impact on the bidding behaviour in different environmental settings, e.g. different numbers of agents or varying information acquisition costs?*
P5: Increasing information costs may reduce social welfare [Hirshleifer and Png, 1989].

(Q5) *How do sealed-bid auctions perform under uncertainty in comparison to an open-cry ascending auction?*
P6: Under uncertainty, English Auctions lead to higher expected prices compared to sealed-bid second price auctions [Milgrom and Weber, 1982].
P7: First-price auctions induce a higher incentive to acquire information than second price auctions [Persico, 2000].

The propositions are derived from comparative statics and neglect dynamic auction behaviour and the fact that agents do not always act fully rational. To the author's knowledge, there is neither a study of (dynamic) behaviour of bidders in the described situation of uncertainty, nor research considering bounded rational agents. This is why the present work uses another approach by applying agent-based computational economics to the problem. Adaptive agents are used to simulate bounded rational agents acting in different environments. The subsequent section develops the simulation model and is followed by the simulative approach. The chapter closes with the description of the simulative approach, including the used parameter settings and a discussion of the applied strategy adaptation techniques.

6.1 The Simulation Model

Agents participate in single sided electronic auctions of two types, an ascending open-cry second-price auction that in the following is called *Ascending Auction (AA)* and a *Second-Price Sealed-Bid Auction (SB)*.

In an ascending open-cry second-price auction, bidders send their bids to the auctioneer. New bids are assessed whether or not they are higher than the actual highest bid. If a new bid is higher, it is accepted as new highest bid. If it is higher than the second highest bid and lower than the highest bid, it is accepted as new second highest bid. The winner of the auction with the highest bid b^* pays the price of the second highest bid b^{2nd}. During the auction the price of the second highest bid is displayed to all bidders, whereas the highest bid remains hidden. In contrast to the sealed-bid auction agents are allowed to increase their bids during the auction.

In the Second Price Sealed Bid Auction, bidders send one bid to the auctioneer. The bidder with the highest bid b^* wins the auction and pays the price of the second highest bid b^{2nd}. It is a dominant strategy to bid one's own valuation. The bidding process of both auction types is explained in more detail in Section 6.1.1.

Figure 6.1 depicts the application flow of the simulation. At the start of each simulation replication, the Simulation Control Agent (SCA) draws the initial seed of the Random Number Generators (RNG) of the participating agents. Having received these initial values, the bidder agents send a "ready for start" signal to the SCA. The SCA starts a round of the simulation and the bidder agents draw their valuations and estimated valuations respectively. The bidder agents set the initial internal state and choose an action. The bid on basis of the chosen action is sent to the auctioneer. Having collected all bids, the auctioneer determines the actual highest bidder and the second highest bid price and sends the result to the bidder agents. The bidders determine the new internal state and the actual reward for the action. They update the reinforcement learner. If the auction has not finished yet, the bidders choose a new action and the bid process starts again.[3] Otherwise, the actual internal state is written to a log file and the SCA is notified about the end of the auction. The auctions are repeated as often as specified in the setting description (this depends on the environmental settings and is explained in Chapter 7). After the end of a simulation, the SCA checks whether a replication of the simulation is specified. In this case, the bidder agents are reset and the simulation is started with new initial seeds for the RNGs of the bidders.

Neither the number nor the type of competing agents in the auction is known to other agents. The auctions are modelled as game of incomplete information since the valuation of the competitors are unknown. There are $N \in \{1, \ldots, N\}$ agents participating in one auction. The agents $i = 1, 2, \ldots, N$ draw valuations v_i from a continuous uniform distribution F_V with support $[a, b]$. The density $f_V(v)$ is given by:

$$f_V(v) = \begin{cases} \frac{1}{(b-a)} & a \leq v \leq b \\ 0 & \text{otherwise} \end{cases} \qquad (6.1)$$

Agents are either *certain* or *uncertain* on their valuation. Those agents being certain on their valuation know the drawn value, whereas uncertain agents do not know this value at the beginning of the a simulation round. Instead, uncertain agents receive an estimated valuation $v_i^E \in [v_i - d; v_i + d])$. The estimated valuation v_i^E is calculated as the sum of the drawn valuation v_i and a uniform distributed

---

[3]The bidder process is described in more detail in Section 6.1.1.

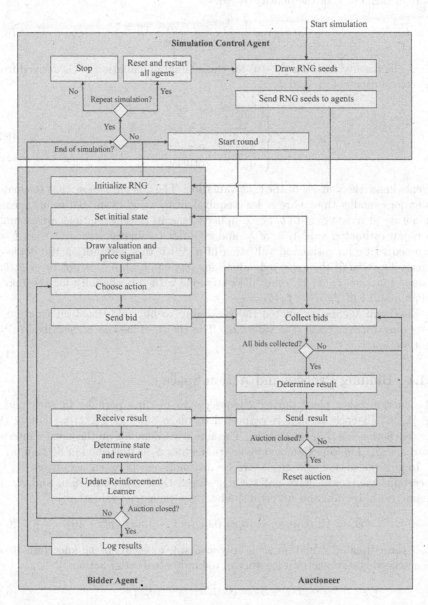

Figure 6.1: Application flow of the simulation model including all agent types: Simulation Control Agent (SCA), Bidder Agents, and Auctioneer.

random variable Y of the density $f_Y(y)$:

$$f_Y(y) = \begin{cases} \frac{1}{2d} & -d \leq y \leq +d \\ 0 & \text{otherwise} \end{cases} \tag{6.2}$$

Thus, the density function $f_{V^E}(v)$ for the estimated valuation v^E is derived from the convolution[4] of f_V and f_Y:

$$f_{V^E}(v) = \begin{cases} \frac{v-a-d}{2d(b-a)} & a-d \leq v < a+d \\ \frac{1}{(b-a)} & a+d \leq v \leq b-d \\ \frac{b+d-v}{2d(b-a)} & b-d < v \leq b+d \\ 0 & \text{otherwise} \end{cases} \tag{6.3}$$

Agents know the density of the true valuation. Thus, agents know that estimated valuations smaller than a are at least equivalent to a and estimated values greater than b are at most equal to b. For simplicity reasons these valuations are assumed to be an estimated valuation of a, and estimated valuations greater than b are assumed to be an estimated valuation of b. With this assumption the depicted density function of the expected valuations (cp. equation 6.3) is not precise. The density function $f_E(x)$ becomes discontinuous with a probability for the border values a and b of $f_E(a) = f_E(b) = \frac{1}{2d}$.

Uncertain agents are offered the possibility to buy additional information at costs c to discover their true valuation. The choice of actions is described in the next section.

6.1.1 · Bidding Process and Action Space

The auction takes place during T consecutive bidding periods. In each period $t \in \{1, \ldots, T\}$ each agent i is requested to place one bid $b_i^t \in B(s_i)$ out of the discrete action set $B(s_i)$ in state s_i. The action set depends on the agent's internal state $s_i \in S_i$. The set of an agent's internal states S_i is described in Section 6.1.2.

In general, action sets $B(s_i)$ can be distinguished between action set B_u for uncertain agents who have not yet discovered their true valuation, and B_c for agents (both, certain and uncertain) who know their true valuation:

$$B_u = \{0, 0.5v_i, v_i - 10, v_i, 0.5v_i^E, v_i^E, v_i^E - 10, v_i^E, v_i^E + 10\} \tag{6.4}$$

Since the estimated valuation v_i^E is only available to agents being uncertain about their true valuation, certain agents can bid only a subset of actions:

$$B_u \supset B_c = \{0, 0.5v_i, v_i - 10, v_i\} \tag{6.5}$$

Uncertain agents can acquire additional information at cost c to discover their true valuation. If uncertain agents have discovered their true valuation, they can not bid v^E any longer and the set of possible actions is reduced to B_c.

---

[4]The convolution is explicitly calculated in the Appendix A.5.

The agents chose one bid and send it to the auctioneer, who collects the bids during one bidding period and sequential assesses the bids as described in the following.[5] Assume b^* is the actual highest bid and b^{2nd} is the actual second highest bid, then three possible cases are to be distinguished:

1. $b_i^t > b^*$
   If the drawn bid b_i^t is greater than the actual highest bid b^*, b^* is the new second highest bid $b^{2nd} = b^*$, b_i^t becomes the new highest bid $b^* = b_i^t$ and agent i is the new highest bidder. This applies also if the bidder i is the actual highest bidder j^* (and $j = i$).

2. $b^* > b_i^t > b^{2nd}$
   The drawn bid b_i^t is smaller than the actual highest bid b^* but greater than the actual second highest bid b^{2nd}. In this case, b_i^t becomes the new second highest bid $b^{2nd} = b_i^t$.

3. $b^{2nd} > b_i^t$
   The drawn bid b_i^t is smaller than the actual second highest bid b^{2nd}. The identity of the actual highest bidder j^*, the value of the actual highest bid b^* and the value of the actual second highest bid b^{2nd} remain unchanged.

At the beginning of an auction, agents draw their valuations and estimated valuations. In time period $t = 1$ the agents have to choose their first action out of their action space and send the bid to the auctioneer. The action selection depends on the type of the agent and is explained in more detail in Section 6.2. The actual highest bidder and the actual second highest bid price are determined. The actual highest bidder i^* is informed about being the actual highest bidder and all agents are informed about the second highest bid price. Dependent on the environmental feedback the action selection process is updated at the end of each bidding period. This procedure is repeated for each bidding period until the end of the auction is reached.

To compare the two auction formats AA and SB, agents participate in both auctions at the same time using equal valuations and estimated valuations but independent action selection processes, and consequently, submitting different bids. The two auctions are treated completely separate from each other, so agents do not apply information from one auction in the other auction. In bidding period $t = 1$ agents submit bids to both auctions, SB and AA. In the subsequent periods agents are only allowed to bid in the AA. The results of both auctions are announced after period $t = T$.

6.1.2 Agents and Environment

There are two basic types of agents, *stationary* and *dynamic*. These basic types implement different sub-behaviour. The stationary agents are certain in their val-

---

[5]The auctioneer draws the bid by random to avoid preferences for certain bids due to processing reasons.

ʌuation and follow one determined strategy regardless what the other agents do. Four stationary agents are available, *early stationary (HE)*, *late stationary (HL)*, *price signalling agents (HP)*, and *random (Monte Carlo) agents (HR)*. Since the stationary agents play their true valuation at some stage, they are also called *honest (H)* agents. Agents of type HE bid their full valuation in bidding period $t = 1$, whereas agents of type HL and HP bid their full valuation as late as possible $(t = T)$. HL agents send a bid of full valuation at the end of the auction and zero bids otherwise. HP agents send an early price signal $b_i^E \in \mathbb{R} : 0 \leq b_i^E < v_i$ in $t = 1$. Actions are chosen randomly by the HR agents in each bidding period.

Dynamic agents adopt a reinforcement learning algorithm to choose appropriate actions. Two types of dynamic agents are used: *certain* and *uncertain* agents. Dynamic agents are able to observe their environment based on the feedback of the auctioneer at the end of each bidding period. These observations lead to a new agent internal state $s_i \in S_i$. The set S_i of agent's i internal states s comprises all tuples $\langle DT, t, CE, H, I \rangle$. The set $S = S_1 \times \ldots \times S_N$ describes the set of system states. The five factors of the tuple that determine the internal state are described in the following:

1. Dynamic agent type $DT \in \{\text{TRUE,FALSE}\}$: This parameter specifies the type of the agent: *certain (TRUE)* or *uncertain (FALSE)*.

2. Bidding period $t \in \{1, \ldots, T\}$: There is just one bidding period in case of a SB format: $(T = 1)$, whereas AA formats usually have more than one bidding period $(T > 1)$.

3. Certainty $CE \in \{\text{TRUE,FALSE}\}$: The information of certainty depends on the previous actions and on the type of the agent. Certain bidders are always certain (TRUE) about their valuation at any time. Uncertain agents however, are either uncertain (FALSE) on their valuation as long as they do not buy additional information to discover their true valuation. After having bought additional information, uncertain agents switch to the internal state certain (CE=TRUE).

4. High bidder status $H \in \{-4, -3, -2, -1, 0, 1, 2, 3, 4, 10\}$: The auctioneer informs all agents whether or not they are the highest bidder at the end of the actual bidding period. If the agent is a high bidder, the high bidder status is positive. If the agent has only submitted zero bids, the high bidder status is zero. A negative high bidder status belongs to all agents that have submitted bids greater than zero and are not the highest bidder. The numbers $0, \ldots, 4$ are assigned to the last actions, whereby 0 is assigned to a zero bid, 1 to $b_i = \frac{1}{2} v_i$ or $b_i = \frac{1}{2} v_i^E$, etc. The agent itself determines its own high bidder status. Uncertain agents receive an error afflicted estimated valuation in the beginning that has a positive probability of being greater than the true valuation. Therefore, it is possible that these agents submit bids above their true valuation. Additionally, uncertain agents are allowed to bid above their estimated valuation (as long as they are uncertain about the valuation)

since there is also a positive probability that the received estimated valuation is lower than the true valuation. Thus, uncertain agents might win the auction at a price above their true valuation leading to a negative reward. In order to capture this information of overbidding at the end of an auction, the high bidder status $H_i = 10$ is introduced. This leads to the following highest bidder states:

$$
H_i = \begin{cases}
-4 & \text{, if } b_i \neq b^* \text{ and last action was } b_i = v_i^E + 10 \\
-3 & \text{, if } b_i \neq b^* \text{ and last action was } b_i = v_i \text{ or } b_i = v_i^E \\
-2 & \text{, if } b_i \neq b^* \text{ and last action was } b_i = v_i - 10 \text{ or } b_i = v_i^E - 10 \\
-1 & \text{, if } b_i \neq b^* \text{ and last action was } b_i = \frac{1}{2}v_i \text{ or } b_i = \frac{1}{2}v_i^E \\
0 & \text{, if } b_i \neq b^* \text{ and last action was } b_i = 0 \\
1 & \text{, if } b_i = b^* \text{ and last action was } b_i = \frac{1}{2}v_i \text{ or } b_i = \frac{1}{2}v_i^E \\
2 & \text{, if } b_i = b^* \text{ and last action was } b_i = v_i - 10 \text{ or } b_i = v_i^E - 10 \\
3 & \text{, if } b_i = b^* \text{ and last action was } b_i = v_i \text{ or } b_i = v_i^E \\
4 & \text{, if } b_i = b^* \text{ and last action was } b_i = v_i \text{ or } b_i = v_i^E + 10 \\
10 & \text{, if } b_i = b^* \wedge t = T \wedge b^{2nd} > v_i
\end{cases}
$$

5. Interval class $I \in \{1, \ldots, 5\}$ of the second highest bid: each bidder compares the second highest bid b^{2nd} to its own valuation. The interval classes are distinguished for certain I^c and uncertain internal states. I^u. The actual second highest bid lies in one of the following interval classes. For the certain bidder, there are four interval classes:

$$
\begin{aligned}
I_{i1}^c &:= [0; \tfrac{1}{2}\max(v_i^*; 65)) \\
I_{i2}^c &:= [\tfrac{1}{2}\max(v_i^*; 65); \max(65; v_i^* - 10)) \\
I_{i3}^c &:= [\max(65; v_i^* - 10); \max(\min(v_i^*; 115), 65)) \\
I_{i4}^c &:= [\max(\min(v_i^*; 115), 65); \infty)
\end{aligned}
$$

For the uncertain bidder, there are five interval classes:

$$
\begin{aligned}
I_{i1}^u &:= [0; \tfrac{1}{2}\max(v_i^*; 65)) \\
I_{i2}^u &:= [\tfrac{1}{2}\max(v_i^*; 65); \max(65; v_i^* - 10)) \\
I_{i3}^u &:= [\max(65; v_i^* - 10); \max(\min(v_i^*; 115); 65)) \\
I_{i4}^u &:= [\max(\min(v_i^*; 115); 65); \min(v_i^* + 10; 115)) \\
I_{i5}^u &:= [\min(v_i^* + 10; 115); \infty)
\end{aligned}
$$

Remember that the valuation $v_i^* = v_i$ is the true valuation for bidders who know their true valuation and $v_i^* = v_i^E$ is the estimated valuation for bidders who have not yet discovered their true valuation.

Each agent has to place a bid in each bidding period, and thus, faces the decision of how much to bid. Uncertain agents additionally have to decide whether or not to buy additional information to discover their true valuation. Uncertain agents who have not yet discovered their true valuation ($CE = \text{FALSE}$), can choose one action out of the action set $B(s) = B_u$ (cp. equation 6.4). This is either not to buy information and place a bid $b \in B_u^E \subset B_u$ with $B_u^E = \{0, \frac{1}{2}v_i^E, v_i^E - 10, v_i^E, v_i^E + 10\}$, or to buy additional information at costs c and bid $b \in \{\frac{1}{2}v_i, v_i - 10, v_i\}$.

A certain agent[6] has the choice of four actions since it is not reasonable to buy information for him. A certain agent can bid $b \in B_c = \{0, \frac{1}{2}v_i, v_i - 10, v_i\}$.

Formally, each agent i possesses a set of actions A_i of all available actions and a set of possible actions $A_i(s) \subseteq A_i$ depending on the current state $s \in S_i$. The described states $s \in S_i$ and the possible actions $a \in A_i(s)$ span the state-action space $S_i \times A_i(S_i)$. The space of possible actions depends on the agent's internal state. Uncertain agents, for example, can acquire information only once. Additionally, agents are only allowed to bid at least as much as their last bid.

6.1.3   The Reinforcement Learning Mechanism

The decision problem of the agents is also known in literature as an *n-armed bandit* problem in analogy to the *one-armed bandit*. In each state, the agents face the situation of choosing amongst different actions of which the outcome is unknown. Reinforcement learning has proven to cope with such a model-free situation.[7] The transition from state $s \in S_i$ to $s' \in S_i$ proceeds according to transition probabilities controlled jointly by all agents $i \in \{1, \ldots, N\}$. The agents influence the transition by choosing an action $a_{ij} \in A_i(s)$, and $j \in \{1, \ldots, |A_i(s)|\}$. Thus, the model environment constitutes a controlled Markov process with the agents being the controller. Agents receive a reward after each transition. The goal of each agent is to maximize the discounted future rewards, and thus, solve the Markov decision process (MDP) by finding an optimal policy $\pi : S \to A$.

Reinforcement learning algorithm are used to implement a decision approach for agents by mapping received rewards of state action pairs into future probabilities of choosing a certain action. Watkins [1989] has introduced Q-Learning as model-free reinforcement learning algorithm with close similarities to MDPs. Erev and Roth [1998] have developed a RL algorithm (ER) according to rules known from psychology and they have tested it in dynamic environments in order to compare the results to human behaviour. For the present model, characteristics of both approaches, Q-learning and ER were integrated. Each agent i possesses a table of Q-values $q_{kl}^i = Q^i(s_{ik}, a_{il})$ for each state-action pair (s_{ik}, a_{il}) with $k \in \{1, \ldots, |S_i|\}$ and $a_{il} \in A_i(s_{ik})$ and $l \in \{1, \ldots, |A(s_{ik})|\}$. The agents receive rewards according

---

[6]This might be an agent of type *certain* or an agent of type *uncertain* that has discovered his true valuation.

[7]Model-free approaches learn optimal policies without building a model on the state transitions and rewards, whereas model-based techniques estimate a model first and afterwards learn optimal policies (cp. refsubsubsec:learningModel).

to the following reward function:

$$R_i(a_i, s') = \begin{cases} b^{2nd} - v_i & \forall a_i \in A_i(s) \wedge s' \in \{S_i | t = T \wedge H > 0 \wedge \\ & [DT = \text{TRUE} \vee (DT = \text{FALSE} \wedge CE = \text{FALSE})]\} \\ b^{2nd} - v_i - c & \forall a_i \in A_i(s) \wedge s' \in \{S_i | t = T \wedge H > 0 \wedge \\ & DT = \text{FALSE} \wedge CE = \text{TRUE})\} \\ -c & \forall a_i \in A_i(s) \wedge s' \in \{S_i | t = T \wedge H \leq 0 \wedge \\ & DT = \text{FALSE} \wedge CE = \text{TRUE}\})\} \\ 0 & \text{otherwise} \end{cases}$$

(6.6)

Recall that the costs c accrue only if an uncertain agents acquires additional information. The costs for information acquisition is equal for every agent. The update rule for the Q-values is the normal Q-learning update rule and is formulated as follows:

$$Q(s,a) = (1 - \beta)Q(s,a) + \beta(R(a,s') + \gamma(\max Q(s',a'))) \tag{6.7}$$

$$\Leftrightarrow Q(s,a) = Q(s,a) + \beta[R(a,s') + \gamma(\max Q(s',a')) - Q(s,a)] \tag{6.8}$$

Erev and Roth [1998] introduce weights for each action that are called *propensities*. These propensities are used to establish a probabilistic choice rule for playing action a_{il} in state s_{ik}. This is expressed in the probability p^i_{kl} which is the weighted propensity by the sum of all actions a_i in state s_{ik}. This approach complies only to positive rewards. Consequently, a different approach for computing the probability was chosen. Basically, the propensity approach rewards higher Q-values with a higher choice probability. Not considering negative Q-values at all causes the effect of losing choices for actions. Especially in cases in which all Q-values of the possible actions are negative, their disregard leads to a dead lock. Therefore, the negative Q-values are weighted and considered for the probability computation with a small proportion. Temporary Q-values $\hat{q}^i$ are computed and weighted to get the probabilities. This is written as follows:

$$\hat{q}^i_{kl} = \begin{cases} q^i_{kl} + \dfrac{q^i_{kl} + \sum_{j=1}^{L} |q^i_{kj}|}{L \sum_{j=1}^{L} |q^i_{kj}| + \sum_{j=1}^{L} q^i_{kj}} & \forall q^i_{kl} \geq 0 \\[4mm] \dfrac{q^i_{kl} + \sum_{j=1}^{L} |q^i_{kj}|}{L \sum_{j=1}^{L} |q^i_{kj}| + \sum_{j=1}^{L} q^i_{kj}} & \forall q^i_{kl} < 0 \end{cases} \tag{6.9}$$

L specifies the number of possible actions in state k, i.e. $L = |A_i(s)|$. This leads to the computation of the choice probabilities p^i_{kl}:

$$p^i_{kl} = \frac{\hat{q}^i_{kl}}{\sum_{j=1}^{L} \hat{q}^i_{kl}} = \begin{cases} q^i_{kl} + \dfrac{q^i_{kl} + \sum_{j=1}^{L} |q^i_{kj}|}{L \sum_{j=1}^{L} |q^i_{kj}| + \sum_{j=1}^{L} q^i_{kj}} \dfrac{1}{\sum_{j=1}^{L} q^{i+}_{kj}} & \forall q^i_{kl} \geq 0; q^{i+}_{kj} > 0 \\[4mm] \dfrac{q^i_{kl} + \sum_{j=1}^{L} |q^i_{kj}|}{L \sum_{j=1}^{L} |q^i_{kj}| + \sum_{j=1}^{L} q^i_{kj}} \dfrac{1}{\sum_{j=1}^{L} q^{i+}_{kj}} & \forall q^i_{kl} < 0; q^{i+}_{kj} > 0 \end{cases}$$

(6.10)

The learning mechanisms controls the action selection of each dynamic agent and thus, influences the state transition of the model. The tuple $\langle S, A, R, T \rangle$ describes the Markov Decision Process, where $S = S_1 \cup \ldots \cup S_N$ is the finite state space as the united set of all internal states, A denotes the finite space of actions available to an agent, $R : S \times A \to \mathbb{R}$ is the payoff function, and $T : S \times A \times S \to [0, 1]$ is a transition function. The components S, A, R have been explained in full length. The transition function T depends on the chosen actions $a_i \forall i \in \{1, \ldots, N\}$ and on the valuations of the agents that is subject to the density function $f_X(x)$ and the error function for the estimated valuation $f_E(x)$. The model is fully described by the number of agents N, the MDP, the valuation and estimated valuation functions f_X, f_E, and the market institution as described in the bidding process.

The next section describes the simulation approach in general, specifying the chosen parameters and the treatments. Hypotheses are formulated to enable a statistical analysis of the research questions which were posed at the beginning of this chapter. Finally, a theoretic analysis of the expected results is performed.

6.2   Simulation Approach

In order to analyse the described scenario regarding the agents' bidding behaviour and the expected outcome, the model is kept as simple as possible by choosing the initial parameters of the model such that the results are not diluted by redundant information. The initial parameter settings are described in detail in Section 6.2.1. The simulation model has been developed by continuously improving and refining the model. The presented model is the result of this development process. At the end of the model development the model was verified by modular testing the single components and the model as a whole. After the model had been verified, the parameter values of the treatments were identified to analyse the impact of uncertainty about the own valuation on the bidding behaviour of the participants, the auctioneer's revenue, the bidders' payoffs, and the social welfare. The treatments are described in Section 6.2.2.

6.2.1   Initial Parameter Values of the Simulation

The density functions for drawing the agents' valuations have been described in Section 6.1. Continuous uniform distributions are used. Since bids were defined on the action set $\{\frac{1}{2}v, v - 10, v, v + 10\}$, the distribution is determined in such a way that the expected bidders' payoffs in a two player game are smaller than 10. Bidders then have the incentive to bid the full valuation rather than 10 units below due to the fact that this would lower the likelihood to win the auction. Thus, the interval for the distribution function of the valuations is determined at $a = 65$ and $b = 115$. This leads to the following density function:

$$f_V(v) = \begin{cases} \frac{1}{50} & \forall v \in \mathbb{R} : 65 \leq v \leq 115 \\ 0 & \text{otherwise} \end{cases} \tag{6.11}$$

The interval for drawing the valuation error is determined at $d = 10$, leading to the density function:

$$f_Y(y) = \begin{cases} \frac{1}{20} & \forall y \in \mathbb{R} : -10 \leq y \leq +10 \\ 0 & \text{otherwise} \end{cases} \tag{6.12}$$

The density function of the estimated valuations is derived from the convolution of the two density functions:

$$f_{V^E}(v) = \begin{cases} \frac{v-55}{1000} & \forall v \in \mathbb{R} : 55 \leq v < 75 \\ \frac{1}{50} & \forall v \in \mathbb{R} : 75 \leq v \leq 105 \\ \frac{125-v}{1000} & \forall v \in \mathbb{R} : 105 < v \leq 125 \\ 0 & \text{otherwise} \end{cases} \tag{6.13}$$

The reinforcement mechanism was described in Section 6.1.3. Its basic method is the update rule:

$$Q(s,a) = Q(s,a) + \beta[R(a) + \gamma(\max Q(s',a')) - Q(s,a)] \tag{6.14}$$

Reinforcement learning presumes that each action receives an immediate reward and agents try to maximize the sum of the discounted future rewards. Recall that auctions determine the winner and the the price to be paid at the end. Thus, an early action might be the cause for winning the auction but the reward is received for the last action taken. It was not the purpose of the model to reward late bidding. That is why the discount factor is set to $\gamma = 1$ that projects the reward onto the course of actions.

The learning rate β weighs the influence of the present action in comparison to previously chosen actions, and thus, has a great impact on the course of a simulation. It can either be fix during the whole course of a simulation or it can be adapted. Generally, at the start of a simulation present actions are considered more relevant compared to the end of a simulation. Some initial experiments with different approaches to a dynamic learning rate suggested to entertain not only one β per agent, but one $\beta(s,a)$ for each state-action pair (s,a). The $\beta(s,a)$ is defined as $\beta(s,a) = \frac{1}{m_{(s,a)}}$ with $m_{(s,a)}$ being the number of times actions a was chosen in state s. This leads to the desired effect of reducing the impact of the present action by computing the average Q-value. The Q-table is initialized with the expected reward in a two player game ($q = 8.3$).

The rewards r_i correspond to the payoff of each agent i that computes as the difference of the true valuation v_i and the price to pay (b^{2nd}) minus the costs c_i for information acquisition (if information was acquired): $r_i = v_i - b^{2nd} - c_i$. If the agent is not the winner of the auction, the reward is zero minus the costs for information acquisition (if information was acquired).

The information costs c_i are fix during one setting and equal for each agent. Variations between the settings help to understand the impact of the costs on the bidding behaviour. Settings with $c_i \in [1.0, 1.5, 2.0, 5.0, 6.0, 7.0, 8.0, 9.0, 10.0]$ are conducted.

The simulation software AMASE uses the Random Number Generator (RNG) *Mersenne Twister* developed by Matsumoto and Nishimura [1998]. It is distributed in the free Java package `cern.jet.random.engine.RandomEngine` of the colt library developed at CERN.[8] Mersenne is one of the strongest pseudo random number generators known so far with a period of $2^{19937-1}(= 10^{6001})$.

The seed of a RNG determines the sequence of random numbers that are generated. Since an RNG produces a sequence of pseudo random numbers, the observation from one simulation run are not independent identically distributed (iid). The simulation run is replicated and each replication ($M_i, i \in \{1,\ldots,10\}$) is using common distributed seeds. The observation from two replications are independent from each other. This is the key for data output analysis, since statistical analysis techniques require independence. The approach taken in this work for output data analysis is explained in more detail in Section 7.

In order to guarantee comparability across different simulation settings, the initial seeds of the replications are identical for the settings, e.g. the initial seeds in setting 1 and 2 each use the same initial seeds for replications $M_1, M_2, \ldots, M_{10}$. For additional information on that issue of output data analysis it is referred to Law and Kelton [2000].

6.2.2   Simulation Settings

The research questions relating to the propositions summarized in Section 2.1.4 were formulated at the beginning of this chapter. In the present section, the problem is structured more precisely and hypotheses are derived in order to evaluate the simulation data.

To analyse the impact of uncertainty on auction results and bidding behaviour different environmental settings are examined. Therefore, the following three environmental parameters are identified:

(a) Institutional rules: sealed-bid auction (SB) versus open-cry ascending auction (AA) (cp. Section 6.1),

(b) group structure: number (two or five) and type of participants, and

(c) cost levels: information costs $c \in \{1.0, 1.5, 2.0, 5.0, 6.0, 7.0, 8.0, 9.0, 10.0\}$.

These three axes span the evaluation space. This is also depicted in Figure 6.2. The group structure differs in the amount of agents and their type. The following abbreviations are introduced to differentiate these different groups:

- HE: Non-learning agent with static action selection (early bidding),

- HP: Non-learning agent with static action selection (price signalling),

- HL: Non-learning agent with static action selection (late bidding),

---

[8]Conseil Europen pour la Recherche Nuclaire (CERN) was founded 1954 by eleven European governments and is located close to Geneva. Today it has 20 European member states. More information is available under `http://public.web.cern.ch`.

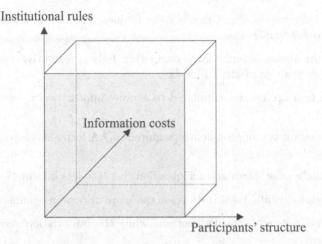

Figure 6.2: The evaluation space spanned by the treatment variables

- HR: Non-learning agent with random action selection,
- C: Learning agent with certain valuation
- U: Learning agent with uncertain valuation

The combination of these letters denominate the particular group structure, e.g. 1HE1C characterizes one stationary early bidder playing versus one bounded rational agent with certain valuation.

At the beginning of this chapter, research questions on the described problem were posed. The questions are interrelated to propositions that were formulated in literature. The research questions as well as the propositions are formulated in general form. This makes a statistically founded analysis difficult. The following hypotheses are proposed to evaluate the simulation data by statistically appropriate means:

H1 The bidders' payoffs are smaller in AA formats compared to SB formats: $\theta_{AA} < \theta_{SB}$.

H2 Auctioneer's revenue is greater in AA formats: $\pi_{AA} > \pi_{SB}$.

H3 Social welfare is greater in AA formats: $\omega_{AA} > \omega_{SB}$.

H4 Social welfare in auctions with certain bidders is greater than in auctions with uncertain bidders: $\omega_C > \omega_U$.

H5 Auctioneers profit from uncertain bidders that means the revenue is greater in auctions with uncertain agents: $\pi_U > \pi_C$.

H6 Certain bidders receive higher payoffs than uncertain bidders: $\theta_C > \theta_U$.

H7 Late information acquisition is more frequent than early information acquisition: $LB > EB$.

H8 Certain agents submit early competing bids (preemptive bids) more frequently than late bids: $EC > LC$.

H9 Uncertain agents are stimulated to acquire information by early competing bids.

H10 Information is more frequently acquired in AA formats compared to SB formats: $B_{AA} > B_{SB}$.

H11 The higher the information acquisition costs the less information is acquired.

H12 Uncertain agents' payoffs decrease the more uncertain agents compete.

H13 Uncertain agents' payoffs decrease while the information acquisition costs increase.

H14 Auctioneer's revenues increase while information costs increase.

H15 Auctioneer's revenues increase the more uncertain agents participate in an auction.

H16 Social welfare decreases while information acquisition costs increase.

The presented hypotheses are investigated in various settings along the axes of the evaluation space of the model. Firstly, the simulation is tested in a relatively controlled environment where the behaviour of the model can be understood more easily. Therefore, settings with one adaptive and one stationary agent under one fixed information acquisition cost level are conducted. This allows for evaluating adaptive agents behaviour in different stationary settings in order to understand the action selection. All four stationary agent types are used. The opposed settings 1U1HE and 1U1HL as well as 1C1HE and 1C1HL are of major interest.

Secondly, five agents settings at one cost level but different degrees of uncertainty are evaluated. That is, five adaptive agents compete in the settings 5C, 4C1U, 1C4U and 5U in different formations.

Thirdly, simulations along the cost level axis are performed, i.e. simulations with two and five agents at different cost levels are conducted. These settings allow the analysis of the impact of information acquisition costs. Before starting to evaluate the simulation, the theoretical predictions results are discussed in the next section, as they serve as a benchmark.

6.2.3   Theoretical Benchmark

The current case assumes that bidders have continuous uniform value functions with density $f(x)$ and support on the interval $[a, b]$. Furthermore, the estimated valuations for uncertain agents are drawn from a uniform distribution with density $f_{VE}(v)$, i.e. the valuation v is drawn from the distribution with density $f_V(v)$ and an additional error y drawn from the density $f_Y(y)$ is added. It is possible to compute the expected social welfare ω, the expected revenue of the auctioneer π, the bidder's expected payoff θ for the case of certainty and for the case of uncertainty (θ_u) without information acquisition (see Appendix A.1, A.2, A.3, and A.4 for a detailed explanation, or Krishna [2002] for additional reading):

$$\omega = b - \frac{b-a}{N+1} \tag{6.15}$$

$$\pi = b - 2\frac{b-a}{N+1} \tag{6.16}$$

$$\theta = \frac{b-a}{N(N+1)} \tag{6.17}$$

$$\theta_u = \frac{1}{2dN(N+1)(N+2)(b-a)^N}\left[(b-a+d)^{N+1}(2(b-a)-Nd)\right.$$
$$\left.+Nd^{N+2}(1-(-1)^{N+2})-(b-a-d)^{N+1}(2(b-a)+Nd)\right] \tag{6.18}$$

It is also possible to derive a bidding function $b(v)$ for the certain bidder (cp. Rasmusen [2005]):

$$b(v) = v \tag{6.19}$$

For the case of uncertainty, it is possible to apply comparative statics to analyse the best bidder behaviour in given situations. If an agent acquires information, the bid function is the same as for the certain agent, otherwise it is advantageous to bid the expected value (the estimated valuation), $b(v^E) = v^E$. The uncertain agents' payoffs depend on the other bidders' actions. Thus, it is possible to compute the expected payoff without information acquisition, i.e. the uncertain bidders submits bids amounting to their estimated valuation.

Four special cases in a SB setting of one uncertain and one certain bidder are identified and the Nash equilibrium solution concept is applied. All Nash equilibrium strategies are identified with restraint to strategies that dominate others. In the following it is assumed that the certain bidder has valuation v_1 and the uncertain bidder received the estimated valuation v^E and has true (unknown) valuation v_2. The Tables 6.1, 6.2, 6.3, and 6.4 display the payoff-matrix in a SB auction for the following four cases:

(a) $v_1 < v_2$ and $v_1 > v^E$

(b) $v_1 < v_2$ and $v_1 < v^E$

(c) $v_1 > v_2$ and $v_1 < v^E$

(d) $v_1 > v_2$ and $v_1 > v^E$

For the certain bidder it is profitable to bid the full valuation in all four settings. There is no other strategy that results in a higher payoff. For the uncertain bidder, it is advantageous in case (a) is to bid 10 units above the current estimated valuation. In that case, the uncertain bidder wins the auction and receives a payoff of at least $v_2 - v_1$.

	0	$0.5v_1$	$v_1 - 10$	v_1
0	$(0;0)$	$(0;v_1)$	$(0;v_1)$	$(0;v_1)$
$0.5v^E$	$(v_2;0)$	$(0; v_1 - 0.5v^E)$	$(0; v_1 - 0.5v^E)$	$(0; v_1 - 0.5v^E)$
$v^E - 10$	$(v_2;0)$	$(v_2 - 0.5v_1;0)$	$(0; v_1 - (v^E - 10))$	$(0; v_1 - (v^E - 10))$
v^E	$(v_2;0)$	$(v_2 - 0.5v_1;0)$	$(v_2 - (v_1 - 10);0)$	$(0, v_1 - v^E)$
$v^E + 10$	$(v_2;0)$	$(v_2 - 0.5v_1;0)$	$(v_2 - (v_1 - 10);0)$	$(v_2 - v_1;0)$
$0.5v_2$	$(v_2 - c;0)$	$(v_2 - 0.5v_1 - c;0)$	$(-c; v_1 - 0.5v_2)$	$(-c; v_1 - 0.5v_2)$
$v_2 - 10$	$(v_2 - c;0)$	$(v_2 - 0.5v_1 - c;0)$	$(v_2 - (v_1 - 10) - c;0)$	$(-c; v_1 - (v_2 - 10))$
v_2	$(v_2 - c;0)$	$(v_2 - 0.5v_1 - c;0)$	$(v_2 - (v_1 - 10) - c;0)$	$(v_2 - v_1 - c;0)$

Table 6.1: Payoff matrix of the certain and uncertain agent for case (a) with $v_1 < v_2$ and $v_1 > v^E$

In case (b), two cases have to be distinguished for the winner determination if agent 1 bids v_1 and agent 2 bids $v^E - 10$. Case (i) applies if $v^E - 10 > v_1$, and case (ii) applies if $v^E - 10 < v_1$. Independent from these situation, it is advantageous for the certain bidder to submit bids at the true valuation, since no other strategy results in higher payoffs. For the case of $v_1 < v^E - 10$ the certain bidder is indifferent between bidding $v_1 - 10$ and v_1. On the other hand, the uncertain bidder is indifferent to submit v^E or $v^E + 10$, since both policies result in the same payoff. Consequently, both strategy dominate the others.

	0.0	$0.5v_1$	$v_1 - 10$	v_1
0.0	$(0;0)$	$(0;v_1)$	$(0;v_1)$	$(0;v_1)$
$0.5v^E$	$(v_2;0)$	$(v_2 - 0.5v_1;0)$	$(0; v_1 - 0.5v^E)$	$(0; v_1 - 0.5v^E)$
$v^E - 10$	$(v_2;0)$	$(v_2 - 0.5v_1;0)$	$(v_2 - (v_1 - 10);0)$	(i)　$(v_2 - v_1)$ (ii)　$(v_1 - v^E)$
v^E	$(v_2;0)$	$(v_2 - 0.5v_1;0)$	$(v_2 - (v_1 - 10);0)$	$(v_2 - v_1;0)$
$v^E + 10$	$(v_2;0)$	$(v_2 - 0.5v_1;0)$	$(v_2 - (v_1 - 10);0)$	$(v_2 - v_1;0)$
$0.5v_2$	$(v_2 - c;0)$	$(v_2 - 0.5v_1 - c;0)$	$(-c; v_1 - 0.5v_2)$	$(-c; v_1 - 0.5v_2)$
$v_2 - 10$	$(v_2 - c;0)$	$(v_2 - 0.5v_1 - c;0)$	$(v_2 - (v_1 - 10) - c;0)$	$(-c; v_1 - (v_2 - 10))$
v_2	$(v_2 - c;0)$	$(v_2 - 0.5v_1 - c;0)$	$(v_2 - (v_1 - 10) - c;0)$	$(v_2 - v_1 - c;0)$

Table 6.2: Payoff matrix of the certain and uncertain agent for case (b) with $v_1 < v_2$ and $v_1 < v^E$

For the case (c) that the uncertain agent's true valuation is lower than the certain agent's valuation but the estimated valuation is above the opponent's valuation, the best strategy is to bid $v^E - 10$. Note that bidding the full estimated valuation v^E or above results in a negative payoff $v_2 - v_1 < 0$, since $v_2 < v_1$ by definition. For the certain agent it is still the best strategy to bid the full valuation.

It is much more difficult to obtain the advantageous strategies for the fourth case (d). A couple of case differentiation have to be made. These cases are:

For the certain bidder it is again advantageous to bid the true valuation. The uncertain bidder receives the best result by bidding the estimated valuation v^E. In case of $v_1 - 10 < v^E < v_1$ and $v_1 - 10 < v_2 < v_1$ the uncertain bidder can receive a positive payoff if the opponent bids $v_1 - 10$. The uncertain bidder might win the auction by bidding $v^E + 10$, but this would result in a negative payoff if the opponent bids the true valuation v_1. Thus, it is advantageous for the uncertain agent to bid v^E.

	0.0	$0.5v_1$	$v_1 - 10$	v_1
0.0	$(0;0)$	$(0;v_1)$	$(0;v_1)$	$(0;v_1)$
$0.5v^E$	$(v_2;0)$	$(v_2-0.5v_1;0)$	$(0;v_1-0.5v^E)$	$(0;v_1-0.5v^E)$
v^E-10	$(v_2;0)$	$(v_2-0.5v_1;0)$	$(v_2-(v_1-10);0)$	$(0;v_1-(s-10))$
v^E	$(v_2;0)$	$(v_2-0.5v_1;0)$	$(v_2-(v_1-10);0)$	$(v_2-v_1;0)$
v^E+10	$(v_2;0)$	$(v_2-0.5v_1;0)$	$(v_2-(v_1-10);0)$	$(v_2-v_1;0)$
$0.5v_2$	$(v_2-c;0)$	$(-c;v_1-0.5v_2)$	$(-c;v_1-0.5v_2)$	$(-c;v_1-0.5v_2)$
v_2-10	$(v_2-c;0)$	$(v_2-0.5v_1-c;0)$	$(-c;v_1-(v_2-10))$	$(-c;v_1-(v_2-10))$
v_2	$(v_2-c;0)$	$(v_2-0.5v_1-c;0)$	$(v_2-(v_1-10)-c;0)$	$-c;(v_1-v_2)$

Table 6.3: Payoff matrix of the certain and uncertain agent for case (c) with $v_1 > v_2$ and $v_1 < v^E$

(i)	$v^E-10 > 0.5v_1$	(ii)	$v^E-10 < 0.5v_1$
(iii)	$v^E > v_1-10$	(iv)	$v^E < v_1-10$
(v)	$v^E+10 > v_1-10$	(vi)	$v^E+10 < v_1-10$
(vii)	$v^E+10 > v_1$	(viii)	$v^E+10 < v_1$
(ix)	$v_2 > 0.5v_1$	(x)	$v_2 < 0.5v_1$
(xi)	$v_2 > v_1-10$	(xii)	$v_2 < v_1-10$

	0.0	$0.5v_1$	$v_1 - 10$	v_1
0.0	$(0;0)$	$(0;v_1)$	$(0;v_1)$	$(0;v_1)$
$0.5v^E$	$(v_2;0)$	$(0;v_1-0.5v^E)$	$(0;v_1-0.5v^E)$	$(0;v_1-0.5v^E)$
v^E-10	$(v_2;0)$	(i) $(v_2-0.5v_1;0)$ (ii)$(0;v_1-(v^E-10))$	$(0;v_1-(v^E-10))$	$(0;v_1-(v^E-10))$
v^E	$(v_2;0)$	$(v_2-0.5v_1;0)$	(iii)$(v_2-(v_1-10);0)$ (iv) $(0;v_1-v^E)$	$(0;v_1-v^E)$
v^E+10	$(v_2;0)$	$(v_2-0.5v_1;0)$	(v) $(v_2-(v_1-10);0)$ (vi)$(0;v_1-(v^E+10))$	(vii) $(v_2-v_1;0)$ (viii)$(0;v_1-(v^E+10))$
$0.5v_2$	$(v_2-c;0)$	$(-c;v_1-0.5v_2)$	$(-c;v_1-0.5v_2)$	$(-c;v_1-0.5v_2)$
v_2-10	$(v_2-c;0)$	(ix) $(v_2-0.5v_1-c;0)$ (x)$(-c;v_1-(v_2-10))$	$(-c;v_1-(v_2-10))$	$(-c;v_1-(v_2-10))$
v_2	$(v_2-c;0)$	$(v_2-0.5v_1-c;0)$	(xi)$(v_2-(v_1-10)-c;0)$ (xii) $(-c;v_1-v_2)$	$-c;(v_1-v_2)$

Table 6.4: Payoff matrix of the certain and uncertain agent for case (d) with $v_1 > v_2$ and $v_1 > v^E$

The separate analysis of the four cases shows that it is optimal for the certain agent in respect to his reward to bid the full valuation in any case and to play the actions v^E-10, v^E, and v^E+10 for the uncertain agent dependent on the valuations v_1, v_2, and the estimated valuation v^E. Analysing these cases separately neglects that the agents do not know the valuation of the opponents, and thus, do not know which of the cases applies. As a result, an uncertain agent might bid v^E+10 assuming to bid the optimal policy of case (a) ($v_1 < v_2$, and $v_1 < v^E$), but receives a negative payoff if it is case (c) ($v_2 < v_1 < v^E$) that applies. Taking this example into account, the agent might be better of to acquire information in order to reduce losses. This depends on the information acquisition costs.

The described model is implemented using AMASE and simulations are conducted. This allows for studying the given situation and to investigate the bidding behaviour of the agents (when to buy information). The simulation results are evaluated and discussed in the next chapter.

Chapter 7

Assessment of the Simulation Results

In this section the results of the agent-based simulation are discussed. Simulation data should be subject to scrutiny for two reasons:

Firstly, the data often is biased since software models use (one and the same) random number generator (RNG). RNGs produce pseudo random numbers that look like being random. In fact these pseudo random numbers are generated by a deterministic algorithm, i.e. the output data of the simulation is per construction biased. This effect can be aggravated if a single RNG generates random numbers for several processes.

Secondly, simulation models that are subject to stochastic processes exhibit the problem of the initial transient also known as the simulation start-up problem. Suppose the stochastic output variable $Y_1, \ldots, Y_m$ is subject to the distribution $F_i(y|I) = P_i(Y_i \leq y|I), \forall i = 1, 2, \ldots, m$ and F_i varies for different values of i where y is a real number and I represents the initial conditions of the simulation run. Furthermore, if for all y and I the conditional probabilities converge to a distribution $F_i(y|I) \overset{i \to \infty}{\Rightarrow} F(y)$, then $F(y)$ is called the steady-state distribution. Often, the distribution function of the observations $Y_1, Y_2, \ldots, Y_m$ are different from F. Consequently, the observations $Y_1, Y_2, \ldots, Y_m$ are not representative (see also Law and Kelton [2000, p. 499f, 519]).

The problem of biased data can be solved by simulation replication. The stochastic output data $Y_{j1}, Y_{j2}, \ldots, Y_{jm}$ is biased due to the explained reasons. The replicated output data of $j = 1, \ldots, n$ simulation runs are not biased as long as the seeds for the RNG differ. Thus, $Y_{1i}, Y_{2i}, \ldots, Y_{ni}$ with $i = 1, \ldots, m$ are independent identically distributed and can be used for estimating $E(Y)$.

In order to assess the steady-state behaviour of the simulation, the graphical approach of Welch [1981, 1983] is applied. The Welch procedure is based on moving averages and requires $n \geq 5$ replications of length m. The average output variables

$\overline{Y} = \sum_{j=1}^{n} \frac{Y_{i,j}}{n}$ for all $i = 1, 2, \ldots, m$ are used to compute the moving average $\overline{Y}_i(w)$ of the window $w \le \lfloor \frac{m}{4} \rfloor$ as follows [Law and Kelton, 2000, p. 521]:

$$\overline{Y}_i(w) = \begin{cases} \frac{\sum_{s=-w}^{w} \overline{Y}_{i+s}}{2w+1} & \text{if } i = w+1, \ldots, m-w \\ \frac{\sum_{s=-(i-1)}^{i-1} \overline{Y}_{i+s}}{2i-1} & \text{if } i = 1, \ldots, w \end{cases} \tag{7.1}$$

The $\overline{Y}_i(w)$ are plotted for $i = 1, 2, \ldots, m - w$. Then, it is possible to identify l as the value from which on $\overline{Y}_l(w), \ldots, \overline{Y}_{m-w}$ appears to have converged. In the current simulation analysis the window is determined at a value of $w = 15$.

Welch's approach is applied to the Q-tables of the simulation due to the fact that the Q-tables comprise the information the action decision is based on. As soon as the Q-values converge to a steady state, the simulation can be assessed.

The absolute frequency of chosen strategies over all repetitions of the steady-state period is extracted to analyse the strategies of the agents. The frequency table of strategies constitutes a distribution of strategies. The independence of the strategy distribution for different settings can be analysed by using a χ^2-test. Note that it is essential for correct application of the χ^2-test to use the nominal data instead of relative frequencies. In most of the tables in this work relative data is displayed. Nevertheless, the test were conducted on the absolute values. Law and Kelton [2000, p. 361] indicate that a χ^2-test is valid and unbiased if at least five observations were made for each interval in a table.

An other focus of interest is on the agents' payoffs and the social welfare. Both varies amongst the different settings. Due to the construction of the model the data is paired. Consequently, paired t-tests can be applied to verify statistical significant differences in the observed data for normally distributed values. A Shapiro-Wilk test can be applied to test, whether or not the data is normally distributed [Shapiro and Wilk, 1965]. In those cases, where the simulation output data is not normally distributed Wilcoxon rank sum tests can be applied [Wilcoxon, 1945].

The different environmental settings are abbreviated as described in Section 6.2.2. There are four types of stationary agents that are abbreviated as follows: early bidding (HE), price signalling (HP), late bidding (HL), and random bidding (HR). The dynamic agents are abbreviated by the first letter: certain (C), and uncertain (U). Thus, a setting can be described with the abbreviations and a leading number characterising how many agents of that type are participating. For example, 1C1U describes a setting with one certain agent playing against one uncertain agent. In settings with more than one agent of one type, the specific agent is denominated by the setting abbreviation and the additional number and type of this agent, e.g. 1C4U-1U denominates uncertain agent number 1 in a setting with 1 certain agent and four uncertain agents.

Since different settings are compared it is necessary to clarify, how to deal with the partially unequal amount of data. For example if the average uncertain agents' payoffs is compared in setting 4C1U and 1C4U, there are $X_{1,1}^{4C1U}, \ldots, X_{1,10}^{4C1U}$ values in setting 4C1U (from the ten replications) and

$$X_{1,1}^{1C4U}, \ldots, X_{1,10}^{1C4U}$$

$$X_{2,1}^{1C4U}, \ldots, X_{2,10}^{1C4U}$$

$$X_{3,1}^{1C4U}, \ldots, X_{3,10}^{1C4U}$$

$$X_{4,1}^{1C4U}, \ldots, X_{4,10}^{1C4U}$$

values in setting 1C4U (ten replications for each of the four agents). In order to compare the settings, the four data series of the four agents are averaged per column. This results in a data series of ten values in which the dependence on the initial values is reduced. Thus, the data can be assumed as independent from the results in the other settings. It is to be noted that the values are not completely independent, but in the following the data is processed as it were independent. This assumption allows the application of the statistical methods.

Section 6.2.2 has presented the evaluation space and the settings that are evaluated. The analysis is structured in two sections starting with the comparison of the institutional rule in Section 7.1. At first the two-agent case is evaluated that also serves as an initial analysis for the models validity. In the second step the five-agent scenario is analysed and compared to the two-agent case. Section 7.2 examines the impact of the information acquisition cost. Here it is also distinguished in the two-agent and five-agent case. This chapter closes with a conclusion of the discussed results.

7.1 Institutional Rules: Sealed Bid versus Ascending Second Price Auction

The literature on auction institutions predicts revenue equivalence for second price sealed-bid and second price ascending auction. This is true for assuming rational and informed participants. Milgrom and Weber [1982] postulate that these auction models are not equivalent under uncertainty. Compte and Jehiel [2000] find that under uncertainty ascending price auctions induce higher expected welfare than sealed-bid auctions. The present section examines the impact of uncertainty under different auction models. At first, a two agent environment is studied distinguishing a mixed setting with stationary and adaptive agents and a dynamic environment with two adaptive agents. Secondly, a five agent environment with solely adaptive agents is analysed.

7.1.1 Two Agent Environment

As outlined in the beginning of the present chapter, it is essential to determine the steady-state phase of the simulation. Therefore, Welch's graphical approach is

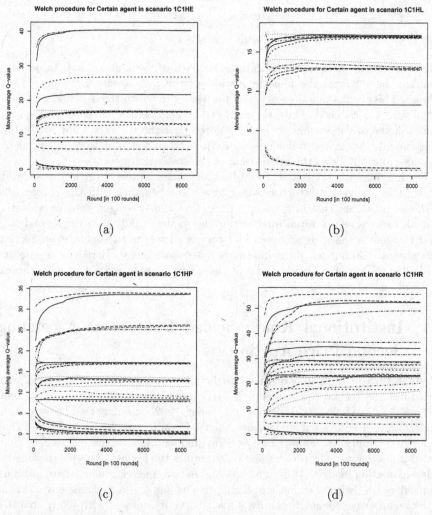

Figure 7.1: Welch diagrams of the Q-tables for a certain agent playing against stationary strategies

applied. Figure 7.1 displays the Welch diagram of the moving average for the Q-tables of a certain agent playing against stationary agents of type HE, HL, HP, and HR. The convergence to a steady state starts relatively early. For the analysis, the last 3000 rounds are used, which certainly lie in the steady-state part of the simulation.

Before starting to simulate different settings, it is essential to evaluate how one adaptive agent copes with one stationary competitor following one fixed strategy. One aspect of interest is to study changes in the frequency of the adaptive agent's chosen strategies amongst different settings with stationary strategies (HE, HL, HP, HR). As outlined in Section 6.2.3 the bidders' expected payoffs in the two bidder case with rational agents is $\theta = 8.\overline{3}$ for certain bidders and $\theta_u = 8.0$ for uncertain bidders. The auctioneer's expected revenue is $\pi = 81.\overline{6}$ and the expected social welfare is $\omega = 98.\overline{3}$ respectively. These values serve as a benchmark for the performance of the bounded rational (adaptive) agents.

		Ascending Auction				Sealed Bid Auction		
	θ_1	Performance	θ_2	Performance	θ_1	Performance	θ_2	Performance
2HE	8.27	99.59%	8.40	101.21%	8.27	99.60%	8.40	101.20%
1C1HE	7.55	90.93%	10.09	121.60%	7.61	91.64%	12.50	150.63%
1C1HL	7.43	89.54%	10.62	127.92%	7.60	91.57%	12.43	149.74%
1C1HP	7.46	89.93%	7.57	91.17%	7.61	91.67%	12.46	150.16%
1C1HR	12.32	148.46%	8.88	107.00%	19.50	234.91%	13.30	160.29%

Table 7.1: Agents' payoffs in the two-agent case with certain agents

Table 7.1 displays the agents' payoffs in both auction models and the performance measured as ratio of the agents' average payoffs and the expected payoffs θ. The column "θ_1" displays the payoff of the agent named first in the setting description. For example, in setting 1C1HE the certain agent's payoff is displayed in column "θ_1" and the payoff of the stationary agent HE is listed in column "θ_2" respectively. All values are computed at a precision of four decimal places and rounded to two decimal places afterwards. The performance of the adaptive agents is around 90% in those cases where the competitor plays the true valuation at some stage.

Remark that the payoff of agents is less in the ascending auction compared to the sealed-bid auction. A left-sided Wilcoxon signed rank test ("less than") is applied since the data is not normally distributed (Shapiro-Wilk test, $p \ll 0.02$) and the data is paired due to the design of the model. The test compares the agents' payoffs in the AA type to the SB type for each setting separately and confirms that agents' payoffs in the ascending auction are lower than in the sealed-bid auction. This result is significant on basis of p-values $p \ll 0.02$ and confirms hypothesis H1. It is interesting to note that the agent who chooses the actions completely on random still performs good. In that scenario the adaptive agent performs best compared to the other stationary settings.

The average auctioneer's revenue in both auction models is exhibited in Table 7.2. The auctioneer's relative success is the ratio of the average auctioneer's revenue to the expected revenue of fully rational agents. The earnings of the auctioneer are higher in the ascending auction compared to the sealed-bid auction with bounded rational agents. This suggests a better result of the ascending auction from the auctioneer's point of view. The revenue is tested for each setting using a Wilcoxon signed rank test that gives strong support for hypothesis H2 on basis of a p-values $p \ll 0.02$ (the tests produced p-values smaller than 0.02 for all settings).

Interestingly, it is setting 1C1HR including the random agent that generates the worst result for the auctioneer.

	Ascending Auction		Sealed Bid Auction	
	Revenue	Rel. Success	Revenue	Rel. Success
2HE	81.76	100.20%	81.76	100.20%
1C1HE	80.50	98.65%	77.66	95.17%
1C1HL	80.00	98.03%	77.73	95.26%
1C1HP	83.02	101.73%	77.70	95.22%
1C1HR	75.66	92.72%	62.09	76.08%

Table 7.2: Average revenue of the Auctioneer in the last 3.000 rounds of the simulation

Regarding the efficiency in terms of social welfare, measured as ratio of the observed welfare compared to the expected welfare $\omega = 98.6$, it can be observed that the ascending auction performs slightly better than the sealed-bid auction as hypothesis H3 supports. Wilcoxon signed rank test for each of the settings (1C1HE, 1C1HL, 1C1HP, and 1C1HR) strongly support H3 on basis of $p \ll 0.02$. Table 7.3 displays the data.

	Ascending Auction		Sealed Bid Auction	
	Welfare	Efficiency	Welfare	Efficiency
2HE	98.43	100.13%	98.43	100.13%
1C1HE	98.14	99.84%	97.77	99.46%
1C1HL	98.05	99.74%	97.76	99.45%
1C1HP	98.05	99.74%	97.77	99.46%
1C1HR	96.86	98.54%	94.89	96.53%

Table 7.3: Average welfare of agents in the last 3.000 rounds of the simulation

For further evaluation of the model it is important to evaluate the behaviour of the adaptive agents. It is of interest if an environmental change has an impact on the action selection of the adaptive agents, and if so, how a particular environmental change affects the strategy. Table 7.4 summarizes the average frequency of the selected strategies during the last 3000 rounds of simulations under different settings. The strategies consist of the two chosen actions during one simulation, whereby "0.0", "0.5", "-10"', and "1.0" correspond to the possible actions $\{0, \frac{1}{2}v, v - 10, v\}$ and "N" determines that no additional information was bought at this step. The actions "0.0N 1.0N", for examples, denominates that bidder i has submitted a bid $b_i^1 = 0$ in the first time step and a bid of the full valuation $b_i^2 = v_i$ in the second time step. The confidence intervals[1] were computed on

---

[1]For the computation of the confidence intervals it is referred to the Chapters 4.4, 4.5 and

basis of $t_{n'-1,1-\frac{\alpha}{2}} \sqrt{\frac{S^2(n')}{n'}}$ where $n' = 10$ corresponds to the number of replications, $t_{9,0.975} = 2.262$ gives the critical point for the t-distribution with 9 degree of freedom (df) and the sample variance computes as $s^2(n') = \frac{\sum_{i=1}^{n'}[X_i - \overline{X}(n)]^2}{n-1}$.

	1C1HE	1C1HL	1C1HP	1C1HR
0.0N 0.0N	0.34 ± 0.06	0.32 ± 0.08	0.43 ± 0.07	0.21 ± 0.06
0.0N 0.5N	0.37 ± 0.07	0.42 ± 0.14	0.39 ± 0.07	2.09 ± 0.53
0.0N -10N	10.34 ± 0.44	11.08 ± 0.69	11.13 ± 0.34	10.70 ± 0.45
0.0N 1.0N	13.90 ± 0.70	14.42 ± 0.86	14.84 ± 0.68	12.97 ± 0.54
0.5N 0.5N	0.41 ± 0.10	0.39 ± 0.09	0.53 ± 0.12	1.14 ± 0.30
0.5N -10N	10.96 ± 0.62	11.43 ± 0.36	10.97 ± 0.46	10.75 ± 0.55
0.5N 1.0N	13.94 ± 0.73	14.70 ± 0.58	14.48 ± 0.51	13.21 ± 0.74
-10N -10N	5.88 ± 0.35	10.59 ± 0.52	9.31 ± 0.37	9.20 ± 0.32
-10N 1.0N	19.15 ± 0.64	10.66 ± 0.50	11.64 ± 0.51	14.69 ± 0.42
1.0N 1.0N	24.72 ± 0.63	25.99 ± 0.87	26.29 ± 0.45	25.04 ± 0.77

Table 7.4: Average frequency and confidence interval of actions chosen in the last 3000 rounds by the certain agent during the ascending auction

The observed frequency has only a small error probability as the confidence intervals suggest. Generally, agents play the full valuation most frequently, followed by strategies bidding 10 currency units below the true valuation. It can be noticed that agents change their strategy dependent on the competitors actions. A χ^2-test pairwise applied on the actions frequency table strongly supports this observation for settings 1C1HE and 1C1HL on the basis of a p-value of $p \ll 0.01$. It rejects independence between settings 1C1HL and 1C1HP.

Figure 7.2 exhibits the data of the table in a bar chart. For each strategy the frequency bars are grouped by the four settings. Observing the two diametrical settings 1C1HE and 1C1HL where the stationary agents play the full valuation either at the beginning of the auction (HE) or at the end (HL), there is a noticeable change in the frequency of the strategies "-10N -10N" and "-10N 1.0N". This appears reasoned, since in the 1C1HE setting a high competing bid is perceived at the beginning. The agent decides on that basis either to rise the own bid to full valuation "1.0N" or to keep the former valuation "-10N" if the adaptive agent is the highest bidder anyway. This observation can be affirmed with the detailed data of Table B.3 in the appendix which displays the frequency of state-action occurrence. As discussed in Section 6.2.3, certain agents bid their true valuation most frequently. It is surprising that the certain agent places $b_i = v_i - 10$ as highest bid relatively often in the late bidding setting (1C1HL), because the expected bidder's payoff is at $8.\overline{3}$ and thus, smaller than 10. Since the payoff computes as $v - b^{2nd}$, it is expected that in average $v - 10$ is smaller than the second highest valuation, and thus, will not result in winning the auction. Nevertheless, agents playing this strategy perform almost as good as those agents bidding the full valuation. The only intuitive explanation is that there is at least a small overall positive average reward for bidders playing this strategy.

9.5 of Law and Kelton [2000].

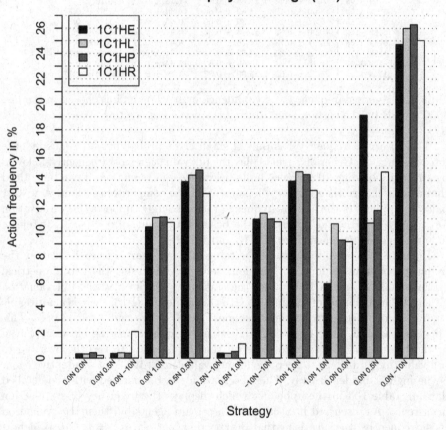

Figure 7.2: Average frequency of the certain agent's strategies chosen in the last 3000 rounds of the settings playing against a stationary agent in an ascending auction

Looking on the selected actions' frequencies in a sealed-bid auction, it can be remarked that the frequency of bidding $v - 10$ is quite high at around 45%. Of course, there is no difference between the settings, since there is just one shot in a sealed-bid auction in which all stationary agents play the true valuation. It is only the random agent who chooses the action stochastically. This has an impact on the action selection of the adaptive agent who can win the auction by bidding less than the full valuation. The data is displayed in Table 7.5.

	1C1HE	1C1HL	1C1HP	1C1HR
0.0N	1.57 ± 0.18	1.44 ± 0.12	1.52 ± 0.13	0.61 ± 0.09
0.5N	1.54 ± 0.21	1.56 ± 0.12	1.55 ± 0.16	18.10 ± 0.80
-10N	44.78 ± 0.77	45.72 ± 0.74	45.88 ± 0.69	39.74 ± 0.93
1.0N	52.11 ± 0.90	51.28 ± 0.90	51.05 ± 0.72	41.56 ± 1.15

Table 7.5: Average frequency of actions chosen in the last 3000 rounds by the certain agent during the sealed-bid auction

At next, the same approach is applied for an uncertain agent with information acquisition costs of $c = 1$ currency unit. The results of the simulations are exhibited in Table 7.6. The performance of the uncertain (adaptive) agents is between 76% - 78% in those settings with competitors playing stationary strategies. In comparison to the performance of the certain agents, uncertain agents perform worse. This can be explained with the lack of information leading to bad action choices and the information acquisition costs that reduce the agents' payoff. Similarly to the scenario with certain agents and according to H1, agents perform better in sealed-bid auctions compared to ascending auctions in the settings with bounded rational agents. According to the settings with certain agents, Wilcoxon signed rank tests are applied for each setting (1U1HE, 1U1HL, 1U1HP, 1U1HR). All test produce p-values $p \ll 0.02$, and thus, support H1 that the bidder's payoff being less in ascending auctions compared to sealed-bid auctions.

	Ascending Auction				Sealed Bid Auction			
	Agent 1	Performance	Agent 2	Performance	Agent 1	Performance	Agent 2	Performance
2HE	8.27	99.59%	8.40	101.21%	8.27	99.60%	8.40	101.20%
1U1HE	6.49	78.22%	8.74	105.28%	7.21	86.86%	10.44	125.77%
1U1HL	6.32	76.20%	8.96	107.97%	7.21	86.90%	10.38	125.02%
1U1HP	6.36	76.59%	6.50	78.27%	7.21	86.85%	10.55	127.06%
1U1HR	11.16	134.46%	7.21	86.84%	19.49	234.86%	11.45	137.91%

Table 7.6: Average payoff of agents in the last 3000 rounds of the simulation

The auctioneer's revenue is displayed in Table 7.7. It is interesting to note that the average revenue of the auctioneer is around 100% for the ascending auction compared to the theoretic expected revenue and in sealed-bid auctions it is around 98%. In the setting with an agent playing actions at random, the revenue of the auctioneer is significantly lower. This can be explained with the not deterministic and as such not rational behaviour of the random agent. As in the settings with one certain agent and according to H2, ascending auctions produce a higher revenue for the aucioneer compared to the SB format. Wilcoxon signed rank test gives strong support for this observation on basis of p-values smaller than 2% ($p \ll 0.02$).

In H5 it was stated that the auctioneer profits from uncertain bidders. In order to test this hypothesis, it is necessary to compare the auctioneers revenue of the settings with certain agents to the settings with uncertain agents. Wilcoxon rank sum test are applied here, since the data of different settings are not paired. Thus, the setting 1C1HE is compared to setting 1U1HE and the other settings are compared respectively. The Wilcoxon tests confirm H5 on basis of p-values all significantly less than 2%.

	Ascending Auction		Sealed Bid Auction	
	Revenue	Rel. Success	Revenue	Rel. Success
2HE	81.76	100.20%	81.76	100.20%
1U1HE	82.12	100.63%	79.72	97.70%
1U1HL	81.96	100.45%	79.78	97.77%
1U1HP	84.46	103.50%	79.62	97.57%
1U1HR	77.75	95.28%	63.46	77.77%

Table 7.7: Average revenue of the Auctioneer in the last 3000 rounds of the simulation

Although the performance of the uncertain agents is at only 77%, the efficiency of both auction models is close to 100% regarding the social welfare. Unfortunately, there is no statistical significant support for a difference in the social welfare of the two auction models if uncertain agents are participating (1U1HE: $p = 0.98$, 1U1HL: $p = 1.00$, 1U1HP: $p = 0.98$). It is only setting 1U1HR that supports H3 on basis of a p-value of $p \ll 0.02$. Table 7.8 summarizes the average social welfare of the simulation with one uncertain and one stationary agent.

Hypothesis H4 proposes that social welfare is greater for settings with certain agents compared to settings with uncertain agents. Therefore, it is necessary to compare the settings of certain and uncertain agents playing against a stationary agent of the same type. That is, the welfare of the settings 1C1HE and 1U1HE is compared. The Wilcoxon rank sum test produce p-values that are less than 2%. This is a significant support for H4.

	Ascending Auction		Sealed Bid Auction	
	Welfare	Efficiency	Welfare	Efficiency
2HE	98.43	100.13%	98.43	100.13%
1U1HE	97.35	99.03%	97.37	99.05%
1U1HL	97.25	98.93%	97.37	99.06%
1U1HP	97.31	99.00%	97.37	99.05%
1U1HR	96.12	97.78%	94.40	96.04%

Table 7.8: Average welfare of agents in the last 3000 rounds of the simulation

The strategy space of the uncertain agents is larger than the set of strategy for certain agents. Evaluating the average frequency of strategies of the last 3000 rounds of the simulated settings, a similar behaviour as observed by the certain agents can be determined. Table 7.9 shows the average frequency including the confidence intervals for the uncertain agent settings. The precision of the simulated estimate is sufficient as the confidence intervals suggest. The most frequent strategy in all settings is to acquire information and play the true valuation ("1.0B 1.0N").[2] Comparing the opposed settings "1U1HE" and "1U1HL" a similar change in the action selection as amongst the certain agents can be observed: There is significant reduction of agents choosing strategy "-10B 1.0N" in favour of bidding 10 units below the true valuation (χ^2-test with $p \ll 0.01$). Again, this can be explained with the lack of information about the competitors valuation. The strategy frequency is depicted as a bar chart in Figure 7.3.

	1U1HE	1U1HL	1U1HP	1U1HR
0.0N 0.0N	0.14 ± 0.07	0.15 ± 0.05	0.13 ± 0.05	0.08 ± 0.06
0.0N 0.5N	0.11 ± 0.04	0.14 ± 0.04	0.11 ± 0.05	0.35 ± 0.19
0.0N 0.5B	0.02 ± 0.03	0.03 ± 0.02	0.04 ± 0.03	0.09 ± 0.10
0.0N -10N	2.62 ± 0.30	2.84 ± 0.27	2.61 ± 0.45	2.70 ± 0.26
0.0N -10B	2.12 ± 0.43	2.03 ± 0.25	1.65 ± 0.64	2.28 ± 0.32
0.0N 1.0N	3.19 ± 0.45	3.12 ± 0.40	3.29 ± 0.23	2.92 ± 0.24
0.0N 1.0B	3.11 ± 0.43	3.12 ± 0.35	2.68 ± 0.73	2.78 ± 0.20
0.0N +10N	2.54 ± 0.67	3.01 ± 0.32	3.21 ± 0.34	2.71 ± 0.30
0.5N 0.5N	0.37 ± 0.11	0.11 ± 0.03	0.20 ± 0.07	0.44 ± 0.11
0.5N 0.5B	0.02 ± 0.01	0.03 ± 0.02	0.04 ± 0.04	0.14 ± 0.08
0.5N -10N	2.76 ± 0.25	2.64 ± 0.40	3.21 ± 0.27	2.94 ± 0.46
0.5N -10B	2.15 ± 0.15	2.17 ± 0.17	2.22 ± 0.44	2.10 ± 0.74
0.5N 1.0N	3.28 ± 0.24	3.08 ± 0.42	3.82 ± 0.50	3.43 ± 0.36
0.5N 1.0B	2.83 ± 0.37	3.13 ± 0.29	3.46 ± 0.38	2.96 ± 0.34
0.5N +10N	2.41 ± 0.64	2.69 ± 0.61	2.60 ± 0.71	2.37 ± 0.82
0.5B 0.5N	0.14 ± 0.05	0.09 ± 0.07	0.16 ± 0.03	0.43 ± 0.13
0.5B -10N	4.98 ± 0.32	4.97 ± 0.47	4.27 ± 0.42	4.64 ± 0.26
0.5B 1.0N	6.91 ± 0.66	6.91 ± 0.65	6.33 ± 0.43	5.98 ± 0.28
-10N -10N	1.58 ± 0.16	2.96 ± 0.38	2.87 ± 0.16	2.37 ± 0.22
-10N -10B	1.24 ± 0.22	2.17 ± 0.57	2.19 ± 0.25	1.89 ± 0.35
-10N 1.0N	3.60 ± 0.44	2.45 ± 0.19	2.76 ± 0.26	2.77 ± 0.58
-10N 1.0B	3.37 ± 0.76	2.17 ± 0.28	2.38 ± 0.39	3.02 ± 0.52
-10N +10N	2.39 ± 0.74	2.36 ± 0.31	1.94 ± 0.31	2.52 ± 0.44
-10B -10N	2.86 ± 0.27	4.51 ± 0.32	4.42 ± 0.55	4.00 ± 0.37
-10B 1.0N	8.54 ± 0.44	4.65 ± 0.44	4.95 ± 0.31	7.01 ± 0.55
1.0N 1.0N	6.41 ± 0.61	6.97 ± 0.48	6.89 ± 0.77	6.19 ± 0.31
1.0N 1.0B	4.82 ± 0.67	4.96 ± 0.41	4.67 ± 0.21	4.70 ± 0.84
1.0N +10N	1.54 ± 0.58	1.30 ± 0.60	2.02 ± 0.30	1.65 ± 0.58
1.0B 1.0N	11.99 ± 0.58	12.70 ± 0.75	11.95 ± 0.46	11.99 ± 0.70
+10N +10N	8.14 ± 0.35	6.77 ± 0.47	8.06 ± 0.35	7.70 ± 0.47
+10N 1.0B	3.81 ± 0.30	5.79 ± 0.31	4.87 ± 0.36	4.85 ± 0.34

Table 7.9: Average frequency of actions chosen in the last 3000 rounds by the uncertain agent during the ascending auction

An other interesting issue in this context is the point of time for information acquisition. In the "1U1HE" setting 23.5% decide on a late acquisition, whereas 35.4% buy information right at the beginning. In the setting playing against a late bidder, uncertain agents more frequently decide to wait with information acquisition until the end (25.6%) and less frequent acquire information at the beginning of the auction (33.8%). On basis of a χ^2-test with an error probability of $p = 5.7\%$ this is a significant change in the strategy selection. However, this is no support for H9, since it was expected that late information acquisition is

---

[2] The letter "B" denote that the uncertain agent has bought information. For example, the actions "1.0B 1.0N" state, that the agent has bought information in the first time step and submitted a bid of $b_i = v_i$. In the second time step, the full valuation was submitted again.

more frequent than early acquisition. This might be dependent on the cost level for information acquisition which is at $c = 1$ for the present setting and as such relatively low compared to the expected agent's payoff. The results also show that agents more frequently acquire information instead of bidding the estimated valuation. In Section 6.2.3 it was shown that it is an optimal policy to bid the estimated valuation in some cases. Recall, that in the analysis of Section 6.2.3 the dynamic environment and the cost levels were not considered.

The first steps of the simulation were to compare adaptive agents playing against agents with stationary strategies. A more realistic scenario is a dynamic environment where several adaptive agents compete against each other. In order to determine, how well adaptive agents are capable to cope with such an extremely dynamic environment, simulations with two adaptive agents were conducted. These simulation results can be compared to the settings with stationary agents. If the adaptive agents perform well in the dynamic setting, scenarios with more than two adaptive agents can be evaluated.

Table 7.10 displays the payoffs of the agents in the dynamic setting compared to the stationary settings. It is remarkable, that the average payoff of both adaptive agent types is higher in the dynamic setting compared to the stationary settings. For the explanation it is necessary to have a look on the descriptive stochastic parameters of the rewards. The statistical spread and thus, the variance is larger on average in the setting with two dynamic agents since the maximum is larger compared to the other settings. This emerges due to the fact that the second highest bid in the "1C1U" setting is often below the true valuation of this agent. Therefore, the winner pays a lower price compared to the settings where stationary agents bid their true valuation. The results suggest a good performance of adaptive agents in a dynamic environment with more than one adaptive agent.

For this setting H1 can also be confirmed on basis of a Wilcoxon signed rank test ($p << 0.02$). Additionally, H6 can be investigated stating that the certain bidder's payoff is greater than the uncertain agent's payoff. Unfortunately, this hypothesis is not supported by one-sided Wilcoxon signed rank tests (AA: $p = 0.97$, SB: $p = 1.00$).

	Payoff	Performance	Min	Max	Var	Payoff	Performance	Min	Max	Var
1C1HE	7.55	90.93%	0.00	48.64	128.27	7.61	91.64%	0.00	48.70	138.82
1C1HL	7.43	89.54%	0.00	48.64	128.80	7.60	91.57%	0.00	48.60	139.15
1C1U-C	8.06	97.10%	0.00	107.43	155.22	11.97	144.20%	0.00	110.50	313.84
1U1HE	6.49	78.22%	-18.26	47.94	130.84	7.21	86.86%	-17.70	48.40	143.61
1U1HL	6.32	76.20%	-18.36	48.57	130.61	7.21	86.90%	-18.40	48.50	143.75
1C1U-U	8.38	100.93%	-17.93	106.83	190.24	13.49	162.51%	-18.10	113.00	369.52

Table 7.10: Statistical parameters of the rewards of adaptive agents in the last 3.000 rounds of the simulation

The auctioneer's revenue in the dynamic setting turns out to be not significantly different in the ascending auction, but much lower in the sealed-bid auction compared to the stationary settings evaluated earlier. This effect was not expected in so far that the bidders' payoffs was on average higher in the dynamic setting. The sealed-bid auction is conform to the expectation of being less profitable for the

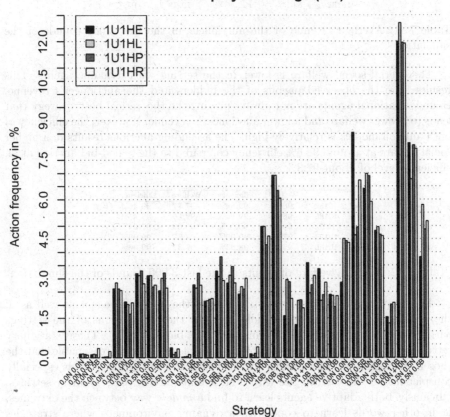

**Frequency of actions of an uncertain agent
in two player settings (AA)**

Figure 7.3: Average frequency of the certain agent's strategies chosen in the last 3000 rounds of the settings playing against a stationary agent in an ascending auction

auctioneer than the AA format in the dynamic case. Thus, H2 can be confirmed on basis of a one-sided Wilcoxon signed rank test with $p \ll 0.02$. The ascending auction still performs well from the auctioneer's perspective.

	Revenue	Rel. Success	Revenue	Rel. Success
1C1HE	80.50	98.65%	77.66	95.17%
1C1HL	80.00	98.03%	77.73	95.26%
1C1U	80.45	98.59%	70.23	86.07%
1U1HE	82.12	100.63%	79.72	97.70%
1U1HL	81.96	100.45%	79.78	97.77%

Table 7.11: Average revenue of the auctioneer in the last 3.000 rounds of the simulation

The overall social welfare is lower in the setting with dynamic agents. This results from the observed payoffs of the bidders and the auctioneer's revenue. Bounded rational agents are not always playing the theoretical best strategy that leads to a lower welfare and a lower auctioneer's revenue. However, the efficiency of both auction models is relatively high. The ascending auctions results in a higher social welfare at around 98.6% efficiency compared to the sealed-bid auction at an efficiency level of about 97.3%.

	Welfare	Efficiency	Welfare	Efficiency
1C1HE	98.14	99.84%	97.77	99.46%
1C1HL	98.05	99.74%	97.76	99.45%
1C1U	96.89	98.57%	95.69	97.34%
1U1HE	97.35	99.03%	97.37	99.05%
1U1HL	97.25	98.93%	97.37	99.06%

Table 7.12: Average welfare of agents in the last 3.000 rounds of the simulation

The frequency of the selected strategies of the uncertain agent as well as of the certain agent rank in the middle between the observations of the settings with one stationary early (1HE) and one late bidder (1HL). These stationary settings mark the extreme cases for bidding, insofar it appears reasonable that the chosen strategies for the dynamic scenario rank in the middle. This is especially conspicuous for those strategies with a large difference in the stationary settings. Obviously, both adaptive agents learn to find a *middle* way between the extremes, or in other words learn to cope with a dynamic environment where strategies change from early bidding to late bidding. The data is found in the appendix (Figure B.1, B.2, and Tables B.2, B.1).

Concluding, it can be stated that agents' payoffs are higher in SB auctions compared to AA auctions, whereas auctioneer's revenue is higher in AA formats. There is no support for a systematic higher or lower social welfare comparing the two auction formats. The auctioneer's revenue is higher in those auctions in which uncertain agents participate compared to auctions with certain agents. The next section investigates simulations results with five adaptive agents.

7.1.2 Five Agent Environment

This subsection investigates settings with five dynamic agents. In such a dynamic environment it takes longer for the agents to adapt. Thus, the auction games were repeated 20000 times instead of 10000. The Welch tests show convergence for the Q-values after 15000, consequently the last 3000 rounds are used for the evaluation. It is to be remarked that not all Q-values show clear convergence after 15000 rounds. This is due to the dynamic environment, in which the agents are exposed to higher competition. It is more difficult for uncertain agents to cope with this dynamic situation. Nevertheless, the majority of the Q-table values converge, and thus, the last 3000 rounds of the simulation can be used for the evaluation.

The participation of five agents reduces the expected payoff of one certain agent from $8.\overline{3}$ to $1.\overline{6}$, the payoff of an uncertain agent from 8.0 to 1.3, and increases the auctioneer's expected revenue from $81.\overline{6}$ to $98.\overline{3}$. The decrease in the agents' expected payoffs effects an increase of the ratio of information acquisition costs to expected payoff. Information is relatively more expensive in comparison to the two player setting which might result in less frequently information acquisition compared to the two-agent settings.

In order to study the auctions under different states of uncertainty, the number of uncertain agents participating in the auction is varied. Four different environmental settings are investigated: 5C, 4C1U, 1C4U, and 5U. Table 7.13 displays the average agents' payoffs θ for both auction formats, ascending auction (AA) and sealed-bid auction (SB). Furthermore, the auctioneer's average revenue and the average social welfare is depicted. Table B.4 in Appendix B.1 shows the results as ratio to the theoretical expected outcome under rational behaviour and full information.

	payoff certain		payoff uncertain		revenue		welfare	
	θ_{AA}^C	θ_{SB}^C	θ_{AA}^U	θ_{SB}^U	π_{AA}	π_{SB}	ω_{AA}	ω_{SB}
5C	1.96	2.44	NA	NA	95.98	92.98	105.81	105.16
4C1U	1.81	2.24	1.16	2.07	96.61	93.47	104.99	104.49
1C4U	1.42	1.73	0.81	1.53	98.33	95.16	102.98	103.01
5U	NA	NA	0.70	1.39	98.93	95.68	102.46	102.65

Table 7.13: Overview on the agents' average payoff, auctioneer's average revenue, and average social welfare over the last 3.000 rounds of the simulation with five adaptive agents

Comparing the results of the SB format and the AA format it is to be noted that bidders, regardless of being certain or uncertain, achieve better results in sealed-bid auctions compared to ascending auctions. This was also shown for the two-agent setting. Hypothesis H1 can be picked up here that $\theta_{SB} > \theta_{AA}$. A Shapiro-Wilk test confirms that the data is not normally distributed. Therefore, the hypothesis is confirmed by a Wilcoxon rank sum test for both, certain and uncertain agents, on a basis of a p-value $p \ll 0.02$.

On the other hand, ascending auctions lead to higher revenue for the auctioneer as it was shown for the two-agent setting. This is also confirmed by a Wilcoxon rank sum test on basis of $p \ll 0.02$ that supports H2. There is no statistical support on basis of a Wilcoxon rank sum test for H3 that also the social welfare of AA auctions is higher compared to the SB format ($p = 0.23$).

At next, the impact of uncertainty is highlighted more thoroughly. Looking at the progression of the auction outcome subject to the number of uncertain participants, a clear trend is noticeable for both auction formats: agents' payoffs decreases as the number of uncertain agents raises, whereas auctioneer's revenues increase. The trend is illustrated in Figure 7.4 (a) for the bidders' payoffs and in (b) for the auctioneer's revenue. This is in accordance to H12 and H15, stating that auctioneers will profit from uncertain bidders. These trends are supported by one-sided Wilcoxon rank sum tests comparing the certain and uncertain agents' averaged payoffs for each setting as well as the auctioneer's revenue in these settings. That is, the certain agents' averaged payoffs in setting 5C are consecutively compared with the averaged payoffs for the certain agents of both settings, 4C1U and 1C4U. As well, the averaged uncertain payoff in setting 4C1U, 1C4U and 5U are compared. All tests (in AA and SB auction formats) produce p values $p \ll 0.02$, and thus, support the hypothesis that payoffs decrease while the number of uncertain agents increase. The auctioneer's revenue of these settings is compared also. On basis of p-values smaller than 0.02 one-sided Wilcoxon rank sum tests support H15 that revenues increase if the ration of uncertain to certain agents increases.

Regarding the social welfare, it is expected that an increasing ratio of uncertain to certain bidders reduces the social welfare (H4). Figure 7.5 depicts the averaged social welfare for the four settings in both, AA and SB auctions. A Wilcoxon rank sum test comparing the social welfare of the 10 replications confirms the proposition for both auction formats on the basis of p-values all significantly smaller than 0.02.

Comparing the social welfare between the two auction formats (H3), there are small differences observable. In the settings 5C and 4C1U the social welfare is greater in the AA format compared to the SB format. This can be confirmed with a Wilcoxon rank sum test on basis of p-values significantly smaller than 0.02. For the setting 1C4U there is no support for a difference in the averaged social welfare ($p = 0.97$ for a two sided Wilcoxon ranks sum test). In the setting with five uncertain agents (5U) the social welfare is higher in the SB format. This is statistically significant on basis of a p-value $p \ll 0.02$ in a Wilcoxon rank sum test. This observation indicates that sealed-bid auctions lead to higher social welfare the more uncertain agents participate. Since only one setting supports this proposition, this issue should be further investigated and is picked up in Section 7.2.2.

At next, the strategies are evaluated. The tables that display the frequency of strategy selection are depicted in Appendix B.1.2. Regarding the selected strategies of the certain bidders in the AA format it is remarked that in the majority (approx. 69%) the full valuation is submitted at one stage of the auction. This is according

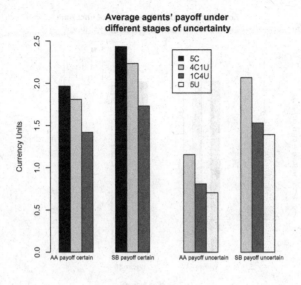

(a)

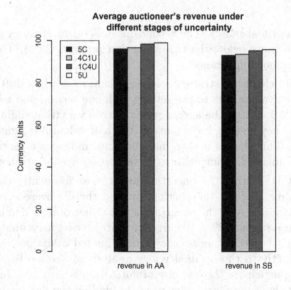

(b)

Figure 7.4: Average agents' payoffs and auctioneer's revenue in the last 3000 rounds of five agents settings under different stages of uncertainty

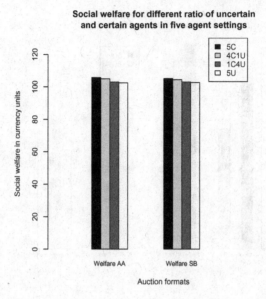

Figure 7.5: Average social welfare for both auction types in five agent settings

to the expected optimal policy. The second most frequent strategy is to submit a bid 10 currency units below the true valuation (approx. 23%). The remaining strategies are of minor importance.

There is a slight change in strategy selection identifiable when shifting from the setting with five certain agents to the setting with one certain and four uncertain agents. In the 1C4U setting the agents play the true valuation slightly less often (-1.8%). Instead, they submit lower bids at the half valuation slightly more frequently (+1.7%). This change is marginal and thus, indicates a marginal impact of the number of uncertain competitors on the certain agents' strategy selection.

During the 4C1U setting the uncertain agent most frequently choose to buy information at some stage of the auction and bid the discovered true valuation (approx. 37%). Alternatively, the uncertain agent either bids as maximum the estimated valuation (approx. 22%), 10 currency units above the estimated valuation (approx. 16%), or 10 currency units below the estimated valuation (approx. 16%). This complies exactly to the optimal policy analysis of Section 6.2.3. The more uncertain agents participate the less often information is acquired. In the 5U setting, only 30% of the chosen strategies result in bidding the discovered valuation. There is no clear alternative strategy identifiable. This indicates that the uncertain agents become more indifferent in the strategy selection the more uncertain agents participate.

The same is noticeable for the SB format. Here the uncertain agent in the 4C1U setting most frequently bid the estimated valuation (25%), 10 currency units less than the estimated valuation (20%), or decide to acquire information and bid the full valuation (20%). There are small changes observable for the settings with more uncertain agents, but these changes are of minor importance. Nevertheless, the frequency of selected strategies complies to the expected results analysis.

The certain agents do not show significant changing strategy selection in the SB format between the settings 4C1U and 1C4U. The most frequent strategy is to play the true valuation (52%) or 10 currency units below the true valuation (40%). In the remainder of this section, the hypothesis concerning the strategy selection are evaluated in detail.

Research question Q1 aims on the bidding behaviour of uncertain bidders. Recall, proposition H7 that suggests that bidders will wait with information acquisition as long as possible. Part (b) of Figure 7.6 illustrates the frequency of early versus late information acquisition for the three settings with uncertain agents (4C1U, 1C4U, 5U). The more uncertain agents participate in the auction, the less often information is acquired in general and at the beginning in particular. This observation is supported by three t-tests pairwise comparing the three settings. All t-test produce a p-value $p << 0.02$. A t-test was applied, since the Shapiro-Wilk test for the data suggests that the data is normally distributed.

Comparing the frequency of information acquisition in the AA and the SB format (H10), it is to be noted that information is more frequently bought in the AA format. Again, this is statistically supported by t-tests ($p << 0.02$) pairwise comparing the three settings. This suggests that information is more valuable in ascending auctions.

Additionally, it is of interest if an early price signal stimulate value discovery (H9). Therefore, the frequency of those strategies are regarded that contain the response on an early price signal. This issue is also depicted in part (b) of Figure 7.6. Note that the fraction of late information acquisition after having perceived an early competing bid compared to the total frequency of late information acquisition is around 73%. This is a high percentage and indicates a relation between early competing bids and late information acquisition. It has been shown for the two agent case comparing the frequency of late information acquisition in the settings 1U1HE and 1U1HL that there is a significant decrease in late information buying if competitors bid late. These findings suggest that uncertain agents are stimulated to buy information if they perceive an early competing bid. This relation found for the two player case will certainly apply in the five agent setting, and thus, the high percentage of late information acquisition indicates support for H9.

On the other hand it is interesting to look at the strategies of the certain agents. It was suggested in Q2 that it might be profitable for certain agents to stimulate value discovery through early bidding. The term "early bidding" subsumes all strategies that include a bid $b > 0$ at the beginning of the auction. "Late bidding" denominates all strategies with one single bid $b > 0$ at the end of the auction. Part (a) of Figure 7.6 displays the amount of early and late bidding in the three settings

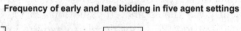

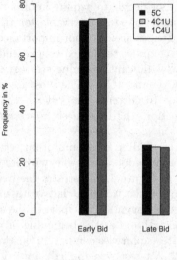

(a)

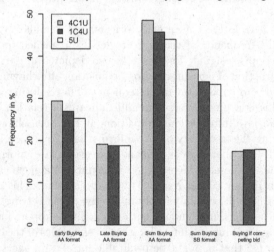

(b)

Figure 7.6: Frequency of early and late bidding (a) and frequency of information buying (b) in five agents settings

with certain agents participating. There is much less late bidding (approx. 26%) observable in comparison to early bidding (approx. 74%). Additionally, it appears that there is a small decrease of late bidding coupled with a small increase of early bidding while the number of certain agents decrease amongst the settings. A Wilcoxon rank sum test confirms a decrease of late bidding from setting 5C to 4C1U ($p < 0.02$), but has not significant support for the comparison of 4C1U and 1C4U ($p = 0.30$).

The difference in frequency of early and late bidding is significantly large. This observation supports H8 and suggests that it is more profitable to bid early in the present auction environment.

As in the two-agent games, it is observed that agents receive higher payoffs in SB formats compared to AA formats. Auctioneer's revenue is higher in AA formats and auctioneers profit from uncertain agents. There is no support for statistical systematic higher or lower social welfare in one of the two auction formats.

Having compared the two auction formats in depth, the next section investigates the impact of different information acquisition cost levels on the bidders' behaviour and the auction outcome.

7.2 Impact of Information Acquisition Cost

This subsection studies the impact of the information acquisition costs on the bidding behaviour of the agents and on the auction outcome including the agents' payoff, the auctioneer's revenue and the social welfare. In both environmental settings, the two agents and the five agents setting, the information acquisition costs are varied. The number of competitors impact the bidders' expected payoff. Thus, the information acquisition cost level plays an important role. Since the expected agents' payoffs in the two player setting amounts to 8.3 (according to equation 6.17) it is of major interest to study the settings with costs between 5 and 10 currency units. The expected payoff in the five agent setting computes to $1.\bar{6}$ for certain agents and to 1.3 for uncertain agents respectively. Consequently, it is of interest to investigate settings with cost levels at $1.0, 1.5, 2.0$ in the close neighbourhood of the expected payoff and at cost level 5.0 exemplary for high costs.

Intuitively, it is to be expected that an increase in the information acquisition costs results in decreasing payoffs for the uncertain agents (H13). It is expected that the agents acquire less information (H11) and wait with the information acquisition the more expensive the information is (H9). The following two subsections will study the issue of information costs in more depth starting with the two agents environment in Section 7.2.1, followed by the evaluation of the five agents environment in Section 7.2.2.

7.2.1 Two Agent Environment

In the two agent environment four settings are evaluated. In order to better insulate the behaviour of agents and impact of early and late bidding, an uncertain agent plays against an early and a late bidder. Additionally, one setting with an uncertain agent and a price signalling agent was chosen. The price signalling agent randomly draws a first bid for the first round and bids the true valuation in the last round. The fourth setting comprises both adaptive agent types, certain and uncertain.

Figure 7.7 displays the uncertain agents' payoffs for the different settings under varying information acquisition costs for both, the ascending (a) and the sealed-bid auction (b). The picture shows a large decrease of the agents' payoffs in the AA format while increasing the information costs from 1 to 5 currency units. For a further increase of information costs it appears that the payoffs increase also, but there is no statistical evidence for this (Wilcoxon rank sum test for pairwise comparison of the settings with different costs does not support the stated proposition). This trend is not observable for the sealed-bid auction. As such, there is just weak support for H13 in the AA format and no support at all for the SB format.

Concerning H14, one sided Wilcoxon rank sum tests were conducted in order to test the auctioneer's revenues for ascending cost levels. In the majority of the settings, there is no support for H14. Table B.9 summarises the p-values of these tests and is found in Appendix B.1. Table B.7 and Table B.8 in Appendix B.1 summarize the average agents' payoff, auctioneer's revenue and social welfare of these simulation settings.

Independent from the information acquisition costs agents achieve better payoffs in the SB format compared to the ascending format. This is supported by a Wilcoxon rank sum test for all four environments (uncertain vs. early bidder, uncertain vs. price signalling bidder, uncertain vs. late bidder, and uncertain vs. certain bidder) on basis of a p-value significantly small ($p << 0.02$). This is support for H1.

According to the results in Section 7.1, the auctioneer receives higher payoff in the AA format compared to the SB format in all four environments (on basis of a Wilcoxon rank sum test with p-values $p << 0.02$). This is support for H2.

Regarding the social welfare, there is not enough statistical support for H3 that social welfare is greater in ascending auctions compared to sealed-bid auctions. There is only a weak support for that proposition in the dynamic setting with one certain and one uncertain agent (p-values for the settings: 1U1HE: $p = 0.99$, 1U1HP: $p = 0.70$, 1U1HL: $p = 0.068$, 1U1C: $p << 0.02$).

Hypothesis H6 suggest that the uncertain agents' payoffs is less than the certain agents' payoff. Therefore, the payoffs of the stationary agents and the uncertain agents are compared for all cost levels. Since the data is not normally distributed (Shapiro-Wilk test: $p < 0.02$), one-sided Wilcoxon signed rank tests are applied. The early and late stationary bidders always perform better

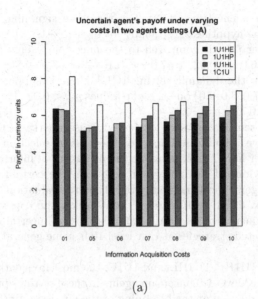

(a)

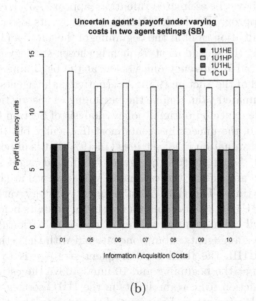

(b)

Figure 7.7: Average uncertain agents' payoffs in the last 3000 rounds under varying information costs in (a) the ascending and (b) sealed-bid auction competing against early, random, late and certain agents.

than the uncertain agent ($p < 0.02$). For the price signalling agent, the test does not support the hypothesis, especially for higher costs, where the stationary agents receives lower payoffs compared to the uncertain agents ($c=1.0$: $p=0.08$; $c=5.0$: $p<0.02$; $c=6.0$: $p<0.02$; $c=7.0$: $p=0.16$; $c=8.0$: $p=0.84$; $c=9.0$: $p=0.86$; $c=10.0$: $p=0.99$). In the dynamic setting 1C1U, there is support for H6 at cost levels $c \in \{5.0, 6.0, 7.0, 8.0, 9.0\}$ on basis of p-values $p \ll 0.02$. There is no support at cost levels $c = 1.0$ and $c = 10.0$.

At next, the chosen strategies are evaluated. It is remarkable that information acquisition costs have a significant impact on the strategy selection of the uncertain agents. On the other hand, there is only a minor impact of information costs and the changing behaviour of the uncertain agents on the certain agents strategy selection. Certain agents most frequently bid their true valuation at some stage in the auction (approx. 67%), or 10 currency units below the true valuation (30%). Comparing the frequency of selected strategies by the uncertain agents at cost level 1.0 to the selected strategies at cost level 10.0, some general remarks can be made.

For the settings 1U1HP, 1U1HL, and 1U1C, the most frequently chosen strategies are equal. At cost level 1.0 uncertain agents in these settings prefer to discover and play the true valuation at the beginning of the auction (approx. 12%), to bid 10 currency units above the estimated valuation (approx. 7.5%), or to bid the estimated valuation (approx. 7%). In the 1U1HE setting agents also prefer to discover and play the true valuation right at the beginning of the auction (12%). In contrast to the other settings, the second most frequently chosen strategy is to discover the true valuation and bid 10 currency units below at the beginning and bid the true valuation at the end of the auction (9%). Alternatively, the agents bid 10 currency units above the estimated valuation at the beginning of the auction (8%). This is in accordance to the expected optimal policy analysis of Section 6.2.3.

At cost level 10.0, the uncertain agents most frequently bid 10 currency units above the estimated valuation in all settings (16-19% that is almost twice as often as at cost level 1.0). As alternative the agents submit bids right at the beginning of the auction that amount to the estimated valuation value (12-17%). This is observed for all settings. The third most frequent strategy varies amongst the settings. In setting 1U1HE agents submit a first bid at 10 units below the estimated valuation and a final bid amounting to the estimated valuation (9%), whereas in setting 1U1HE uncertain agents submit one late bid with the estimated valuation (8%). In setting 1U1HL the third most frequent strategy is to bid half of the estimated valuation at the beginning and 10 units above the estimated valuation at the end of the auction. Uncertain agents in the 1U1C setting also submit half of the estimated valuation at the beginning of the auction and the full estimated valuation at the end. In the analysis of the optimal policies, three policies were identified: To bid $s-10$, s, or $s+10$. Thus, the found results match the expectations.

These observations indicate a strong impact of the information cost level on the strategy selection. The remainder of this section is dedicated to the analysis of the strategy selection.

H7 proposes that late information acquisition dominates early information buying. Figure 7.8 depicts the frequency of early and late information acquisition under different information costs for the settings playing versus an (a) early bidder, (b) price signalling bidder. Figure 7.9 displays the same information for an uncertain agent competing with (a) a late bidder, and (b) an adaptive certain bidder.

It is interesting to note that the frequency of information acquisition in general reduces while the costs increase (cp. hypothesis H11). This observation appears reasonable, since the costs reduce the expected value. The decrease in early information acquisition is significant in all settings on basis of one-sided t-tests with p-values $p < 0.05$ pairwise comparing the settings. There are two exceptions, the comparison of settings 1U1HE at cost level 9.0 and 10.0 in the scenario with one stationary early bidder has no significant support ($p = 0.11$) and the comparison of setting 1U1HL at cost level 8.0 and 9.0 in the scenario with one stationary late bidder produces only weak statistical support ($p = 0.056$).[3] The decrease of late information acquisition is statistically significant for all pairwise comparisons of settings on basis of one-sided t-tests with p-values $p < 0.05$. An overview on all p-values is given in Table B.16 in Appendix B.1. Recapitulating, both tests give significant support for H11.

Furthermore, it is to be remarked that the frequency of early information acquisition decreases quicker compared to the late information acquisition. I.e. the uncertain agent waits with information acquisition more frequently the more expensive the information is. This is an interesting observation, since H7 suggests that late information acquisition is in general better than early acquisition. In contrast, the simulation suggest that it depends on the costs for information acquisition if the bidder acquire information early or late. It is expected that there is a switch from early to late information acquisition in the two player setting for cost levels that are greater than the expected payoff, i.e. costs $c > 8.0$ currency units. The Tables B.10, B.11, B.12, and B.13 in Appendix B.1 display the frequency of early and late information acquisition in the four environmental settings.

In fact, the data suggest a more differentiated interpretation. In the setting with one stationary early bidder the threshold for the switch from early to late information acquisition is indeed at costs $c = 8.0$. This can be confirmed by conducting one-sided t-tests for the frequency of early and late bidding for each cost level ($p << 0.02$). At the cost levels $c = 7.0$ and $c = 8.0$ the t-test does not support a clear proposition, whether there is more frequent early information acquisition compared to late information buying ($p = 0.32, p = 1.00$).

In the setting with one HP agent, it is at cost level $c = 6.0$ where the frequency of early and late information buying is almost equal, since the one sided test does confirm that late buying is more frequent than ($p = 0.36$). At cost levels greater than $c > 6.0$ there is more late information acquisition compared to early acquisition $p < 0.05$).

In the environmental setting with one stationary late bidder, the uncertain bid-

---

[3]The p-values are fully displayed in Table B.15 in Appendix B.1.

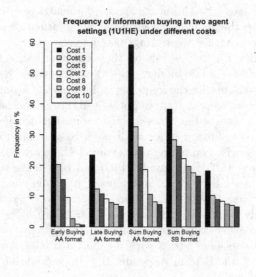

(a)

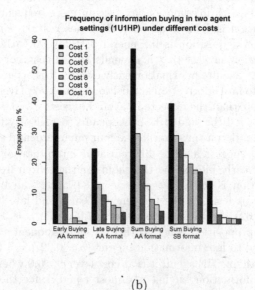

(b)

Figure 7.8: Frequency of early and late information acquisition in two agent settings with an early and a price signal bidder under different costs

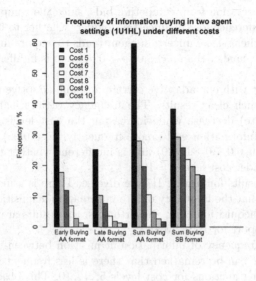

(a)

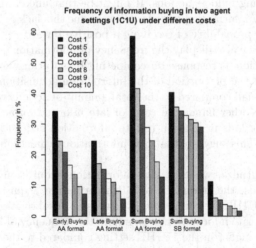

(b)

Figure 7.9: Frequency of early and late information acquisition in two agent settings with a late and a certain agent under different costs

der cannot gain information from competing bids, since the competitor bids late. Thus, there is no difference for the uncertain bidder, whether to buy information early or late. Nevertheless, the uncertain agent tends to acquire information early under the cost levels smaller than $c < 8.0$ ($p < 0.02$) and is indifferent for the cost levels 8.0, 9.0, 10.0.

The environment with one adaptive certain and one adaptive uncertain agent does not produce such clear results. The frequency of information acquisition (both, early and late) decrease while increasing the cost levels. The uncertain agent tend to buy information early more frequently ($p < 0.02$) under the cost levels of $c \in \{1.0, 5.0, 6.0, 7.0, 8.0, 9.0\}$ and is indifferent whether to buy information early or late under cost level $c = 10.0$.

The described results for testing H7 are diverse. There is a majority of situations that indicate that the frequency of late information acquisition also depends on the information acquisition costs. Nevertheless, the results are not unambiguous, so that the support for H7 is weak.

Comparing the frequency of information acquisition between the auction formats AA and SB, it can be remarked that there is less frequent information acquisition in ascending auctions for cost levels $5, \ldots, 10$. This observation can be confirmed by one-sided t-tests for all environmental settings on basis of p-values $p << 0.02$. This is contradicting to H10. In the SB format, agents receive no feedback of the competing bidders actions. It might be that uncertain agents tend to more frequently buy information in order to overcome this lack of information and still have a positive probability of receiving a positive reward.

Figures 7.8 and 7.9 also display the frequency of information acquisition in the last tick of the auction as response on competing bids during the first tick (H9). It is noticeable that the proportion of the information acquisition as response on competing bids is small compared to the total amount of actions with information buying. But on the other hand, the ratio of late information acquisition due to perceived competing bids in relation to late information acquisition in general is on average at 83%. This suggests that late information acquisition was stimulated by early bids.

In order to scrutinize, whether late information acquisition was caused by early competing bids, the frequency of late information acquisition in the settings 1U1HE and 1U1HL are compared. If there is a causal relation between early competing bids and late information acquisition, the frequency of late information acquisition must be higher in the 1U1HE setting compared to the 1U1HL setting. Therefore, a one-sided paired t-test is conducted for the frequency of late information acquisition on the two settings that confirms this hypothesis on the basis of a p-value significantly smaller than 0.02. These findings indicate support for H9.

The bidding behaviour of the certain bidder might carry more information about this aspect. Figure 7.10 depicts the frequency of early and late bidding of the certain agent for the settings with one uncertain agent under different information cost levels. Early bidding is more frequent (73%) than bidding late (27%) and there is no trend noticeable for a change in the frequency of late bids

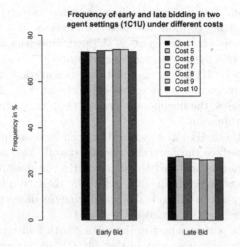

Figure 7.10: Frequency of early and late bidding of a certain agent in the last 3000 rounds under varying information costs in the ascending auction competing against one uncertain agent.

between the different settings. This clear difference in the frequency of early and late bidding confirms hypothesis H8.

Having investigated the impact of the information acquisition costs for two agents, the next section studies a group of five agents under varying information cost levels.

7.2.2 Five Agent Environment

This section studies the impact of information acquisition costs in a setting with five competing bidders. According to equations 6.17 and 6.18, the bidder's expected payoff for certain bidders in an environment with five agents decreases to $\theta = 1.\overline{6}$ currency units and the payoffs of uncertain agents decrease to $\theta_u = 1.3$. The auctioneer's revenue amounts to $\pi = 98.\overline{3}$ (according to equation 6.16) and the social welfare to $\omega = 106.\overline{6}$ (equation 6.15).

The reduced expected payoffs of the agents makes it more difficult to decide, whether or not to acquire information. The agents play in a highly competitive environment, in which all agents are adaptive. Since it takes longer for the Q-learning algorithm to adapt in such a dynamic environment, the auction game is repeated 20000 rounds.

Three environmental settings are evaluated, in which the amount of uncertain agents is increased, starting with one uncertain agent competing against four certain agents. The second setting includes four uncertain agents and one certain agent, and the third setting contains five uncertain agents. In contrast to Section 7.1.2, the setting with five certain agents is skipped, since the information costs have no impact on certain agents in such an environment.

Concerning hypothesis H12, it is assumed that the average uncertain agent's payoff decrease while more uncertain agents enter the auction. If the number of uncertain agents increases, the likelihood increases that competing agents submit bids above their true valuation.

In respect to hypothesis H13 it is assumed that an increase in the information acquisition costs will reduce the uncertain agents' payoff. This is due to the fact that the less information is acquired the more costly the information is, and as a result, uncertain agents more frequently bid above their true valuation. Figure 7.11 depicts the average uncertain agents' payoff during the different environmental settings for both, ascending and sealed-bid auctions.

The uncertain agent performs best in the setting with four certain agents. The payoff decreases significantly from this setting (4C1U) to setting 1C4U in which four uncertain agents and one certain agent are involved and to setting 5U with five uncertain agents. This proposition is tested with a Wilcoxon rank sum test, since the values are not normal distributed (tested with a Shapiro-Wilk test with a p-values $p \ll 0.02$). The averaged payoff for the settings are compared as described at the beginning of this chapter. The Wilcoxon rank sum test is applied to 4C1U vs. 1C4U for all cost levels, 4C1U vs. 5U for all cost levels, and to 1C4U vs. 5U for all cost levels. It turns out that hypothesis H12 can be confirmed for all described comparisons with a p-values $p \ll 0.02$ that the uncertain agents' payoffs decrease the more uncertain agents participate in the auction game.

A Wilcoxon rank sum test is also performed to test H13 which proposes that increasing cost levels reduces the uncertain agent's payoff. For this test the observed average payoff of the uncertain agent are compared within the same environmental setting for different cost levels, i.e. the 10 observations for the uncertain agent in setting 4C1U are compared for the cost levels 1.0 vs. 1.5, 1.5 vs. 2.0, 2.0 vs. 5.0. For the settings with more than one uncertain agents the averaged values over the uncertain agents are used as basis for the test. The data of the corresponding p-values is found in Table B.19 in Appendix B.1. It turns out that there is no support for the hypothesis in the setting 4C1U, neither in the AA format, nor in the SB format. There is support for the hypothesis for the AA format in setting 1C4U, but no significant support for the SB setting. The picture in the 5U setting is mixed, meaning that there is support for both, AA format and SB format, while comparing 1.0 vs. 1.5 and 2.0 vs. 5.0. There is no support for a decrease in payoffs while comparing 1.5 vs. 2.0. Due to these non-uniform results of the tests, it is difficult to give a non-ambiguous proposition. The impact of the information costs is obviously smaller as expected.

Figure 7.12 shows the average auctioneer's revenue for the four cost levels and the three environmental settings. The revenue varies for the different cost levels. The application of a Shapiro-Wilk test (4C1U: $p = 0.84$, 1C4U: $p = 0.34$,

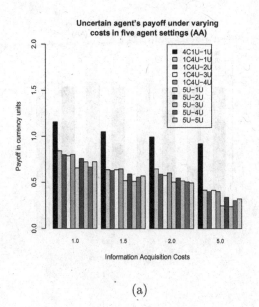

(a)

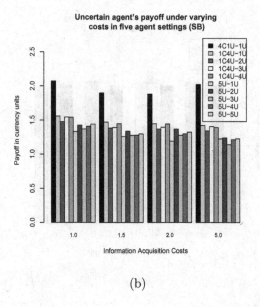

(b)

Figure 7.11: Average uncertain agents' payoffs in the last 3000 rounds under varying information costs in (a) the ascending and (b) sealed-bid auction in settings 4C1U, 1C4U and 5U.

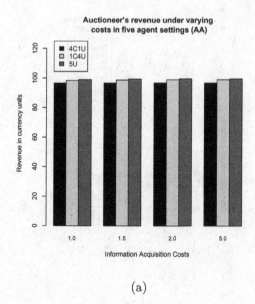

(a)

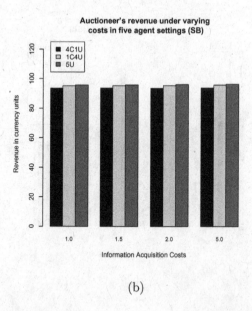

(b)

Figure 7.12: Average auctioneer's revenue in the last 3000 rounds under varying information costs in (a) the ascending and (b) sealed-bid auction in settings 4C1U, 1C4U and 5U.

5U: $p = 0.14$) confirms normally distributed data for the auctioneer's revenue. Consequently, a one-sided paired t-test is applied to scrutinise the proposition that an increase of information acquisition costs has an positive impact on the auctioneer's revenue. Table 7.14 shows the p-values for these tests.

	AA format			SB format		
	1.0 vs. 1.5	1.5 vs. 2.0	2.0 vs. 5.0	1.0 vs. 1.5	1.5 vs. 2.0	2.0 vs. 5.0
4C1U	0.04	0.01	0.38	0.03	0.81	0.01
1C4U	<<0.02	0.01	0.14	0.04	0.01	<<0.02
5U	<<0.02	0.04	0.58	0.13	<<0.02	<<0.02

Table 7.14: Overview on the p-values of one-sided paired t-test with $H_0 : \pi_i \neq \pi_j$ and $H_1 : \pi_i - \pi_j < 0$

It can be remarked that there is a significant positive impact on the revenue for increasing information costs from 1.0 to 2.0 during the AA format. For a larger increase of the cost, the t-test do not prove the proposition for the AA format. In the SB format the results are ambiguous, since there is a significant positive impact on the revenue in the 4C1U and 1C4U settings while increasing the information costs from 1.0 to 1.5. This can not be proved for the 5U setting. Comparing the cost levels 1.5 and 2.0 there is statistical support for the proposition in the settings 1C4U and 5U and no support in setting 4C1U. The t-test supports the proposition for the further increase of the information costs from 2.0 to 5.0 for all environmental settings. Recapitulating, in the majority of the analysed settings, there is support for a dependency between the information costs and the auctioneer's revenue. This supports the proposition that auctioneers can profit from increasing information cost.

It appears that the auctioneer profits from uncertain bidders, since there is a slight increase in revenue while the number of uncertain agents increase. This was also suggested in P3 of research question Q3 and summarized in hypothesis H15. A one-sided paired t-test is applied that on a basis of p-values $p << 0.02$ confirms the expected increase of the auctioneer's revenue from setting 4C1U to 1C4U and from 1C4U to 5U for all cost levels. This observation is made for both auction formats, sealed-bid as well as ascending auction.

Research question Q4 concerns the impact of information costs on the auction's outcome. P4 proposes a reduction of social welfare for increasing information costs. Figure 7.13 shows the social welfare for all three environmental settings and the four cost levels. In order to test hypothesis H16, hat increasing information costs reduce social welfare one-sided paired t-tests are applied. Table 7.15 presents the p-values of these tests for $H_0: \omega_i \neq \omega_j$ and $H_1: \omega_i - \omega_j > 0$, testing for the alternative hypothesis that the difference in social welfare means of the compared settings is greater than 0. There is significant support for the proposition while increasing the costs from level 1.0 to 1.5 and from 2.0 to 5.0 in all three environmental settings (4C1U, 1C4U, 5U) of the AA format. The switch from cost level 1.5 to 2.0 in the AA format has no impact in settings 1C4U and 5U, but also leads to a significant welfare decrease in setting 4C1U. In the SB format there is no support for the

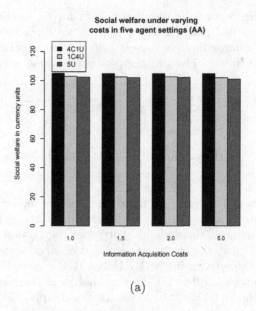

(a)

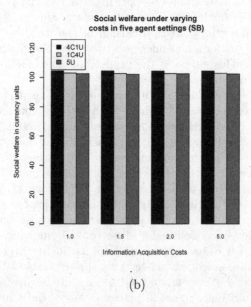

(b)

Figure 7.13: Average auctioneer's revenue in the last 3000 rounds under varying information costs in (a) the ascending and (b) sealed-bid auction in settings 4C1U, 1C4U and 5U.

proposition in most of the test. It is only the switch from cost 1.0 to 1.5 in settings 1C4U and 5U, and the switch from 2.0 to 5.0 in the 5U setting that supports the proposition. These findings suggest that SB auctions are much more robust against the height of information costs than AA auctions.

	AA format			SB format		
	1.0 vs. 1.5	1.5 vs. 2.0	2.0 vs. 5.0	1.0 vs. 1.5	1.5 vs. 2.0	2.0 vs. 5.0
4C1U	<<0.02	<<0.02	0.04	0.08	0.14	0.87
1C4U	<<0.02	0.86	<<0.02	<<0.02	0.60	1.00
5U	<<0.02	0.65	<<0.02	<<0.02	0.99	<<0.02

Table 7.15: Overview on the p-values of one-sided paired t-test with $H_0 : \omega_i \neq \omega_j$ and $H_1 : \omega_i - \omega_j > 0$

It is also interesting to note that the agents' payoffs is greater in the SB format compared to the AA format. Wilcoxon rank sum test support H1 for all settings over all cost levels on basis of $p << 0.02$. The same applies to H2. The performed Wilcoxon rank sum tests conducted for all settings and cost levels strongly support H2 on a basis of p-values $p << 0.02$.

According to the previously analysed settings, there is no distinct statement possible for H3. In the setting with four certain agents and one uncertain agent (4C1U), H3 is rejected on basis of a $p = 1.00$. For the settings with more uncertain agents, H3 can be accepted at p-values of 1C4U: $p << 0.02$ and 5U: $p << 0.02$. The impact of information acquisition costs on the social welfare is evaluated in more detail in the following.

Regarding the question, whether uncertainty negatively influences the social welfare, it is to be expected that social welfare decrease the more uncertain agents are involved (H4). Therefore, it is necessary to compare the social welfare of the settings 4C1U, 1C4U and 5U for all cost levels. Again, a one-sided paired t-test is used to scrutinize this proposition for comparing setting 4C1U and 1C4U, as well as 1C4U and 5U at all cost levels. It turns out that the proposition can be confirmed for all settings and cost levels on the basis of p-values below 0.02 (H_0: $\omega_i \neq \omega_j$ and H_1: $\omega_i - \omega_j > 0$).

In Section 7.1.2 the proposition was investigated whether SB auctions result in a higher social welfare the more uncertain agents participate. There was statistical support for this proposition in the setting with 5 uncertain agents (5U) and no support for setting 1C4U. In order to further scrutinise this proposition, the social welfare of the two auction formats is compared for each setting and cost level. It is expected that the social welfare for the 4C1U settings is higher in the AA format compared to the SB format and vice versa for the 5U settings. There is probably no distinct support for the 1C4U settings.

In fact, one sided Wilcoxon rank sum tests comparing the social welfare in the two auction formats show support for this proposition. Table 7.16 depicts the p-values for the test for each setting and cost level. There is significant support that social welfare is higher in AA formats for the 4C1U setting in all cost levels. Setting 1C4U is ambiguous, since there is support for the proposition that social welfare is higher in SB compared to AA format in the cost levels 1.5 and 5.0, but no support for the cost levels 1.0 and 2.0. There is full support for the proposition of higher social welfare in SB formats for setting 5U in each cost level. This indicates the trend that it is preferable to use SB-format auctions the more uncertain agents are expected to participate in an auction. In respect to H6, it is analysed, whether

	4C1U	1C4U	5U
	$H_1: \omega_{AA} > \omega_{SB}$	$H_1: \omega_{AA} < \omega_{SB}$	$H_1: \omega_{AA} < \omega_{SB}$
1.0	$\ll 0.02$	0.18	$\ll 0.02$
1.5	$\ll 0.02$	0.01	0.02
2.0	$\ll 0.02$	0.07	$\ll 0.02$
5.0	$\ll 0.02$	$\ll 0.02$	$\ll 0.02$

Table 7.16: Overview on the p-values of one-sided paired t-test comparing the social welfare of AA and SB auctions in five agent settings

the certain agents receive a higher payoff on average compared to the uncertain agents. Therefore, the payoffs within one setting and cost level are compared using a one sided Wilcoxon rank sum test. The tests are applied to the setting 4C1U and 1C4U for all cost levels. On basis of the test results ($p \ll 0.02$ for all settings and cost levels), H6 can be confirmed.

At next, the strategy selection of uncertain and certain agents is evaluated. As already observed in the previous section, the impact of information acquisition costs on the certain agents action selection is marginal for both auction formats. As in the settings evaluated so far, certain agents most frequently choose to bid the full valuation at some stage of the ascending auction (68%), mostly right at the beginning of the auction (25%). The second most frequent strategy (23%) is to bid 10 units below the true valuation as the maximum bid during the auction. Agents only deviate marginally from these main strategies.

This is not the same for the uncertain agents that react sensitive on changes of the information cost levels. It can be observed that uncertain agents most frequently decide to discover and play the true valuation at the beginning of the auction if the information acquisition costs are low compared to the expected reward. For example, in a setting with five competing agents and cost level 1.0 uncertain agents choose the described strategy in 10% of the played games. The second most frequent strategy is to submit bids at the auction start at the estimated valuation (8%). Alternatively, uncertain agents submits bids 10 units above the estimated valuation (7%). In general, uncertain agents discover and bid the true valuation at some stage of the auction at a frequency of 25%.

Comparing these results to the strategy table at cost level 5.0, there are significant changes identifiable. In 15% of the games uncertain agents submit a bid that amounts to the estimated valuation right at the beginning, or they submit bids at the beginning with values of 10 units above the estimated valuation (13%). The third most frequent played strategy (8%) is to submit a bid at 10 units below the estimated valuation at the beginning and a bid amounting to the estimated valuation at the end of the auction. In general, it can be stated that agents less often

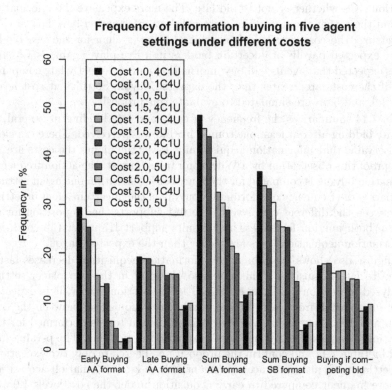

Figure 7.14: Frequency of early and late information acquisition of the uncertain agents in the last 3000 rounds under varying information costs in different environmental settings.

discover the true valuation the more expensive the information acquisition is. In these cases, the most frequently played strategies comply with the expected optimal policies. Consequently, it can be stated that the agents learn to play optimal policies. In the following, the action selection is analysed in more depth.

Hypothesis H7 addresses the strategy of the uncertain bidder who is supposed to bid late. As the results of the two player setting suggest, it depends on the information cost, whether or not to bid late. The more expensive the information acquisition the rather the uncertain agent will buy information late. For the five agents settings the cost threshold is considerably lower than for the two bidder case. The expected payoffs of uncertain bidders in a five player game is 1.3, and thus, it is expected that agents will buy information more frequently late compared to early if the costs are greater than the expected payoff. Settings at cost levels 1.0, 1.5, 2.0, and 5.0 were simulated to evaluate this proposition.

Figure 7.14 summarizes the frequency of early and late bidding in general, as well as late bidding after at least one competing bid was perceived. There is a clear trend observable that information acquisition is lower the higher the costs are. In order to proof this observation by a Wilcoxon rank sum test, the action frequency of information buying is compared for the four cost levels within one agent setting. I.e. comparing the frequency of information buying of the uncertain agent in setting 4C1U between the different cost levels. The test supports the proposition for all settings in both auction formats. These results support H7 under the condition that information acquisition costs are higher than the expected payoff.

The figure also shows that the early information acquisition decreases faster compared to late acquisition. This was also observed in the two player setting and analysed in Section 7.2.1. As explained in the section earlier, it is expected that there is a switch from early to late information acquisition between the cost levels 1.0 and 1.5. Consequently, a Wilcoxon rank sum test is performed for the three settings comparing early and late information acquisition. The p-values are depicted in Table 7.17 and confirm the proposition. There are only two exceptions for the setting with just one uncertain agent, where late information acquisition is not more frequent compared to early acquisition under the cost levels 1.0 and 2.0. Nevertheless, these results support hypothesis H11.

	Cost 1.0: H_1: EB¡LB	Cost 1.5: H_1: EB¡LB	Cost 2.0: H_1: EB¡LB	Cost 5.0: H_1: EB¡LB
4C1U	<<0.02	1.00	0.19	<<0.02
1C4U	<<0.02	0.01	<<0.02	<<0.02
5U	<<0.02	<<0.02	<<0.02	<<0.02

Table 7.17: P-values for comparing early (EB) and late (LB) information acquisition for the three environmental settings under different information costs

Comparing information acquisition in AA and SB format, it is interesting to note that information acquisition is more frequent in AA formats. This is not in accordance to the findings in the two player case, where information was more frequently bought in SB auctions. This observation is significant on basis of Wilcoxon rank sum tests for all settings resulting in p-values $p << 0.02$ except of setting 4C1U at cost level 5.0 with a p-value of $p = 0.04$. Thus, the findings are a strong support for H10.

Figure 7.14 also shows the frequency of information acquisition after competing bids were perceived. It can be noted that on average 72% of late information acquisition was performed after the bidder perceived competing bids. The question arises if the agents acquire information *because* a competing bid was placed, or if this observation is just a coincidence. It is referred to Section 7.2.1 where exactly this question was investigated. The results of the analysis suggest that the information acquisition is stimulated by early competing bids. Consequently, this applies also to the present setting and gives support for hypothesis H9.

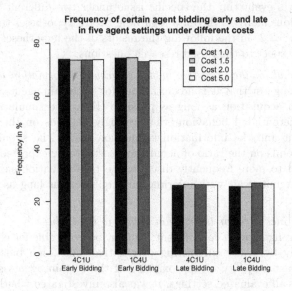

Figure 7.15: Frequency of early and late bidding of the certain agents in the last 3000 rounds under varying information costs in different environmental settings.

Regarding the frequency of early and late bidding of the certain agents, according to the settings evaluated in the previous sections it is to be remarked that early bidding is preferred (73.5%) to late bidding (26.5%). Figure 7.15 shows the frequency of early and late bidding of uncertain agents. This data confirm hypothesis H8 and indicate that it is more profitable for certain agents to bid early, and thus, submitting early price signals. There was some evidence shown in the present section as well as in Section 7.2.1 that early price signals stimulate information acquisition of uncertain agents.

7.3   Summary

The present chapter evaluates the impact of valuation uncertainty on the bidder behaviour and the auction outcome. The presence of uncertainty over one's own valuation raises a couple of questions concerning e.g. the point of time for submitting the bid, whether or not to acquire additional information, or the impact on the bidders' payoffs and auctioneer's revenue. Section 6.2.2 has introduced the evaluation space of the present model that is spanned by three axis along which the model is evaluated. These axis represent the auction format, the structure of the participants, and the information acquisition costs. The axis implicitly determine the structure of the present chapter. The two subsections analyse the impact of the auction format and the information acquisition costs. Both subsections are structured in two parts evaluating the specific issue under two different group types. Each of the sections analyses the data regarding the 16 hypotheses that were proposed in Section 6.2.2. In the following the results of the hypotheses analysis are summarised in respect to the raised research questions.

(Q1) *Is it beneficial for the uncertain bidder to acquire information late?*
Literature suggest that it is advantageous for uncertain agents to wait with information acquisition as long as possible (H7). The simulation produces a more differentiated behaviour that strongly depends on the competitive environment and the information acquisition costs. The simulation shows that it depends on the ratio of acquisition costs to the expected payoff. The agents tend to more frequently discover the true valuation early the lower the ratio. Agents wait with information acquisition as long as possible the greater the ratio.

(Q2) *Is there an incentive for the certain bidder to bid early?*
There is strong support for H8 that it might be profitable for certain agents to bid early by either submitting preemptive bids (high bids) or a price signal. A vast majority of approx. 73% of the certain agents submit early bids during all evaluated settings. It was also investigated whether the early bids stimulate value discovery or not (H9). There is some evidence that this is the case especially for increasing information acquisition costs.

(Q3) *How does uncertainty influence revenues of bidders and the auctioneer?*
There was strong support amongst all evaluated settings for hypothesis H1 that proposes higher payoffs for bidders in SB compared to AA formats, and hypothesis H2 that expects lower revenues for the auctioneer in SB compared to AA formats. This observation contradicts theory that proves revenue equivalence for both auction formats. Additionally, the findings correspond to observations on internet auction markets, where ascending price auctions result in higher revenues for the auctioneer.
    Hypotheses H4, H5, and H6 scrutinise the impact of uncertainty on the social welfare (H4), the auctioneer's revenue (H5), and the bidders' payoffs (H6). It is expected that the social welfare is higher under certainty compared

to settings with uncertainty. On the other hand, auctioneer's revenues may be greater in settings with uncertain agents, whereas the uncertain bidders' payoffs is expected to be smaller than the certain bidders' payoff. Significant support was found for H4 and H5. The results for the bidders' payoffs are non-uniform in respect to H6. Most of the settings confirm that uncertain agents receive lower payoffs than their certain competitors. In a few settings with just two bidders, there was not enough support for the hypothesis. Nevertheless, in competitive environments, uncertain agents perform worse compared to their certain competitors.

Regarding the auctioneer's revenue, H14 proposes increasing revenue for increasing information costs. There is no support for this hypothesis in the two bidder case and only weak support in the five bidder scenarios. Unlike to this issue, there is strong support for H15 that suggests an increase of the auctioneer's revenue for an increasing number of uncertain agents participating in the simulation.

(Q4) *Is there an impact on the bidding behaviour in different environmental settings, e.g. different numbers of agents or varying information acquisition costs?*

In general, it is observed that the frequency of value discovery decreases while the acquisition costs raise. This is support for H11 on basis of significant tests.

H12 proposes a decreasing payoff of uncertain bidder for an increase in the number of uncertain bidders. The simulation data shows support for that hypothesis. Decreasing uncertain agents' payoffs was also expected for increasing information costs in H13. The simulation did not find enough support for this hypothesis.

Hypothesis H16 concerns the impact of information acquisition costs on the social welfare. It proposes a negative impact of increasing information costs on the social welfare. This hypothesis can be confirmed on the basis of the simulation data.

In general, it is observed on basis of the simulation that uncertain agents tend to buy information immediately if the costs are adequate low. The greater the information acquisition costs are the less frequent information is acquired. In cases of high information costs, uncertain agents most frequently play their estimated valuation or slightly above the estimated valuation. This is conform to the theoretical benchmark as described in Section 6.2.3 and helps to understand overbidding in auctions. Certain agents generally prefer to submit early bids at their true valuation or slightly below and bid the true valuation at some stage during the auction.

(Q5) *How do sealed-bid auction perform under uncertainty in comparison to an*
     open-cry ascending auction?
     Regarding the social welfare, it is not possible to confirm hypothesis H3
     that suggests higher social welfare in AA formats compared to SB formats.
     This hypothesis is rejected in most of the settings. This indicates that the
     distribution of the social surplus between auctioneer and bidder differs for the
     two auction formats. Thus, it depends on the purpose of the auction, which
     format to apply. If it is the auctioneer's revenue that is to be maximised than
     the AA format performs better. If the bidder's payoff is to be maximised, the
     SB format appears to better suit this purpose.
         Comparing the frequency of value discovery in AA and SB formats,
     hypothesis H10 expects more frequent information acquisition in AA formats.
     This can be confirmed for the competitive environments with five bidders,
     but not for the two agent games.

Apart from the economic analysis of the simulation, it is to be regarded if the chosen evolutionary approach is appropriate for the present problem. The central issue
is, whether or not equilibrium policies are found during the simulation. Therefore,
four special cases were ex ante analysed in Section 6.2.3 and some optimal policies
were identified. The simulation results show that the agents most frequently learn
to play these theoretical optimal policies, i.e. the learning algorithm converges
to the optimal policies. This is an important finding, since it is mathematically
not founded that reinforcement learning converges in a multi-learning environment. The present results suggest that this is the case – at least in the present
simulation. This observation makes the simulation results even more reliable.

The simulation has shown interesting insights in both, the behaviour of bidding
agents in two different auction formats and in the applicability of multi-agent
learning. The results are to a large extend in accordance to the relevant literature.
In some cases as for example the point of time for information acquisition, the
simulation indicates a more differentiated agent behaviour than literature assumes.
Overall, it can be remarked that the chosen simulation approach is an appropriate
mean for the evaluation of such a complex problem in Market Engineering

The next part summarises the main contributions of this book, discusses the
limitations of the applied agent-based simulation approach and point out how to
build on the present book for further research.

Part IV

Concluding Discussion and Future Research

Chapter 8

Conclusion

Electronic auctions have received much attention in recent years. It is known that auction rules can have a great impact on the bidders' behaviour and the auction outcome. Nevertheless, just a small part of effects has been studied so far. This is the reason why a structured approach for the development of electronic markets appears valuable. Such an approach was proposed by Weinhardt et al. [2003] as Market Engineering. The present work puts the focus on the evaluation of electronic markets on the basis of agent-based simulations.

At the beginning of this book, three main research questions have been raised that implicitly determine the structure of the work and lead through the book. The first question concerns the appropriateness of agent-based simulation approaches in economics and the validity of such simulations. As such its answer contributes to methodological issues in market engineering. The second and the third question concern the economic impact of valuation uncertainty on the bidders' behaviour and the outcome of two different auction formats. The answers to these questions are manifold.

In the next section, answers which were developed during the course of this book are given to the questions raised at the beginning. The main contributions of this work are summarised and the limitations of the applied agent-based simulation approach are discussed in Section 8.2 and an outlook to further research is given in Section 8.3.

8.1 Summary of the Main Contributions

Regarding the overall research questions raised in the introduction of this book, there are two main contributions. One concerns the first research question asking how to conduct valid agent-based market simulations. The second contribution summarises the answers to research questions 2 and 3 that regard the impact of valuation uncertainty on the bidders' behaviour and the auction's outcome. The main contributions are summarised in the following:

1. Application of agent-based market simulations
   The most important methodological approaches for agent-based simulations and their interrelations to economic theory were reviewed. In order to easily apply agent-based market simulations, the market simulation environment AMASE was developed. The possibility of both, developing appropriate simulation models by using the described methodological approaches and implementing the models to conduct simulation on AMASE and meet2trade, is a major advancement towards computer aided market engineering.

2. Evaluation of two auction models with uncertain bidders
   The problem of valuation uncertainty was only theoretically analysed so far. The simulation results of this work give more insight to the problem since it also regards dynamic aspects of the game and allows to investigate the impact of a set of parameter values. Hence, the simulation studies the bidders' behaviour of certain and uncertain agents as well as the outcome of two auction formats, open-cry ascending second-price auction (AA) and second-price sealed-bid auction (SB). The findings contribute to economic market research.

It was pointed out that the application of agent-based simulations is often not well theoretically founded. In Section 4, the main agent-based simulation methods were reviewed and the current related work was presented on the theoretical foundation of agent-based simulations and its analogy to economic theory. It is differentiated in pure agent-based approaches, Monte Carlo techniques, evolutionary methods, and reinforcement learning. The latter method was picked up for research on the problem of valuation uncertainty. In case of two participants, reinforcement learning is one method to solve Markov games. This was not yet theoretically verified for multi-agent learning environments. The main contribution of the review on agent-based simulation techniques is the overview on the methods used and their bridges to link economic theory and computational approaches in order to develop appropriate models that allow economic interpretation. This work applies a reinforcement learning approach to a Markov Game in one-, two-, and five-agent learning environments. The algorithm converges in all environments. The results can to large extend explain equilibrium behaviour. This is the reason why the algorithm is considered to also produce valuable results in a multi-agent environment.

The generic electronic market platform meet2trade was developed to enable the configuration of various electronic auctions. With the possibility to easy configurate electronic auctions meet2trade can serve as a core for electronic market research. An experimental and a simulation system facilitate the evaluation of markets. The agent-based simulation environment AMASE was developed to enable market simulations in both systems, AMASE and meet2trade. AMASE and meet2trade are important building blocks for computer aided market engineering as it is discussed in Section 2.3.

A simulation model was developed and implemented to study the impact of valuation uncertainty on the bidders' behaviour and the auction outcome. The model builds on the independent private values assumptions and is modelled as a Markov game. Agents are equipped with a reinforcement learning algorithm to optimise their action selection. Reinforcement learning algorithms are used to find optimal policies in Markov games. As mentioned above, two auction formats were investigated: an open-cry ascending second-price auction (AA) and a second-price sealed-bid auction (SB). The main findings are summarised in the following.

There was strong support for the hypothesis that agents receive higher payoffs in the AA format compared to the SB format. It was also found that auctioneer's revenue is higher in AA formats. This is contradicting to economic theory that can prove revenue equivalence for both auction formats. There is no evidence for higher or lower social welfare in one of the two auction formats.

The participation of uncertain bidders results in increasing auctioneer's revenue and decreasing social welfare in both auction formats. Uncertain agents mostly perform worse than certain agents. It is interesting to note that uncertain agents' payoffs does not decrease due to increasing information acquisition costs but due to an increasing number of uncertain agents. Accordingly, it appears that auctioneers do not profit from increasing information acquisition costs. There is only weak support for increasing auctioneer's revenue in the five agent scenario.

Regarding the strategy selection, uncertain agents tend to early information acquisition if the acquisition costs are low compared to the expected payoff. The more expensive the information costs the less frequently information is acquired. Agents will wait with value discovery if the information costs are high. In the case of high information acquisition costs uncertain agents most frequently bid the expected valuation or above the expected valuation. This is conform to the optimal policies analysis in Section 6.2.3 and helps to understand overbidding in auctions.

Certain agents prefer to bid early independent from the information acquisition costs for uncertain agents. There is some evidence that early bidding stimulates value discovery of uncertain agents. Certain agents learn to submit their full valuation at some stage of the bidding process. In many online auctions it can be observed that participants bid late. Some studies have been done on that issue (cp. Ünver [2003] and Ockenfels and Roth [2005]) that differ from the discussed model in so far that there is a probability $p > 0$ that late bids (submitted shortly before the end of an ascending auction) don't access the system.

Apart from the findings that support the theoretic expectations there are also observations that are not in accordance to the expected characteristics. Certain bidders surprisingly often submit bids below their valuation. It was expected that this is not profitable due to the construction of the model. The second highest possible bid to submit is 10 units below the full valuation. The expected payoff in the two player game is $8.\overline{3}$ currency units, and thus, smaller than the difference of second highest bid action and full valuation. Therefore, there is no incentive to bid below the full valuation. It is interesting to note that this can also be observed in experimental studies, see for example Seifert [2005, p. 144].

Concluding, it can be stated that it is possible to explain observations from online auctions at least partially with the applied model of valuation uncertainty. It is often observed in online auctions that bidders raise their bids – sometimes above fixed price offers of other online shops. Such behaviour can be explained with valuation uncertainty. In some cases it is an optimal policy of uncertain bidders to bid above their valuation. The applied simulative approach shows promising results for further applications. Nevertheless, it also has some limitations that are discussed in the next section.

8.2   Limitations of the Approach

Although simulations often produce valuable results limitations of the approach have to be remarked. In general, there is the possibility of having implemented a wrong model without noticing that it is incorrect. It was possible to show that the current model works well since the expected results were met during the calibration. Nevertheless, the suggested simulation model has some particular limitations that may not allow to generalise the results. The model studied is rather simplified. The strategy space is limited by discrete actions that can only be carried out at discrete points of time.

Firstly, the assumptions of the model are strict, and thus, may not be fully transferable to reality. Recall that the symmetric independent private values model is assumed, i.e. the agents' valuations are drawn from the same distribution function which is known to all agents. In reality, it can neither be assumed that agents know the distribution function from which competitors draw their valuations, nor that this distribution function is the same for all participants. Additionally, the described auction formats are a simplification of the real world auction formats, e.g. on eBay. For the simulation, second-price auctions were chosen whereas eBay implements a proxy auction. Such a proxy auction results in a second-price auction plus an increment. Regarding the bidding process, the model implements bidding at discrete points of time in order to study effects of early and late bidding. In most of the single-sided electronic auctions continuous bidding is allowed.

Secondly, the learning model of the agents was applied to single and multi agent learning settings. Convergence was theoretically proved in literature for single agent learning settings, i.e. just one agent in the simulation is equipped with a learning method. In this setting, the approach is also applied to settings with five agents. There is no mathematical foundation on convergence in a multi-agent learning case but the simulation results are in accordance to the theoretically expected values. This indicates that reinforcement learning might also work in multi-agent learning scenarios. In fact, the learning algorithm complies with research in psychology and has been successfully applied in literature to reproduce experimental data collected during experiments with humans. Nevertheless, it can not fully represent human behaviour, but is a well suited approach to find equilibria in Markov games.

Thirdly, the present model is just one view on the problem of valuation uncertainty in order to explain the phenomenon of observing bidders who bid above their true valuation. The model does not consider other aspects, e.g. psychological factors. On the other hand, this weakness is also an advantage since the model's parameters are in full control of the simulator. Consequently, the results are not influenced by unknown causes. In the next section, an outlook on further research is given.

8.3 Outlook

In the course of this work, it has been pointed out how to conduct agent-based market simulations and which methods to apply in order to build valid models. The results of the conducted simulation are promising for further research. In the following some ideas for future research are presented.

Firstly, it is possible to improve and to extend the model. The previous section has described some limitations of the model regarding its simplicity. It is possible to overcome these limitations by changing the model, e.g. by replacing discrete time steps for order submission by continuous time, increasing the action space, introducing different levels of risk-awareness, adding other human-like behaviour, and changing the valuations model. In the present model an independent private values model is applied. In reality, it is more likely to observe also common components, i.e. the agents' valuations are at least partly dependent on the competitors' valuations.

Secondly, experiments with human participants can give evidence about the found results as e.g. the simulated behaviour. Experiments may result in a different auction outcome caused by other factors (e.g. psychological factors as a shopping spree) that were not studied during the simulation. An additional interesting alternative is to combine simulations and experiments. Software agents are trained in a controlled environment, and afterwards, they take part in an experiment with humans. Such mixed experiments can be used to compare the results with pure experiments and pure simulations. This can help to study, if the presence of software agents has an impact on the human participants' bidding behaviour and how software agents perform while playing the trained strategies.

Thirdly, the agent-based simulation approach studied in the present book can be adapted and applied to other models, e.g. markets that have been already evaluated experimentally. On the one hand, this can help to evaluate the applicability of such a simulative approach, and on the other hand, it can be tried to better insulate the experimentally investigated effects.

Finally, the applied reinforcement learning approach can be compared to other agent-based approaches such as evolutionary algorithms. Since genetic algorithms are widely used in science it is interesting if the approaches produce the same results and if one of the approaches performs better. This can help researchers in the decision of choosing an appropriate adaptive mechanism for the simulation of human behaviour.

This work has contributed to better understand the behaviour of agents who are uncertain about their valuation. It has become evident that, if appropriately applied, agent-based simulation approaches can contribute valuable results to market engineering. Agent-based computational economics complements theoretical and experimental approaches. There are still many open questions in the understanding of markets where agent-based simulations may be a promising approach to see behind the curtain.

Appendices and Bibliography

Appendix A

Appendix: Mathematical Proofs

A.1 Expected Social Welfare

The expected social welfare computes as the sum for all x weighted by the probability for x being the highest drawn value. The probability is the density of the first order statics $g_{1,N}(x)$ for N bidders. Since g being the first derivative of the first order distribution $G_{1,N}(x)$ and $G_{1,N}(x) = (G_1(x))^N = G_1(x)^N$, the density can easily be computed to $g_{1,N} = N \left(\frac{x-a}{b-a} \right)^{N-1} \frac{1}{b-a}$. So, it can be written:

$$
\begin{aligned}
E(\omega) &= \int_a^b g_{1,N}(x)dx \\
&= \frac{N}{b-a} \int_a^b \left(\frac{x-a}{b-a} \right)^{N-1} x\,dx
\end{aligned}
$$

Applying partial integration:

$$
\begin{aligned}
E(\omega) &= \frac{N}{b-a} \left\{ \left[\frac{b-a}{N} \left(\frac{x-a}{b-a} \right)^N x \right]_a^b - \int_a^b \frac{b-a}{N} \left(\frac{x-a}{b-a} \right)^N dx \right\} \\
&= b - \left[\frac{b-a}{N+1} \left(\frac{x-a}{b-a} \right)^{N+1} \right]_a^b \\
&= b - \frac{b-a}{N+1}
\end{aligned}
$$

A.2   Auctioneer's Expected Revenue

The auctioneer's profit π in the second price auction is equal to the second highest bid. Thus, the auctioneer's expected profit $E(\pi)$ is sum of all y being the the second highest value weighted by its probability which is the second order statistics. Krishna [2002, p. 266] computes the second order statistics as *"the union of the following disjoint events: (i) all X_k's are less than or equal to y, and (ii) $N-1$ of the X_k's are less than or equal to y and one is greater than y. There are N different ways in which (ii) can occur, so we have that"*

$$G_{2,N}(y) \;=\; \underbrace{G(y)^N}_{(i)} + \underbrace{nG(y)^{N-1}(1-G(y))}_{(ii)}$$

$$=\; nG(y)^{N-1} - (n-1)G(y)^N$$

The associated density function computes to:

$$g_{2,N}(y) = N(N-1)(1-G(y))G(y)^{N-2}g(y)$$

Thus, the expected auctioneer's profit is written as follows:

$$E(\pi) \;=\; \frac{N(N-1)}{b-a}\int_a^b \left(1-\frac{x-a}{b-a}\right)\left(\frac{x-a}{b-a}\right)^{N-2} x\,dx$$

$$=\; \frac{N(N-1)}{b-a}\int_a^b \frac{bx-x^2}{b-a}\left(\frac{x-a}{b-a}\right)^{N-2}dx$$

Applying the partial integration rule:

$$E(\pi) \;=\; N(N-1)b - a\left\{\underbrace{\left[\frac{bx-x^2}{b-a}\frac{b-a}{N-1}\left(\frac{x-a}{b-a}\right)^{N-1}\right]_a^b}_{0} - \int_a^b \frac{b-2x}{b-a}\frac{b-a}{N-1}\left(\frac{x-a}{b-a}\right)^{N-1}dx\right\}$$

$$=\; -N\left\{\underbrace{\left[\frac{b-2x}{b-a}\frac{b-a}{N}\left(\frac{x-a}{b-a}\right)^N\right]_a^b}_{-\frac{b}{N}} - \int_a^b \frac{-2}{b-a}\frac{b-a}{N}\left(\frac{x-a}{b-a}\right)^N dx\right\}$$

$$=\; N\left\{\frac{b}{N} - \frac{2}{N}\frac{b-a}{N+1}\left[\left(\frac{x-a}{b-a}\right)^{N+1}\right]_a^b\right\}$$

$$=\; b - 2\frac{b-a}{N+1}$$

A.3 Bidders' Expected Payoff

The bidders' profit θ is computed as the difference of the own valuation x and the price to be paid which is the second highest bid y. Thus, the expected bidders' profit is the sum of all $\theta = (x - y)$ weighted by the probability of x being the highest bid and y being the highest of all $N - 1$ competing bids:

$$E(\theta) = \int_a^b \int_a^x (x - y)g_{1,N-1}(y)dy f(x)dx$$

With $g_{1,N-1}(y)$ being the first order statistics of the remaining $N - 1$ bidders, and $g_{1,N-1}(y) = G'_{1,N-1}(y)$. The distribution of the first order statistics is equal to $G_{1,N-1} = (G_1(y))^{N-1} = G_1(y)^{N-1}$. It is easy to derive the density of the first order statistics as the first derivative of the distribution:

$$g_{1,N-1} = G'_1(y)^{N-1} = \left(\frac{y-a}{b-a}\right)^{N-1} \frac{d}{dx} = \frac{N-1}{b-a}\left(\frac{y-a}{b-a}\right)^{N-2}$$

So, it can be written:

$$E(\theta) = g_{1,N-1} = \int_a^b \int_a^x (x-y)\frac{N-1}{b-a}\left(\frac{y-a}{b-a}\right)^{N-2}\frac{1}{b-a}dydx$$

Applying partial integration:

$$
\begin{aligned}
E(\theta) &= \frac{N-1}{(b-a)^2}\int_a^b \left\{ \underbrace{\left[(x-y)\frac{b-a}{N-1}\left(\frac{y-a}{b-a}\right)^{N-1}\right]_a^x}_{0} - \int_a^x -1\frac{b-a}{N-1}\left(\frac{y-a}{b-a}\right)^{N-1}dy \right\}dx \\
&= \frac{1}{N}\int_a^b \left[\left(\frac{y-a}{b-a}\right)^N\right]_a^x dx = \frac{1}{N}\int_a^b \left(\frac{x-a}{b-a}\right)^N dx \\
&= \left[\frac{1}{N}\frac{b-a}{N+1}\left(\frac{x-a}{b-a}\right)^{N+1}\right]_a^b = \frac{b-a}{N(N+1)}
\end{aligned}
$$

A.4　Uncertain Bidders' Expected Payoff

In the following, we compute the expected payoff θ_u of uncertain bidders that bid the received estimated valuation in a setting with N bidders in total. It computes as the difference of the drawn valuation x and the second highest bid y under the side condition that the signal $s = x + z > y$. Thus, the expected uncertain bidders' payoff is the sum of all $\theta_u = (x - y)$ weighted by the probability of $x + z$ being the highest bid and y being the highest bid of all $N - 1$ competing bids:

$$
\begin{aligned}
E(\theta_u) &= \int_a^b f(x) \int_{-d}^d f(z) \int_a^{x+z} g_{1,N-1}(x-y)dydzdx \\
&= \int_a^b \frac{1}{b-a} \int_{-d}^d \frac{1}{2d} \int_a^{x+z} \frac{N-1}{(b-a)^{N-1}}(y-a)^{N-2}(x-y)dydzdx \\
&= \frac{N-1}{2d(b-a)^N} \int_a^b \int_{-d}^d \int_a^{x+z} (y-a)^{N-2}(x-y)dydzdx
\end{aligned}
$$

Applying partial integration:

$$
\begin{aligned}
E(\theta_u) &= \frac{N-1}{2d(b-a)^N} \int_a^b \int_{-d}^d \left\{ \left[\frac{(x-y)(y-a)^{N-1}}{N-1} \right]_a^{x+z} - \int_a^{x+z} (-1)\frac{y-a)^{N-1}}{N-1}dy \right\} dzdx \\
&= \frac{N-1}{2d(b-a)^N} \int_a^b \int_{-d}^d \left\{ \frac{(-z)(x-a+z)^{N-1}}{N-1} + \left[\frac{y-a)^N}{N(N+1)} \right]_a^{x+z} \right\} dzdx \\
&= \frac{1}{2dN(b-a)^N} \int_a^b \int_{-d}^d (x-a+z)^{N-1}(x-a-(N-1)z)dzdx
\end{aligned}
$$

Again, applying partial integration:

$$
\begin{aligned}
E(\theta_u) &= \frac{1}{2dN(b-a)^N} \int_a^b \left\{ \left[\frac{1}{N}(x-a+z)^N (x-a-(N-1)z) \right]_{-d}^d \right. \\
&\quad \left. + \int_{-d}^d \frac{(N-1)}{N}(x-a+z)^N dz \right\} dx \\
&= \frac{1}{2dN(b-a)^N} \int_a^b \left\{ \frac{1}{N}(x-a+d)^N (x-a-(N-1)d) \right. \\
&\quad - \frac{1}{N}(x-a-d)^N (x-a+(N-1)d) \\
&\quad \left. + \left[\frac{N-1}{N(N+1)}(x-a+z)^{N+1} \right]_{-d}^d \right\} dx \\
&= \frac{1}{2dN^2(b-a)^N} \int_a^b \left\{ (x-a+d)^N \left[\frac{N-1}{N+1}(x-a+d) + x-a-(N-1)d \right] \right. \\
&\quad \left. -(x-a-d)^N \left[\frac{N-1}{N+1}(x-a-d) + x-a+(N-1)d \right] \right\} dx \\
&= \frac{1}{2dN(N+1)(b-a)^N} \int_a^b \left\{ (x-a+d)^N (2(x-a)) \right. \\
&\quad \left. -(N-1)d) - (x-a-d)^N (2(x-a)+(N-1)d) \right\} dx
\end{aligned}
$$

Again, applying partial integration:

$$
\begin{aligned}
E(\theta_u) &= \frac{1}{2dN(N+1)(b-a)^N} \left\{ \left[\frac{1}{N+1}(x-a+d)^{N+1}(2(x-a)-(N-1)d) \right]_a^b \right. \\
&\quad -2\int_a^b \frac{1}{N+1}(x-a+d)^{N+1}dx - \left[\frac{1}{N+1}(x-a-d)^{N+1}(2(x-a)+(N-1)d) \right]_a^b \\
&\quad \left. +2\int_a^b \frac{1}{N+1}(x-a-d)^{N+1}dx \right\} \\
&= \frac{1}{2dN(N+1)(b-a)^N} \left\{ \frac{1}{N+1}(b-a+d)^{N+1}(2(b-a)-(N-1)d) \right. \\
&\quad +\frac{N-1}{N+1}d^{N+2} - 2\left[\frac{(x-a-d)^{N+2}}{(N+1)(N+2)} \right]_a^b \\
&\quad -\left[\frac{1}{N+1}(b-a-d)^{N+1}(2(b-a)+(N-1)d) + \frac{N-1}{N+1}(-d)^{N+2} \right] \\
&\quad \left. +2\left[\frac{(x-a-d)^{N+2}}{(N+1)(N+2)} \right]_a^b \right\} \\
&= \frac{1}{2dN(N+1)^2(b-a)^N} \left\{ (b-a+d)^{N+1}(2(b-a)-(N-1)d) + (N-1)d^{N+2} \right. \\
&\quad -\frac{2}{N+2}(b-a+d)^{N+2} + \frac{2}{N+2}d^{N+2} - (b-a-d)^{N+1}(2(b-a)+(N-1)d) \\
&\quad \left. -(N-1)(-d)^{N+2} + \frac{2}{N+2}(b-a-d)^{N+2} - \frac{2}{N+2}(-d)^{N+2} \right\} \\
&= \frac{1}{2dN(N+1)(N+2)(b-a)^N} \left[(b-a+d)^{N+1}(2(b-a)-Nd) + Nd^{N+2}(1-(-1)^{N+2}) \right. \\
&\quad \left. -(b-a-d)^{N+1}(2(b-a)+Nd) \right]
\end{aligned}
$$

A.5 Density Function for the Estimated Valuations

The estimated valuation v^E calculates from $X + Y$ where X and Y are uniform distributed random variables. X is drawn from the valuation density function f_X and Y is drawn from the density function g_Y. In the general case these functions are defined as follows:

$$f_X(x) = \begin{cases} \frac{1}{b-a} & \forall x \in \mathbb{R} : a \leq x \leq b \\ 0 & \text{otherwise} \end{cases}$$

$$g_Y(y) = \begin{cases} \frac{1}{2d} & \forall y \in \mathbb{R} : -d \leq y \leq d \\ 0 & \text{otherwise} \end{cases}$$

The convolution computes to:

$$h_E(z) = \int_{-\infty}^{\infty} f_X(x) g_Y(z - x) dx$$

Since $f_X = \frac{1}{b-a}$ for all $x \in [a; b]$:

$$\int_a^b \frac{1}{b-a} g_Y(z - x) dx$$

It is $g_Y(z - x) = \frac{1}{2d}$ for all $-d \leq z - x \leq d$ and thus, the integral is split in:

$$h_E(z) = \begin{cases} \int_{a-d}^{z} \frac{1}{2d(b-a)} dx & = \frac{z-a+d}{2d(b-a)} & \forall z \in [a - d; a + d) \\ \int_{z-d}^{s+d} \frac{1}{2d(b-a)} dx & = \frac{1}{b-a} & \forall z \in [a + d; b - d] \\ \int_{z}^{b+c} \frac{1}{2d(b-a)} dx & = \frac{b+d-z}{2d(b-a)} & \forall z \in (b - d; b + d] \end{cases}$$

Appendix B

Appendix: Simulation Data and Figures

B.1   Data

B.1.1   Institutional Rules: Two Bidder

	1C1HE	1C1U-C	1C1HL
0.0N 0.0N	0.34 ± 0.06	0.50 ± 0.22	0.32 ± 0.08
0.0N 0.5N	0.37 ± 0.07	0.61 ± 0.43	0.42 ± 0.14
0.0N -10N	10.34 ± 0.44	11.20 ± 0.69	11.08 ± 0.69
0.0N 1.0N	13.90 ± 0.70	14.37 ± 0.93	14.42 ± 0.86
0.5N 0.5N	0.41 ± 0.10	0.70 ± 0.21	0.39 ± 0.09
0.5N -10N	10.96 ± 0.62	11.15 ± 0.44	11.43 ± 0.36
0.5N 1.0N	13.94 ± 0.73	14.57 ± 0.79	14.70 ± 0.58
-10N -10N	5.88 ± 0.35	8.48 ± 0.45	10.59 ± 0.52
-10N 1.0N	19.15 ± 0.64	14.00 ± 0.63	10.66 ± 0.50
1.0N 1.0N	24.72 ± 0.63	24.42 ± 0.76	25.99 ± 0.87

Table B.1: Average frequency of actions chosen in the last 3000 rounds by the certain agent during the ascending auction

	1U1HE	1C1U-U	1U1HL
0.0N 0.0N	0.14 ± 0.07	0.18 ± 0.10	0.15 ± 0.05
0.0N 0.5N	0.11 ± 0.04	0.19 ± 0.09	0.14 ± 0.04
0.0N 0.5B	0.02 ± 0.03	0.17 ± 0.18	0.03 ± 0.02
0.0N -10N	2.62 ± 0.30	2.82 ± 0.22	2.84 ± 0.27
0.0N -10B	2.12 ± 0.43	1.89 ± 0.61	2.03 ± 0.25
0.0N 1.0N	3.19 ± 0.45	3.09 ± 0.29	3.12 ± 0.40
0.0N 1.0B	3.11 ± 0.43	2.75 ± 0.28	3.12 ± 0.35
0.0N +10N	2.54 ± 0.67	3.01 ± 0.48	3.01 ± 0.32
0.5N 0.5N	0.37 ± 0.11	0.25 ± 0.11	0.11 ± 0.03
0.5N 0.5B	0.02 ± 0.01	0.09 ± 0.09	0.03 ± 0.02
0.5N -10N	2.76 ± 0.25	2.71 ± 0.53	2.64 ± 0.40
0.5N -10B	2.15 ± 0.15	2.40 ± 0.26	2.17 ± 0.17
0.5N 1.0N	3.28 ± 0.24	3.28 ± 0.37	3.08 ± 0.42
0.5N 1.0B	2.83 ± 0.37	2.66 ± 0.15	3.13 ± 0.29
0.5N +10N	2.41 ± 0.64	3.17 ± 0.31	2.69 ± 0.61
0.5B 0.5N	0.14 ± 0.05	0.12 ± 0.07	0.09 ± 0.07
0.5B -10N	4.98 ± 0.32	4.68 ± 0.85	4.97 ± 0.47
0.5B 1.0N	6.91 ± 0.66	6.41 ± 1.13	6.91 ± 0.65
-10N -10N	1.58 ± 0.16	2.41 ± 0.23	2.96 ± 0.38
-10N -10B	1.24 ± 0.22	1.94 ± 0.26	2.17 ± 0.57
-10N 1.0N	3.60 ± 0.44	2.44 ± 0.48	2.45 ± 0.19
-10N 1.0B	3.37 ± 0.76	3.10 ± 0.30	2.17 ± 0.28
-10N +10N	2.39 ± 0.74	2.55 ± 0.46	2.36 ± 0.31
-10B -10N	2.86 ± 0.27	4.42 ± 0.24	4.51 ± 0.32
-10B 1.0N	8.54 ± 0.44	6.06 ± 0.34	4.65 ± 0.44
1.0N 1.0N	6.41 ± 0.61	6.36 ± 0.38	6.97 ± 0.48
1.0N 1.0B	4.82 ± 0.67	4.81 ± 0.49	4.96 ± 0.41
1.0N +10N	1.54 ± 0.58	1.27 ± 0.38	1.30 ± 0.60
1.0B 1.0N	11.99 ± 0.58	11.85 ± 0.57	12.70 ± 0.75
+10N +10N	8.14 ± 0.35	7.79 ± 0.89	6.77 ± 0.47
+10N 1.0B	3.81 ± 0.30	5.10 ± 0.74	5.79 ± 0.31

Table B.2: Average frequency of actions chosen in the last 3000 rounds by the uncertain agent during the ascending auction

	1C1HE	1C1HL	1C1HP	1C1HR	1C1U	1C1C-1	1C1C-2
-10N|1C2H1|-10N|CH|	0.00	3.19	1.66	2.25	1.85	2.82	2.73
-10N|1C2H1|-10N|CL|	0.00	7.40	0.97	0.32	1.55	1.93	2.20
-10N|1C2H1|1.0N|CH|	0.00	5.22	2.55	1.46	1.88	2.74	2.96
-10N|1C2H1|1.0N|CL|	0.00	5.45	0.00	0.00	0.87	1.05	1.16
-10N|1C2H2|-10N|CH|	4.79	0.00	1.54	4.13	2.25	1.93	1.86
-10N|1C2H2|-10N|CL|	0.00	0.00	3.62	1.83	2.08	1.82	1.76
-10N|1C2H2|1.0N|CH|	3.14	0.00	2.63	3.37	2.43	2.26	2.09
-10N|1C2H2|1.0N|CL|	0.00	0.00	2.54	0.88	1.20	1.10	1.20
-10N|1C2H3|-10N|CH|	0.00	0.00	0.00	0.04	0.01	0.00	0.01
-10N|1C2H3|-10N|CL|	0.00	0.00	0.03	0.01	0.03	0.03	0.03
-10N|1C2H3|1.0N|CH|	0.00	0.00	0.08	0.11	0.04	0.05	0.05
-10N|1C2H3|1.0N|CL|	0.00	0.00	0.09	0.01	0.04	0.03	0.04
-10N|1C2L3|-10N|CL|	1.09	0.00	1.49	0.62	0.71	0.53	0.46
-10N|1C2L3|1.0N|CH|	4.29	0.00	0.07	2.24	1.59	1.36	1.34
-10N|1C2L3|1.0N|CL|	11.72	0.00	3.68	6.61	5.95	4.47	4.59
-10N|1C2L4|-10N|CL|	0.00	0.00	0.00	0.00	0.00	0.00	0.00
-10N|1C2L4|1.0N|CL|	0.00	0.00	0.00	0.00	0.00	0.00	0.00
0.0N|1C0L1|-10N|CH|	3.35	3.52	3.58	4.74	3.88	4.69	4.32
0.0N|1C0L1|-10N|CL|	6.99	7.56	7.55	5.96	7.32	6.59	6.72
0.0N|1C0L1|0.0N|CL|	0.34	0.32	0.43	0.21	0.50	0.37	0.37
0.0N|1C0L1|0.5N|CH|	0.00	0.00	0.00	0.10	0.01	0.03	0.02
0.0N|1C0L1|0.5N|CL|	0.37	0.42	0.39	1.99	0.61	1.54	1.36
0.0N|1C0L1|1.0N|CH|	6.91	7.32	7.26	8.01	7.35	8.19	7.84
0.0N|1C0L1|1.0N|CL|	7.00	7.10	7.58	4.96	7.02	5.94	5.50
0.5N|1C1H1|-10N|CH|	0.00	3.53	1.80	1.41	1.85	2.17	2.21
0.5N|1C1H1|-10N|CL|	0.00	7.90	1.01	0.24	1.45	1.89	2.01
0.5N|1C1H1|0.5N|CH|	0.00	0.00	0.00	0.26	0.00	0.01	0.05
0.5N|1C1H1|0.5N|CL|	0.00	0.39	0.09	0.58	0.37	0.40	0.75
0.5N|1C1H1|1.0N|CH|	0.00	7.30	3.54	1.92	2.65	3.83	3.89
0.5N|1C1H1|1.0N|CL|	0.00	7.39	0.00	0.00	1.02	1.32	1.35
0.5N|1C1H2|0.5N|CL|	0.00	0.00	0.00	0.00	0.00	0.00	0.00
0.5N|1C1H2|1.0N|CL|	0.00	0.00	0.00	0.00	0.00	0.00	0.00
0.5N|1C1L2|-10N|CH|	3.48	0.00	1.69	3.22	1.98	1.81	2.00
0.5N|1C1L2|-10N|CL|	7.48	0.00	6.47	5.87	5.87	4.43	4.58
0.5N|1C1L2|0.5N|CL|	0.41	0.00	0.44	0.30	0.33	0.38	0.24
0.5N|1C1L2|1.0N|CH|	6.77	0.00	3.68	5.96	4.84	4.26	3.95
0.5N|1C1L2|1.0N|CL|	7.17	0.00	7.25	5.33	6.06	4.85	4.72
1.0N|1C3H1|1.0N|CH|	0.00	13.07	6.47	4.04	4.63	7.51	7.70
1.0N|1C3H1|1.0N|CL|	0.00	12.93	0.00	0.00	1.61	2.57	2.67
1.0N|1C3H2|1.0N|CH|	7.95	0.00	6.40	8.53	5.69	5.30	5.31
1.0N|1C3H2|1.0N|CL|	0.00	0.00	6.58	2.30	2.78	2.67	2.64
1.0N|1C3H3|1.0N|CH|	4.42	0.00	0.28	2.75	1.63	1.44	1.29
1.0N|1C3H3|1.0N|CL|	0.00	0.00	2.41	0.42	1.10	0.94	0.93
1.0N|1C3H4|1.0N|CH|	0.00	0.00	0.00	0.00	0.00	0.00	0.00
1.0N|1C3L4|1.0N|CL|	12.35	0.00	4.14	6.99	6.97	4.76	5.11

Table B.3: Frequency of strategies of the certain agent in the last 3.000 rounds in two player settings

B.1.2   Institutional Rules: Five Bidder

	payoff certain		payoff uncertain		revenue		welfare	
	θ^C_{AA}	θ^C_{SB}	θ^U_{AA}	θ^U_{SB}	π_{AA}	π_{SB}	ω_{AA}	ω_{SB}
5C	122.79	152.25	NA	NA	97.64	94.59	99.26	98.65
4C1U	113.00	139.84	72.22	129.51	98.28	95.09	98.49	98.02
1C4U	88.66	108.23	50.56	95.66	100.03	96.81	96.60	96.64
4U	NA	NA	44.05	87.13	100.64	97.33	96.11	96.29

Table B.4: Overview on the agents' average relative payoff, auctioneer's average relative revenue, and average relative social welfare over the last 3.000 rounds of the simulation with five adaptive agents

	Early Bid	Late Bid
5C	73.57	26.43
4C1U	74.22	25.78
1C4U	74.42	25.58

Table B.5: Overview on the average frequency of early and late bid of certain agents during the last 3000 rounds within five agent settings

	Early Buying AA	Late Buying AA	Sum Buying AA	Sum Buying SB	Buying if competing bid	No buying if competing bid
4C1U	29.38	19.14	48.52	36.88	14.34	39.87
1C4U	26.95	18.81	45.75	33.95	13.76	42.09
5U	25.27	18.80	44.07	33.35	13.71	43.45

Table B.6: Overview on the average frequency of actions where agents buy information chosen in the last 3000 rounds during five agent settings

B.1.3 Information Acquisition Costs: Two Bidder

	θ^H_{1U1HE}	θ^H_{1U1HP}	θ^H_{1U1HL}	θ^C_{1C1U}	θ^U_{1U1HE}	θ^U_{1U1HP}	θ^U_{1U1HL}	θ^U_{1C1U}
Cost 1.0	8.60	6.49	8.94	8.00	6.35	6.32	6.25	8.11
Cost 5.0	8.00	6.18	8.32	7.73	5.16	5.31	5.38	6.58
Cost 6.0	7.89	6.02	8.27	7.69	5.11	5.56	5.58	6.67
Cost 7.0	7.84	5.97	8.19	7.55	5.37	5.80	5.97	6.64
Cost 8.0	7.71	5.93	8.10	7.55	5.66	6.01	6.26	6.75
Cost 9.0	7.66	5.96	8.15	7.53	5.84	6.11	6.48	7.11
Cost 10.0	7.73	5.91	8.03	7.51	5.87	6.24	6.53	7.33

	π_{1U1HE}	π_{1U1HP}	π_{1U1HL}	π_{1C1U}	ω_{1U1HE}	ω_{1U1HP}	ω_{1U1HL}	ω_{1C1U}
Cost 1.0	82.28	84.37	81.95	80.72	97.23	97.18	97.14	96.82
Cost 5.0	82.85	84.66	82.50	80.87	96.00	96.16	96.20	95.18
Cost 6.0	82.99	84.85	82.56	80.63	96.04	96.18	96.21	94.90
Cost 7.0	83.03	84.89	82.62	80.99	96.02	96.17	96.19	95.12
Cost 8.0	83.27	84.91	82.75	80.88	96.13	96.15	96.24	95.01
Cost 9.0	83.24	84.89	82.64	80.88	96.05	96.16	96.17	94.98
Cost 10.0	83.15	84.92	82.74	80.88	96.03	96.14	96.15	94.97

Table B.7: Overview on the average outcome of the AA format during the last 3000 rounds of two agent settings under varying costs

	θ^H_{1U1HE}	θ^H_{1U1HP}	θ^H_{1U1HL}	θ^C_{1C1U}	θ^U_{1U1HE}	θ^U_{1U1HP}	θ^U_{1U1HL}	θ^U_{1C1U}
Cost 1.0	10.25	10.27	10.26	12.12	7.17	7.16	7.15	13.52
Cost 5.0	10.40	10.36	10.32	12.15	6.56	6.57	6.52	12.22
Cost 6.0	10.36	10.46	10.45	12.20	6.51	6.50	6.51	12.48
Cost 7.0	10.48	10.52	10.49	12.05	6.61	6.60	6.60	12.18
Cost 8.0	10.42	10.44	10.46	12.30	6.72	6.70	6.68	12.23
Cost 9.0	10.51	10.46	10.42	12.37	6.71	6.74	6.74	12.10
Cost 10.0	10.43	10.51	10.44	12.59	6.71	6.68	6.73	12.15

	π_{1U1HE}	π_{1U1HP}	π_{1U1HL}	π_{1C1U}	ω_{1U1HE}	ω_{1U1HP}	ω_{1U1HL}	ω_{1C1U}
Cost 1.0	79.87	79.85	79.86	69.92	97.29	97.28	97.27	95.56
Cost 5.0	79.72	79.76	79.80	70.44	96.68	96.69	96.64	94.81
Cost 6.0	79.76	79.66	79.67	69.71	96.68	96.69	96.64	94.14
Cost 7.0	79.64	79.60	79.63	70.17	96.68	96.69	96.64	94.44
Cost 8.0	79.70	79.68	79.66	69.75	96.68	96.69	96.64	94.27
Cost 9.0	79.61	79.66	79.69	69.72	96.68	96.69	96.64	94.30
Cost 10.0	79.69	79.61	79.68	69.28	96.68	96.69	96.64	94.09

Table B.8: Overview on the average outcome of SB format during the last 3000 rounds of two agent settings under varying costs

	1.0 vs. 5.0	5.0 vs. 6.0	6.0 vs. 7.0	7.0 vs. 8.0	8.0 vs. 9.0	9.0 vs. 10.0
1U1HE	<<0.02	0.07	0.99	<<0.02	0.42	0.86
1U1HP	<<0.02	0.05	0.42	0.42	0.62	0.19
1U1HL	<<0.02	0.35	0.25	0.02	0.81	0.16
1C1U	0.07	0.96	0.01	0.88	0.62	0.50

Table B.9: Summary of p-values for H14 in two agent settings under different costs

	Early Buying AA format	Late Buying AA format	Sum Buying AA format	Sum Buying SB format	Buying if competing bid	No buying if competing bid
Cost 1.0	35.87	23.36	59.23	38.34	18.21	31.33
Cost 5.0	20.25	12.34	32.59	28.45	10.25	51.85
Cost 6.0	15.36	10.71	26.07	26.25	8.93	57.63
Cost 7.0	9.55	9.14	18.69	22.22	8.38	62.93
Cost 8.0	2.68	7.93	10.61	19.69	7.49	69.52
Cost 9.0	0.87	7.33	8.21	17.61	7.04	70.51
Cost 10.0	0.62	6.68	7.30	16.50	6.51	71.83

Table B.10: Overview on the average frequency of actions where agents buy information chosen in the last 3000 rounds during two agent settings with one early bidder under different costs

	Early Buying AA format	Late Buying AA format	Sum Buying AA format	Sum Buying SB format	Buying if competing bid	No buying if competing bid
Cost 1.0	32.60	24.40	57.01	39.18	13.91	25.61
Cost 5.0	16.50	12.86	29.36	28.74	5.26	43.38
Cost 6.0	9.70	9.39	19.08	26.53	2.90	50.05
Cost 7.0	5.15	7.26	12.41	22.29	2.04	53.59
Cost 8.0	1.93	6.05	7.98	19.47	1.85	55.55
Cost 9.0	0.92	5.30	6.22	17.49	1.71	56.06
Cost 10.0	0.43	3.69	4.11	16.93	1.59	56.27

Table B.11: Overview on the average frequency of actions where agents buy information chosen in the last 3000 rounds during two agent settings with one price signalling agent under different costs

	Early Buying AA format	Late Buying AA format	Sum Buying AA format	Sum Buying SB format	Buying if competing bid	No buying if competing bid
Cost 1.0	34.45	25.16	59.61	38.37	0.00	0.00
Cost 5.0	17.75	10.31	28.05	29.30	0.00	0.00
Cost 6.0	11.95	7.72	19.66	25.79	0.00	0.00
Cost 7.0	6.91	3.64	10.55	21.96	0.00	0.00
Cost 8.0	2.81	1.93	4.74	19.66	0.00	0.00
Cost 9.0	1.35	1.35	2.69	17.01	0.00	0.00
Cost 10.0	0.61	1.07	1.69	16.74	0.00	0.00

Table B.12: Overview on the average frequency of actions where agents buy information chosen in the last 3000 rounds during two agent settings with one late bidder under different costs

	Early Buying AA format	Late Buying AA format	Sum Buying AA format	Sum Buying SB format	Buying if competing bid	No buying if competing bid
Cost 1.0	34.11	24.41	58.52	40.28	11.19	19.44
Cost 5.0	24.43	17.09	41.52	35.52	5.90	28.70
Cost 6.0	20.83	15.24	36.07	34.16	5.26	31.82
Cost 7.0	16.64	12.18	28.81	32.75	3.73	35.41
Cost 8.0	13.59	10.96	24.55	31.42	3.29	37.24
Cost 9.0	9.60	8.09	17.69	30.34	2.47	39.82
Cost 10.0	7.19	5.54	12.73	28.95	1.64	41.76

Table B.13: Overview on the average frequency of actions where agents buy information chosen in the last 3000 rounds during two agent settings with one certain bidder under different costs

	Early Bid	Late Bid
Cost 01	72.86	27.14
Cost 05	72.53	27.47
Cost 06	73.45	26.55
Cost 07	73.5	26.5
Cost 08	73.98	26.02
Cost 09	73.94	26.06
Cost 10	73.03	26.97

Table B.14: Overview on the average frequency of early and late bid of certain agents during the last 3000 rounds within two agent settings with different costs

	1U1HE	1U1HP	1U1HL	1U1C
cost: 1 vs. 5	$\ll 0.02$	$\ll 0.02$	$\ll 0.02$	$\ll 0.02$
cost: 5 vs. 6	$\ll 0.02$	$\ll 0.02$	$\ll 0.02$	$\ll 0.02$
cost: 6 vs. 7	$\ll 0.02$	$\ll 0.02$	$\ll 0.02$	$\ll 0.02$
cost: 7 vs. 8	$\ll 0.02$	$\ll 0.02$	$\ll 0.02$	0.04
cost: 8 vs. 9	0.01	0.01	0.05	$\ll 0.02$
cost: 9 vs. 10	0.11	0.01	0.02	0.01

Table B.15: P-values for pairwise comparison of the frequency of early information acquisition on basis of one-sided t-test.

	1U1HE	1U1HP	1U1HL	1U1C
cost: 1 vs. 5	$\ll 0.02$	$\ll 0.02$	$\ll 0.02$	$\ll 0.02$
cost: 5 vs. 6	$\ll 0.02$	$\ll 0.02$	$\ll 0.02$	$\ll 0.02$
cost: 6 vs. 7	$\ll 0.02$	$\ll 0.02$	$\ll 0.02$	$\ll 0.02$
cost: 7 vs. 8	$\ll 0.02$	$\ll 0.02$	$\ll 0.02$	0.04
cost: 8 vs. 9	$\ll 0.02$	$\ll 0.02$	$\ll 0.02$	$\ll 0.02$
cost: 9 vs. 10	$\ll 0.02$	$\ll 0.02$	$\ll 0.02$	$\ll 0.02$

Table B.16: P-values for pairwise comparison of the frequency of late information acquisition on basis of one-sided t-test.

B.1.4 Information Acquisition Cost: Five Bidder

	θ^{1C}_{1U4C}	θ^{2C}_{1U4C}	θ^{3C}_{1U4C}	θ^{4C}_{1U4C}	θ^{1U}_{1U4C}	θ^{1U}_{4U1C}	θ^{2U}_{4U1C}	θ^{3U}_{4U1C}	θ^{4U}_{4U1C}	θ^{1C}_{4U1C}
1.0	1.78	1.87	1.80	1.78	1.16	1.42	0.84	0.80	0.79	0.80
1.5	1.77	1.83	1.74	1.76	1.05	1.33	0.64	0.63	0.64	0.65
2.0	1.71	1.82	1.72	1.76	0.99	1.28	0.65	0.59	0.57	0.60
5.0	1.71	1.80	1.71	1.76	0.92	1.25	0.42	0.40	0.41	0.40

	θ^{1U}_{5U}	θ^{2U}_{5U}	θ^{3U}_{5U}	θ^{4U}_{5U}	θ^{5U}_{5U}	π_{1U4C}	π_{4U1C}	π_{5U}	ω_{1U4C}	ω_{4U1C}	ω_{5U}
1.0	0.65	0.76	0.72	0.66	0.72	96.60	98.33	98.93	104.99	102.98	102.46
1.5	0.52	0.59	0.51	0.56	0.57	96.71	98.72	99.35	104.87	102.60	102.10
2.0	0.50	0.55	0.52	0.50	0.49	96.79	98.98	99.57	104.80	102.67	102.13
5.0	0.25	0.34	0.24	0.30	0.32	96.81	99.05	99.55	104.70	101.93	101.00

Table B.17: Overview on the average outcome during the last 3000 rounds of five agent settings under varying costs (AA)

	θ^{1C}_{1U4C}	θ^{2C}_{1U4C}	θ^{3C}_{1U4C}	θ^{4C}_{1U4C}	θ^{1U}_{1U4C}	θ^{1U}_{4U1C}	θ^{2U}_{4U1C}	θ^{3U}_{4U1C}	θ^{4U}_{4U1C}	θ^{1C}_{4U1C}
1.0	2.22	2.32	2.18	2.23	2.07	1.73	1.56	1.48	1.54	1.54
1.5	2.21	2.28	2.21	2.25	1.90	1.76	1.47	1.38	1.39	1.45
2.0	2.21	2.31	2.22	2.24	1.88	1.72	1.45	1.37	1.40	1.44
5.0	2.17	2.24	2.16	2.14	2.02	1.62	1.42	1.34	1.40	1.39

	θ^{1U}_{5U}	θ^{2U}_{5U}	θ^{3U}_{5U}	θ^{4U}_{5U}	θ^{5U}_{5U}	π_{1U4C}	π_{4U1C}	π_{5U}	ω_{1U4C}	ω_{4U1C}	ω_{5U}
1.0	1.33	1.43	1.37	1.41	1.44	93.47	95.16	95.68	104.49	103.01	102.65
1.5	1.26	1.34	1.28	1.28	1.30	93.59	95.27	95.76	104.44	102.72	102.21
2.0	1.19	1.37	1.28	1.30	1.32	93.53	95.37	96.06	104.39	102.74	102.52
5.0	1.22	1.24	1.14	1.21	1.23	93.69	95.71	96.32	104.43	102.89	102.37

Table B.18: Overview on the average outcome during the last 3000 rounds of five agent settings under varying costs (SB)

	AA format			SB format		
	1.0:1.5	**1.5:2.0**	**2.0:5.0**	**1.0:1.5**	**1.5:2.0**	**2.0:5.0**
4C1U	0.07	0.20	0.12	0.01	0.40	0.97
1C4U	<< 0.02	0.03	<< 0.02	<< 0.02	0.22	0.18
5U	<< 0.02	0.06	<< 0.02	<< 0.02	0.54	<< 0.02

Table B.19: P-values of the Wilcoxon rank sum test for pairwise comparison of the settings with different information costs in both auction formats, ascending auction and sealed-bid auction

	Early Bid	Late Bid
Cost 01	73.72	26.28
Cost 1.5	73.89	26.11
Cost 02	73.79	26.21
Cost 05	73.95	26.05

Table B.20: Overview on the average frequency of early and late bid of certain agent 1 during the last 3000 rounds within five agent settings with different costs and 1 uncertain and 4 certain bidders

	Early Bid	Late Bid
Cost 01	73.85	26.15
Cost 1.5	73.65	26.35
Cost 02	73.69	26.31
Cost 05	73.36	26.64

Table B.21: Overview on the average frequency of early and late bid of certain agent 2 during the last 3000 rounds within five agent settings with different costs and 1 uncertain and 4 certain bidders

	Early Bid	Late Bid
Cost 01	73.85	26.15
Cost 1.5	73.65	26.35
Cost 02	73.69	26.31
Cost 05	73.36	26.64

Table B.22: Overview on the average frequency of early and late bid of certain agent 3 during the last 3000 rounds within five agent settings with different costs and 1 uncertain and 4 certain bidders

	Early Bid	Late Bid
Cost 01	74.36	25.64
Cost 1.5	73.15	26.85
Cost 02	73.63	26.37
Cost 05	74.47	25.53

Table B.23: Overview on the average frequency of early and late bid of certain agent 4 during the last 3000 rounds within five agent settings with different costs and 1 uncertain and 4 certain bidders

	Early Buying AA format	Late Buying AA format	Sum Buying AA format	Sum Buying SB format	Buying if competing bid	No buying if competing bid
Cost 1.0	29.38	19.14	48.52	36.88	17.43	48.43
Cost 1.5	22.23	17.44	39.67	30.48	15.87	56.92
Cost 2.0	13.58	15.29	28.87	25.29	14.14	66.71
Cost 5.0	1.58	8.28	9.86	4.00	8.06	84.32

Table B.24: Overview on the average frequency of actions where the uncertain agent buys information chosen in the last 3000 rounds during five agent settings with 4 certain bidders under different costs

	Early Bid	Late Bid
Cost 1.0	74.42	25.58
Cost 1.5	74.56	25.44
Cost 2.0	73.1	26.9
Cost 5.0	73.45	26.55

Table B.25: Overview on the average frequency of early and late bid of certain agent 1 during the last 3000 rounds within five agent settings with different costs and 4 uncertain and 1 certain bidders

	Early Buying AA format	Late Buying AA format	Sum Buying AA format	Sum Buying SB format	Buying if competing bid	No buying if competing bid
Cost 1.0	27.16	18.75	45.92	33.49	17.76	52.08
Cost 1.5	16.55	17.24	33.79	27.56	16.22	63.52
Cost 2.0	5.40	16.14	21.54	17.43	15.2	74.37
Cost 5.0	2.21	8.97	11.18	5.39	8.79	83.86

Table B.26: Overview on the average frequency of actions where uncertain agent 1 buys information chosen in the last 3000 rounds during five agent settings with 4 uncertain and 1 certain bidder under different costs

	Early Buying AA format	Late Buying AA format	Sum Buying AA format	Sum Buying SB format	Buying if competing bid	No buying if competing bid
Cost 1.0	26.53	19.17	45.70	33.57	18.17	52.28
Cost 1.5	15.13	16.95	32.08	26.63	15.99	64.89
Cost 2.0	5.54	15.90	21.45	17.91	14.80	74.69
Cost 5.0	2.11	8.86	10.97	5.22	8.72	83.97

Table B.27: Overview on the average frequency of actions where uncertain agent 2 buys information chosen in the last 3000 rounds during five agent settings with 4 uncertain and 1 certain bidder under different costs

	Early Buying AA format	Late Buying AA format	Sum Buying AA format	Sum Buying SB format	Buying if competing bid	No buying if competing bid
Cost 1.0	27.51	18.04	45.56	34.45	17.08	52.49
Cost 1.5	14.09	17.68	31.77	26.68	16.51	65.38
Cost 2.0	7.04	14.84	21.88	15.37	14.05	73.86
Cost 5.0	2.27	9.32	11.59	5.15	9.15	83.63

Table B.28: Overview on the average frequency of actions where uncertain agent 3 buys information chosen in the last 3000 rounds during five agent settings with 4 uncertain and 1 certain bidder under different costs

	Early Buying AA format	Late Buying AA format	Sum Buying AA format	Sum Buying SB format	Buying if competing bid	No buying if competing bid
Cost 1.0	26.58	19.26	45.84	34.31	18.23	52.30
Cost 1.5	15.41	17.37	32.78	25.86	16.35	64.37
Cost 2.0	5.31	15.52	20.83	17.77	14.69	74.77
Cost 5.0	2.26	9.24	11.50	5.03	9.06	83.73

Table B.29: Overview on the average frequency of actions where uncertain agent 4 buys information chosen in the last 3000 rounds during five agent settings with 4 uncertain and 1 certain bidder under different costs

	Early Buying AA format	Late Buying AA format	Sum Buying AA format	Sum Buying SB format	Buying if competing bid	No buying if competing bid
Cost 1.0	23.86	19.54	43.40	33.51	18.51	54.86
Cost 1.5	12.87	18.00	30.87	25.13	16.92	66.51
Cost 2.0	4.30	15.90	20.20	14.62	15.04	75.79
Cost 5.0	2.28	9.73	12.01	5.57	9.55	82.93

Table B.30: Overview on the average frequency of actions where agent 1 buys information chosen in the last 3000 rounds during five agent settings with 5 uncertain bidders under different costs

	Early Buying AA format	Late Buying AA format	Sum Buying AA format	Sum Buying SB format	Buying if competing bid	No buying if competing bid
Cost 1.0	24.69	18.97	43.67	32.35	18.24	54.39
Cost 1.5	13.07	16.69	29.76	25.20	15.77	67.44
Cost 2.0	5.11	15.91	21.02	13.40	14.80	75.18
Cost 5.0	2.37	9.60	11.97	5.80	9.39	83.31

Table B.31: Overview on the average frequency of actions where agent 2 buys information chosen in the last 3000 rounds during five agent settings with 5 uncertain bidders under different costs

	Early Buying AA format	Late Buying AA format	Sum Buying AA format	Sum Buying SB format	Buying if competing bid	No buying if competing bid
Cost 1.0	25.58	18.46	44.04	33.52	17.55	54.28
Cost 1.5	13.75	17.40	31.15	24.64	16.35	66.08
Cost 2.0	3.86	14.78	18.64	13.74	13.79	77.34
Cost 5.0	2.25	9.63	11.88	5.85	9.48	83.48

Table B.32: Overview on the average frequency of actions where agent 3 buys information chosen in the last 3000 rounds during five agent settings with 5 uncertain bidders under different costs

	Early Buying AA format	Late Buying AA format	Sum Buying AA format	Sum Buying SB format	Buying if competing bid	No buying if competing bid
Cost 1.0	25.96	18.38	44.35	33.81	17.51	53.97
Cost 1.5	13.28	17.12	30.41	26.83	16.19	66.78
Cost 2.0	4.14	15.52	19.66	14.80	14.35	76.55
Cost 5.0	2.29	9.53	11.82	5.42	9.38	83.33

Table B.33: Overview on the average frequency of actions where agent 4 buys information chosen in the last 3000 rounds during five agent settings with 5 uncertain bidders under different costs

	Early Buying AA format	Late Buying AA format	Sum Buying AA format	Sum Buying SB format	Buying if competing bid	No buying if competing bid
Cost 1.0	26.26	18.63	44.90	33.53	17.70	53.18
Cost 1.5	12.01	17.64	29.64	25.36	16.74	67.46
Cost 2.0	4.28	15.78	20.06	14.04	14.76	75.93
Cost 5.0	2.42	9.58	12.00	5.64	9.37	83.20

Table B.34: Overview on the average frequency of actions where agent 5 buys information chosen in the last 3000 rounds during five agent settings with 5 uncertain bidders under different costs

	1U4C-1U Cost: 1.0	1U4C-1U Cost: 1.5	1U4C-1U Cost: 2.0	1U4C-1U Cost: 5.0
0.0N 0.0N	1.14 ± 0.15	1.34 ± 0.10	1.25 ± 0.12	1.74 ± 0.18
0.0N 0.5N	1.09 ± 0.12	1.23 ± 0.12	1.34 ± 0.16	1.56 ± 0.18
0.0N 0.5B	0.42 ± 0.07	0.43 ± 0.07	0.47 ± 0.09	0.60 ± 0.05
0.0N -1.0N	3.50 ± 0.27	3.81 ± 0.30	4.46 ± 0.36	5.39 ± 0.32
0.0N -1.0B	0.84 ± 0.20	0.87 ± 0.28	0.81 ± 0.22	0.60 ± 0.12
0.0N 1.0N	4.49 ± 1.08	4.82 ± 0.43	6.12 ± 0.75	7.56 ± 0.61
0.0N 1.0B	2.79 ± 0.67	2.83 ± 0.27	2.03 ± 0.59	0.59 ± 0.15
0.0N +1.0N	2.05 ± 0.81	2.76 ± 0.50	3.15 ± 0.70	4.36 ± 0.69
0.5N 0.5N	1.33 ± 0.22	1.53 ± 0.14	1.48 ± 0.12	1.71 ± 0.19
0.5N 0.5B	0.47 ± 0.12	0.52 ± 0.08	0.62 ± 0.07	0.74 ± 0.10
0.5N -1.0N	3.16 ± 0.32	3.69 ± 0.24	4.78 ± 0.40	5.64 ± 0.49
0.5N -1.0B	1.46 ± 0.23	1.16 ± 0.28	0.77 ± 0.15	0.82 ± 0.12
0.5N 1.0N	4.54 ± 0.43	5.30 ± 0.55	6.35 ± 0.62	7.72 ± 0.81
0.5N 1.0B	2.87 ± 0.40	2.88 ± 0.41	1.96 ± 0.53	0.80 ± 0.11
0.5N +1.0N	2.58 ± 0.53	3.37 ± 0.72	4.14 ± 0.45	4.68 ± 0.40
0.5B 0.5N	1.40 ± 0.14	1.02 ± 0.15	0.76 ± 0.16	0.11 ± 0.03
0.5B -1.0N	3.14 ± 0.52	1.97 ± 0.43	1.13 ± 0.25	0.23 ± 0.06
0.5B 1.0N	6.54 ± 0.84	5.50 ± 0.68	3.79 ± 1.01	0.2 ± 0.05
-1.0N -1.0N	2.69 ± 0.27	2.91 ± 0.29	3.34 ± 0.37	4.69 ± 0.30
-1.0N -1.0B	1.56 ± 0.16	1.38 ± 0.24	1.53 ± 0.23	1.20 ± 0.12
-1.0N 1.0N	5.22 ± 0.47	6.25 ± 0.57	6.78 ± 0.46	8.52 ± 0.77
-1.0N 1.0B	2.41 ± 0.33	1.67 ± 0.14	1.84 ± 0.27	1.16 ± 0.14
-1.0N +1.0N	1.96 ± 0.27	2.18 ± 0.28	2.51 ± 0.39	3.76 ± 0.32
-1.0B -1.0N	2.20 ± 0.35	2.12 ± 0.30	1.32 ± 0.43	0.21 ± 0.08
-1.0B 1.0N	6.03 ± 0.51	3.91 ± 0.81	2.05 ± 0.86	0.37 ± 0.09
1.0N 1.0N	7.88 ± 0.51	9.30 ± 0.77	11.54 ± 0.78	13.92 ± 0.90
1.0N 1.0B	3.70 ± 0.26	3.38 ± 0.41	2.99 ± 0.34	0.96 ± 0.17
1.0N +1.0N	2.50 ± 0.35	3.32 ± 0.39	3.78 ± 0.22	5.51 ± 0.29
1.0B 1.0N	10.08 ± 1.07	7.70 ± 0.81	4.54 ± 1.30	0.46 ± 0.11
+1.0N +1.0N	7.35 ± 0.98	8.53 ± 0.89	10.11 ± 1.17	13.39 ± 1.31
+1.0N 1.0B	2.63 ± 0.48	2.32 ± 0.33	2.29 ± 0.38	0.82 ± 0.14

Table B.35: Average frequency of actions chosen in the last 3000 rounds by the uncertain agents in the AA format in setting 4C1U

B.2   Figures

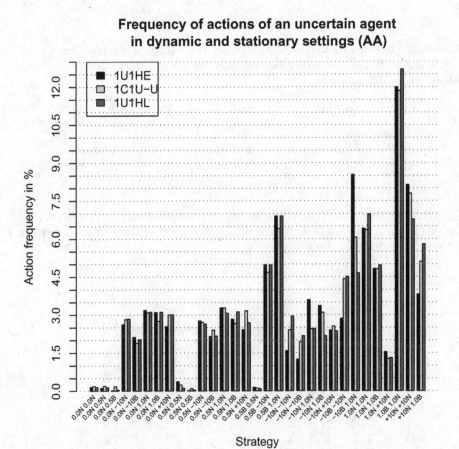

Figure B.1: Average frequency of the certain agent's strategies chosen in the last 3000 rounds of the settings playing against a stationary agent in an ascending auction

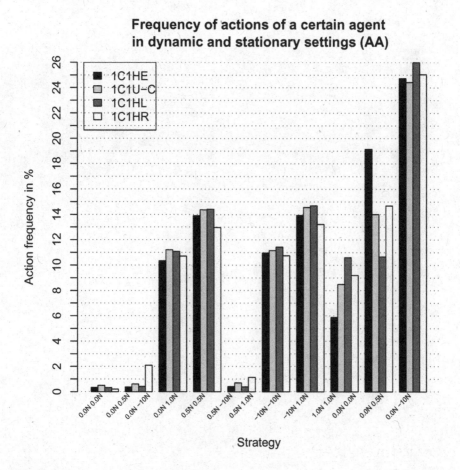

Figure B.2: Average frequency of the certain agent's strategies chosen in the last 3000 rounds of the settings playing against a stationary agent in an ascending auction

Bibliography

H. M. Amman. What is computational economics. *Computational Economics*, 2: 103–105, 1997.

G. Anadalingnam, R. W. Day, and S. Raghavan. The landscape of electronic market design. *Management Science*, 51(3):316–327, 2005.

J. Andreoni and J. H. Miller. Auctions with adaptive artificialy intelligent agents. Santa Fe Institute Working Paper, No. 90-01-004, 1990.

J. Arifovic. Genetic algorithm learning and the cobweb model. *Journal of Economic Dynamics and Control*, 18:3–28, 1994.

W. B. Arthur, J. H. Holland, B. LeBaron, R. Palmer, and P. Tayler. Asset pricing under endogenous expectations in an artificial stock market. Technical report, Santa Fe Institute, December 1996.

R. Axelrod. Advancing the art of simulation in the social science. *Japanese Journal for Management Information System*, 12(3), 2003. Special Issue on Agent-Based Modeling.

R. Axelrod. Evolving new strategies - the evolution of strategies in the iterated prisoner's dilemma. In L. Davis, editor, *Genetic Algorithms and Simulated Annealing*, pages 32–41, London (UK) and Los Altos (CA), 1987. Pitman and Morgan Kaufman.

R. Axtell. Why agents? on the varied motivations for agent computing in the social sciences. In *Proceedings of the Workshop on Agent Simulation: Applications, Models and Tools*, IL, 2000. Argonne National Laboratory.

J. S. Bain. *Industrial Organization*. Wiley, New York, 2nd edition, 1968.

P. Bajari and A. Hortacsu. Winner's curse, reserve prices and endogenous entry: Empirical insights from eBay auctions. In *8th World Congress of the Econometric Society*, Seattly, Washington, 2000. http://fmwww.bc.edu/RePEc/es2000/1927.pdf.

J. Banks. Principles of simulation. In J. Banks, editor, *Handbook of Simulation*, pages 3–31, New York, 1998. John Wiley & Sons, Inc.

F. Bellifemine, A. Poggi, and G. Rimassa. JADA - a FIPA-compliant agent framework. In *Proceedings of the Conference on the Practical Applications of Agents and Multi-Agent Systems (PAAM-99)*, pages 97–108, London, April 1999.

F. Bellifemine, A. Poggi, and G. Rimassa. Developing multi-agent systems with a FIPA-compliant agent framework. *Software - Practice and Experience*, 31: 103–128, 2001.

F. Bellifemine, G. Caire, T. Trucco, and G. Rimassa. *JADE Programmer's Guide*. TILAB, Italy, 2004.

F. L. Bellifemine, G. Caire, A. Poggi, and G. Rimassa. JADE - a white paper. *exp, Telecom Italia Lab*, 3(3):6–19, September 2003. http://exp.telecomitalialab.com/.

R. E. Bellman. *Dynamic Programming*. Princeton University Press, Princeton, 1957a.

R. E. Bellman. A markov decision process. *Journal of Mathematical Mechanics*, 6:679–684, 1957b.

M. Benyoucef, R. K. Keller, S. Kamouroux, J. Robert, and V. Trussant. Towards a generic e-negotiation platform. In *Proceedings of the Sixth International Conference on Re-Technologies for Information Systems*, pages 95–109, 2000.

D. P. Bertsekas. Auction algorithms. In *Encyclopedia of Optimization*. Kluwer, 2001.

M. Bichler, G. E. Kersten, and S. Strecker. Towards a structured design of electronic negotiations. *Group Decision and Negotiation*, 12(4):311–335, July 2003.

J. P. Bigus and J. Bigus. *Constructing Intelligent Agents Using Java: Professional Developer's Guide*. Wiley, 2001.

J. M. Blackburn. Acquisition of skill: An analysis of learning curves. *IHRB Report*, No. 73, 1936.

E. Bonabeau. Agent-based modeling: Methods and techniques for simulating human systems. In *Adaptive Agents, Intelligence, and Emergent Human Organization: Capturing Complexity Through Agent-Based Modeling, Proceedings of the National Academy of Sciences of the USA (PNAS), 99 (3)*, pages 7280–7287, Washington, DC, May 2002. National Academy of Sciences of the USA.

F. Bousquet, I. Bakam, H. Proton, and C. Le Page. Cormas: Common-pool resources and multi-agent systems. *Tasks and Methods in Applied Artificial Intelligence, 11th International Conference on Industrial and Engineering Applications of Artificial Intelligence and Expert Systems, IEA-98-AIE Benicàssim, Castellón, Spain, Lecture Notes in Artificial Intelligence*, 1416:826–837, June 1998, Proceedings Volume II.

M. Bowling and M. M. Veloso. An analysis of stochastic game theory for multiagent reinforcement learning. Technical Report CMU-CS-00-165, Computer Science Department, Carnegie Mellon University, 2000. http://www.cs.ualberta.ca/ bowling/papers/00tr.pdf.

H.-H. Brassel. Flexible modeling with VSEit, the versatile simulation environment for the internet. *Journal of Artificial Societies and Social Simulation*, 4(3), 2001.

W. Brenner, R. Zarnekow, and H. Wittig. *Intelligente Softwareagenten: Grundlagen und Anwendungen*. Springer-Verlag, Berlin, Heidelberg, 1998.

J. Burse. *Quicksilver - Whitepaper*. XLOG, Switzerland, 2000.

S. Bussmann and J. Müller. A negotiation framework for co-operating agents. In S. M. Deen, editor, *Proc CKBS-SIG*, pages 1–17. Dake Centre, University of Keele, 1992.

A. Byde. Applying evolutionary game theory to auction mechanism design. Technical report, Hewlett-Packard Laboratories, Bristol, UK, November 2002.

G. Cai and P. R. Wurman. Monte carlo approximation in incomplete information, sequential auction games. *Decision Support Systems, Special Issue: Decision Theory and Game Theory in agent design*, 39(2):153–168, April 2005.

R. J. Cassady. *Auctions and Auctioneering*. University of California Press, Berkeley, 1967.

C. Castelfranchi. Guarantees for autonomy in cognitive agent architecture. In M. Wooldridge and N. R. Jennings, editors, *Intelligent Agents: Theories, Architectures, and Languages (LNAI Volume 890)*, pages 56–70, Heidelberg, 1995. Springer-Verlag.

A. C. Catania. Thorndike's legacy: Learning, selection, and the law of effect. *Journal of The Experimental Analysis of Behavior*, 72(3):425–428, November 1999.

R. H. Coase. The nature of the firm. *Economica*, 4(16):386–405, November 1937.

N. Collier, T. Howe, and M. North. Onward and upward: The transition to repast 2.0. In *Proceedings of the First Annual North American Association for Computational Social and Organizational Science Conference, Electronic Proceedings*, Pittsburgh, PA, June 2003.

O. Compte and P. Jehiel. On the virtues of the ascending price auction: New insights in the private value setting. http://www.enpc.fr/ceras/compte/ascend.pdf, December 2000. Working Paper, CERAS-ENPC, CNRS, Paris.

C. Czernohous, W. Fichtner, D. Veit, and C. Weinhardt. Management decision support using long-term market simulation. *Journal of Information Systems and e-Business Management*, 1(4):405–423, 2003.

F. Dignum and M. Greaves. Issues in agent communication: An introduction. *Lecture notes in AI (subseries of Lecture notes in computer science)*, 1916:1–16, 2000.

J. E. Doran, S. Franklin, N. R. Jennings, and T. J. Norman. On cooperation in multi-agent systems. *The Knowledge Engineering Review*, 12(3):309–314, 1997. http://www.ecs.soton.ac.uk/ nrj/pubs.html (abgerufen am 31.01.2002).

J. Dugdale. *An Evaluation of Seven Software Simulation Tools for Use in the Social Sciences.* Institut de Recherche en Informatique de Toulouse (IRIT), 2005. http://www.irit.fr/COSI/training/evaluationoftools/Evaluation-Of-Simulation-Tools.htm.

B. Edmonds, S. Moss, and S. Wallis. Logic, reasoning and a programming language for simulating economic and business processes with artificially intelligent agents. In P. Ein-Dor, editor, *Artificial Intelligence in Economics and Management*, pages 221–230, Boston, 1996. Kluwer Academic Publishers.

A. Epstein, R. Wahba, and R. Tau. *StarLogo Tutorial.* MIT Media Lab, 2000.

J. M. Epstein and R. L. Axtell. *Growing Artificial Societies - Social Science From the BottomUp.* MIT Press, Boston, 1996.

I. Erev and A. Roth. Predicting how people play games: Reinforcement learning in experimental games with unique, mixed strategy equilibria. *The American Economic Review*, 88(4):848–881, September 1998.

J. Ferber and O. Gutknecht. A meta-model for the analysis and design of organizations in multi-agent systems. In *Proceedings of the 3rd International Conference on Multi Agent Systems (ICMAS), 2-7 July 1998*, pages 128–135. IEEE Computer Society, 1998.

J. Filar and K. Vrieze. *Competitive Markov Decision Processes.* Springer Verlag, New York, 1997.

K. Fischer and H.-M. Windisch. MAGSY: Ein regelbasiertes multiagentensystem. *KI Zeitschrift*, 1/92:22–26, 1992.

M. J. Fishman. A theory of preemptive takeover bidding. *RAND Journal of Economics*, 19(1):88–101, 1988.

P. A. Fishwick. SIMPACK: Getting started with simulation programmin in C and C++. In *Proceedings of the 1992 Winter Simulation Conference*, pages 154–162, Arlington, VA, December 1992.

L. Foucart. *A Small Multi Agent Systems Review.* Universidad de Granada, 2001. presented as a Complexity in Social Science (COSI) talk, 2-3th March.

FIPA Abstract Architecture Specification. Foundation for Intelligent Physical Agents (FIPA), Geneva, Switzerland, 2002. http://www.fipa.org.

J. R. Galliers. *A Theoretical Framework for Computer Models of Cooperative Dialogue, Acknoledging Multi-Agent Conflict.* PhD thesis, Open University, UK, 1988.

M. R. Genesereth and S. P. Ketchpel. Software agents. *Communications of the ACM*, 37(7):48–53, 1994.

N. Gilbert and S. Bankes. Platform and methods for agent-based modeling. In *Proceedings of the National Academy of Sciences of the USA, Vol. 99, Suppl.*, pages 7197–7198, Washington, DC, USA, May 2002. National Academy of Sciences of the USA.

N. Gilbert and K. G. Troitzsch. *Simulation for the Social Scientist.* Open University Press, FGraw-Hill Education, Berkshire, England, second edition, 2005.

D. K. Gode and S. Sunder. Allocative efficiency of markes with zero-intelligence traders: Market as a partial substitute for individual rationality. *Journal of Political Economy*, 101:119–137, 1993.

P. Gomber. *Elektronische Handelssysteme - Innovative Konzepte und Technologien im Wertpapierhandel.* PhD thesis, Universität Giessen, Germany, 2000.

M. Grunenberg, D. Veit, and C. Weinhardt. Elektronische finanzmärkte und bundle trading. In *Abstract Proceedings of the 66th Annual Conference of the Association of University Professors of Management*, pages 310–313, Universität Graz, 2004. Ursula Schneider and Peter Steiner.

L. Gulyás, T. Kozsik, and J. B. Corliss. The multi-agent modelling language and the model design interface. *Journal of Artificial Societies and Social Simulation*, 2(3), October 1999.

O. Gutknecht and J. Ferber. The MADKIT agent platform architecture. In T. Wagner and O. F. Rana, editors, *Agents Workshop on Infrastructure for Multi-Agent Systems, Barcelona, Spain, June 3-7, 2000, Revised Papers, Lecture Notes in Computer Science, 1887*, pages 48–55, Heidelberg, 2000. Springer.

O. Gutknecht and J. Ferber. The MadKit agent platform architecture. In T. Wagner and O. F. Rana, editors, *Infrastructure for Agents, Multi-Agent Systems, and Scalable Multi-Agent Systems, Proceedings of the International Workshop on Infrastructure for Scalable Multi-Agent Systems, Barcelona, Spain, June 3-7, 2000, Revised Papers*, pages 48–55, Heidelberg, 2001. Springer.

A. Hall. On an experimental determination of pi. *Messeng. Math.*, 2:113–114, 1873.

J. M. Hammersley and D. Handscomb. *Monte Carlo Methods.* Spottiswoode, Ballantyne & Co Ltd, London and Colchester, 1964.

H. Haugeneder and D. Steiner. Cooperating agents: Concepts and applications. In N. Jennings and M. Wooldridge, editors, *Agent Technology: Foundations, Applications, Markets*, pages 175–202, Berlin, Heidelberg, New York, 1998. Springer Verlag.

F. A. Hayek. The use of knowledge in society. *The American Economic Review*, 35(4):519–530, September 1945.

A. Helsinger, R. Lazarus, W. Wright, and J. Zinky. Tools and techniques for performance measurement of large distributed multiagent systems. In *Proceedings of the Second International Joint Conference on Autonomous Agents and Multiagent Systems (AAMAS)*, 2003.

D. Hiebeler. The swarm simulation system and individual-based modeling. In *Proceedings of Decision Support 2001: Advanced Technology for Natural Resource Management*, Toronto, September 1994.

D. Hirshleifer and I. P. L. Png. Facilitation of competing bids and the price of a takover target. *The Review of Financial Studies*, 2(4):587–606, 1989. http://links.jstor.org/sici?sici=0893-9454.0.CO

J. H. Holland. *Adaptation in Natural and Artificial Systems*. MIT Press, Boston, 1st mit-press edition, 1992a. Book was originally published 1975.

J. H. Holland. The echo model. *Proposal for a Research Program in Adaptive Computation*, July 1992b.

J. H. Holland and J. H. Miller. Artificial adaptive agents in economic theory. *American Economic Review, Papers and Proceedings*, 81:365–370, May 1991.

C. Holtmann. *Organisation von Märkten - Market Engineering für den elektronischen Wertpapierhandel*. PhD thesis, Universität Karlsruhe (TH), Karlsruhe, Germany, 2004.

R. A. Howard. *Dynamic Programming and Markov Processes*. The MIT Press, Cambridge, MA, 1960.

J. Hu and M. P. Wellman. Multiagent reinforcement learning: Theoretical framework and an algorithm. In *Proceedings of the 15th International Conference on Machine Learning*, 1998.

M. Huhns and M. P. Singh. CKBS-94 tutorial: Distributed artificial intelligence for information systems. Technical report, Dake Centre,, University of Keele, 1994.

M. N. Huhns and L. M. Stephens. Multiagent systems and society of agents. In G. Weiss, editor, *Mulitagent Systems*, pages 79–120. Cambridge (Massachusetts), London (England), 1999.

L. Hurwicz. Optimality and informational efficiency in resource allocation processes. In K. J. Arrow, S. Karlin, and P. Suppes, editors, *Mathematical Methods in the Social Sciences*, pages 27–46, California, 1960. Stanford University Press.

L. Hurwicz. On the concept and possibility of informational decentralization. *The American Economic Review*, 59(2):513–524, May 1969.

L. Hurwicz. The design of mechanisms for resource allocation. *The American Economic Review*, 63(2):1–30, May 1973.

M. E. Inchiosa and M. T. Parker. Overcoming design and development challenges in agent-based modeling using ASCAPE. In *Adaptive Agents, Intelligence, and Emergent Human Organization: Capturing Complexity Through Agent-Based Modeling, Proceedings of the National Academy of Sciences of the USA, May 14, Vol. 99 (Suppl. 3)*, Washington DC, 2002. National Academy of Sciences of the USA.

N. Jennings and M. Wooldridge. Applications of intelligent agents. In N. Jennings and M. Wooldridge, editors, *Agent Technology: Foundations, Applications, Markets*, pages 3–28, Berlin, Heidelberg, New York, 1998. Springer Verlag.

N. R. Jennings. Coordination techniques for distributed artificial intelligence. In G. M. P. O'Hare and N. R. Jennings, editors, *Foundations of Distributed Artificial Intelligence*, pages 187–210. Wiley, 1996.

T. Jones and S. Forrest. An introduction to SFI echo. Technical Report 93-12-074, Santa Fe Instiute, 1993. ftp://ftp.santafe.edu/pub/echo/how-to.ps.Z.

K. L. Judd. Computational economics and economic theory: Substitutes or complements? *Journal of Economic Dynamics and Control*, 21(6):907–942, 1997.

L. P. Kaelbling, M. L. Littman, and A. W. Moore. Reinforcement learning: A survey. *Journal of Artificial Intelligence Research*, 4:237–285, May 1996.

J. H. Kagel and D. Levin. Independent private value auctions: Bidder behaviour in first-, second- and third-price auctions with varying numbers of bidders. *The Economic Journal*, 103(419):868–879, July 1993.

G. E. Kersten and J. Teich. Are all e-commerce negotiations auctions? In *Proceedings of the Fourth International Conference on the Design of Cooperative Systems, Sophia-Antipolis, France*, 2000.

G. E. Kersten, K. P. Law, and S. Strecker. A software platform for multiprotocol e-negotiations. Technical Report INR04/04, InterNeg, 2004.

A. Kirman. The structure of economic interaction: Individual and collective rationality. In P. Bourgine and J.-P. Nadal, editors, *Cognitive Economics: An Interdisciplinary Approach*, chapter 18, pages 293–312. Springer, Berlin, Heidelberg, 2004.

J. Klein. Breve: A 3d simulation environment for the simulation of decentralized systems and artificial life. In *Proceedings of Artificial Life VIII. the 8th International Conference on the Simulation and Synthesis of Living Systems*, The MIT Press, 2002.

P. Klemperer. *Auctions: Theory and Practice*. Toulouse Lectures in Economics. Princeton University Press, Princeton and Oxford, 1st edition, 2004.

F. Klügel, R. Herrler, and C. Öchslein. From simulated to real environments: How to use SeSAm for software development. In M. Schillo, editor, *Multiagent System Technologies - 1st German Conferences MATES, Lecture Notes in Artificial Intelligence, Vol 2831*, pages 13–24, Heidelberg, 2003. Springer.

F. H. Knight. *Risk, Uncertainty, and Profit*. Hart, Schaffner & Marx, Houghton Mifflin Company, Boston, MA, 1921.

C. D. Kolstad and R. M. Guzman. Auction equilibrium with costly information acquisition. http://www.econ.ucsb.edu/papers/wp17-97.pdf, 1997. California Santa Barbara - Department of Economics, Working Paper no. 17-97.

V. Krishna. *Auction Theory*. Academic Press, San Diego, 2002.

P. Krugman. What economists can learn from evolutionary theorists. http://www.mit.edu/ krugman/evolute.html, November 1996. Talk given to the European Association for Evolutionary Political Economy.

M. Kumar and S. I. Feldman. Business negotiations on the internet. In *INET 98 Conference of the Internet Society*, pages Geneva, Switzerlan, July 1998.

M. Kunzelmann and J. Mäkiö. Pegged and bracket order as a success factor in stock exchange competition. In *Proceedings of the 2nd Conference Finance-Com05*. IEEE, 2005.

I. Lakatos. *Criticism and the Growth of Knowledge*. CUP, Cambridge, 1970.

A. M. Law and W. D. Kelton. *Simulation Modeling and Analysis*. McGraw Hill Higher Education, 3rd edition, 2000.

M. L. Littman. Markov games as a framework for multi-agent reinforcement learning. In *Proceedings of the 11th International Conference on Machine Learning*, pages 157–163, San Francisco, CA, 1994.

S. Luke, G. C. Balan, L. Panait, C. Cioffi-Revilla, and S. Paus. MASON: A java multi-agent simulation library. In *Proceedings of the Agent 2003 Conference*, 2003.

I. S. Lustick. PS-i: A user-friendly agent-based modeling platform for testing theories of political identity and political stability. *Journal of Artificial Societies and Social Simulations*, 5(3), 2002.

J. Mäkiö and I. Weber. Component-based specification and composition of market structures. In M. Bichler, editor, *Coordination and Agent Technology in Value Networks*, pages 127–137, Berlin, 2004a. GITO.

J. Mäkiö and I. Weber. Implementing complex market structures with meta markets. In *Proceedings of the 15th International Workshop on Database and Expert Systems Applications (DEXA)*, Zaragosa, Spain, 2004b.

J. Mäkiö, I. Weber, and C. Weinhardt. Electronic negotiations - a generic approach with action systems. In K. Bauknecht, M. Bichler, and B. Pröll, editors, *E-Commerce and Web Technologies, 5th International Conference EC-Web 20004*, pages 135–143, Berlin, 2004. Springer.

S. Margarita and M. Sonnessa. Sim2Web: An open source system for web-enabling economic and financial simulations. *Journal of Artificial Societies and Social Simulation*, 6(4), October 2003.

M. B. Marietto, N. David, J. S. Sichman, and H. Coelho. Requirements analysis of multi-agent based simulation platforms: State of the art and new prospects. In J. S. Sichman, F. Bousquet, and P. Davidsson, editors, *Multi-Agent-Based Simulation II: Third International Workshop on Multi-Agent Systems and Agent-Based Simulation, MABS 2002, Bologna, Italy, July 15-16, Lecture Notes in Artificial Intelligence, 2581*, pages 125–141, Heidelberg, 2003. Springer.

R. Marimon. Adaptive learning, evolutionary dynamics and equilibrium selection in games. *European Economic Review*, 37:603–611, 1993.

H. Markowitz. Portfolio selection. *Journal of Finance*, 7(1):77–91, 1952.

E. S. Mason. The new competition. *Yale Review*, 1953.

M. Matsumoto and T. Nishimura. Mersenne twister: A 623-dimensionally equidistributed uniform pseudo-random number generator. *ACM Transactions on Modeling and Computer Simulation*, 8(1):3–30, January 1998.

P. McAfee and J. McMillan. Auctions and bidding. *Journal of Economic Literature*, XXV(2):699–738, June 1987.

K. A. McCabe, S. Rassenti, and V. Smith. Designing a uniform-price double auction: An experimental evaluation. In D. Friedman and J. Rust, editors, *The Double Auction Market: Institutions, Theory , and Evidence*, pages 307–322, Cambridge, MA, 1993. Perseus Publishing.

D. McFadzean. SimBioSys: A class framework for biological simulations. Master's thesis, Department of Computer Science, University of Calgary, Canada, Calgary, Alberta, September 1994.

N. Metropolis and S. Ulam. The monte carlo method. *Journal of the American Statistical Association*, 44(247):335–341, 1949.

P. R. Milgrom and R. J. Weber. A theory of auctions and competitive bidding. *Economietrica*, 50(5):1089–1122, September 1982.

J. Miller. A genetic model of adaptive economic behavior. Working paper, University of Michigan, Ann Arbor, 1986.

N. Minar, R. Brukhart, C. Langton, and M. Askenazi. *The Swarm Simulation System: A Toolkit for Building Multi-Agent Simulations*. Santa Fe Institute, 1996.

M. Möhring and R. Ostermann. *MIMOSE: Eine Funktionale Sprache Zur Beschreibung und Simulation Individuellen Verhaltens in Interagierenden Populationen.* Universität Koblenz-Landau, Institut für Sozialwissenschaftliche Informatik, Koblenz, Germany, 1996.

K. G. Müller. Simulating with SimPy. *Pyzine*, 7(6), January 2005.

R. R. Nelson and S. G. Winter. *An Evolutionary Theory of Economic Change.* Belknap Press of Harvard Univ. Press, 1982.

D. Neumann. *Market Engineering - A Structured Design Process for Electronic Markets.* PhD thesis, Universität Karlsruhe (TH), Karlsruhe, Germany, 2004.

J. Nicolaisen, V. Petrov, and L. Tesfatsion. Market power and efficiency in a computational electricity market with discriminatory double-auction pricing. *IEEE Transactions on Evolutionary Computation*, 5(5):504–523, October 2001. www.econ.iastate.edu/tesfatsi/mpeieee.pdf (abgerufen am 11.02.2002).

H. S. Nwana, L. C. Lee, and N. R. Jennings. Coordination in software agent systems. *The British Telecom Technical Journal*, 14(4):79–88, 1996. http://www.ecs.soton.ac.uk/ nrj/pubs.html (abgerufen am 31.01.2002).

A. Ockenfels and A. E. Roth. Late bidding in second price internet auctions: Theory and evidence concerning different rules for ending an auction. *Games and Economic Behavior*, in Press, 2005.

T. M. Ostrom. Computer simulation: The third symbol system. *Journal of Experimental Social Psychology*, 24(5):381–392, June 1988.

G. Owen. *Game Theory.* The MIT Press, Cambridge, MA, second edition, 1982.

M. T. Parker. Ascape: Abstracting complexity. Technical report, Center on Social and Economic Dynamics, The Brookings Institution, March 2000.

M. T. Parker. What is ascape and why should you care? *Journal of Artificial Societies and Social Simulation*, 4(1), January 2001. http://jasss.soc.surrey.ac.uk/4/1/5.html.

N. Persico. Information acquisition in auctions. *Econometrica*, 68(1):135–148, January 2000.

N. Persico. Information acquisition in affiliated decision problems. *Discussion Paper, 1149, Center for Mathematical Studies in Economics and Management Science, Northwestern University*, 1996a.

N. Persico. Information acquisition in auctions. *Working Paper 726, UCLA Department of Economics*, 1996b.

D. Phan and A. Beugnard. Moduleco, a multi-agent modular framework, for the simulation of network effects and population dynamics in social sciences, market and organisations. In *Rencontre Internationale ACSEG (Approches Connexionistes En Sciences Economiques et de Gestion)*. Université de Rennes, 22-23 November 2001.

S. Phelps, P. McBurney, S. Parsons, and E. Sklar. Co-evolutionary auction mechanism design: A preliminary report. In J. Padget, O. Shehory, D. Parkes, N. Sadeh, and W. Walsh, editors, *Agent-Mediated Electronic Commerce IV. Designing Mechanisms and Systems, AAMAS 2002 Workshop on Agent Mediated Electronic Commerce, Bologna, Italy, July 16, 2002, Revised Papers, Lecture Notes in Artificial Intelligence, Vol. 2531*, pages 123–142, Heidelberg, 2002. Springer.

M. Porter. The contributions of industrial organization to strategic management. *Academy of Management Review*, 6(4):609–620, October 1981.

R. Pryor, N. Basu, and T. Quint. *Development of Aspen: A Microanalytic Simulation Model of the U.S. Economy*. Program Development Department, Sandia National Laboratories, Alburquerque, NM 87185, 1996. SAND96-0434.

M. L. Puterman. *Markov Decision Processes - Discrete Stochastic Dynmaic Programming*. Wiley Series in Probability and Statistics. John Wiley & Sons Inc., New York, 1994.

M. L. Puterman and M. C. Shin. Modified policy iteration algorithms for discounted markov decision processes. *Management Science*, 24:1127–1137, 1978.

E. B. Rasmusen. Strategic implications of uncertainty over one's own private value in auctions. *Working Paper, Indiana University Bloomington, Department of Business Economics and Public Policy*, 2005.

B. Reich and I. Ben-Shaul. A componentized architecture for dynamic electronic markets. *SIGMOD Record*, 27(4):40–47, 1998.

S. Reiter. Information and performance in the (new) welfare economics. *The American Economic Review*, 67(1):226–234, February 1977.

A. Repenning. AgentSheets: An interactive simulation environment with end-user programmable agents. In *Interaction 2000*, Tokyo, Japan, 2000.

T. Riechmann. Genetic algorithm learning and economic evolution. In S.-H. Chen, editor, *Evolutionary Computation in Economics and Finance*, pages 45–60. Physica-Verlag, Heidelberg, 2002.

H. J. Rittel and M. Webber. Dilemmas in a general theory of planning. *Policy Science*, 4(2):155–169, 1973.

D. Rolli, D. Neumann, and C. Weinhardt. A minimal market model in ephemeral markets. In *Proceedings of the TheFormEMC*, Toledo, Spain, 2004.

J. S. Rosenschein. *Rational Interaction: Cooperation Among Intelligent Agents*. PhD thesis, Stanford University, 1985.

J. S. Rosenschein and M. R. Genesereth. Deals among rational agents. *Prodeedings of the Ninth International Joint Conference on Artificial Intelligence (IJCAI-85)*, pages 91–99, 1985.

A. E. Roth. The economist as engineer: Game theory, experimentation, and computation as tools of design economics. *Econometrica*, 70:1241–1378, July 2002.

T. C. Schelling. Models of segregation. *The American Economic Review*, 59(2): 488–493, May 1969.

B. Schmid. Was ist neu an der digitalen ökonomie? In M. Sauter and A. Hermanns, editors, *Handbuch Electronic Commerce*. Universität der Bundeswehr München, 1998.

B. Schmid and M. Lindemann. Elements of a reference model for electronic markets. In E. Sprague, editor, *31st Hawaiian International Conference on System Sciences (HICSS)*. IEEE Press, January 1998.

U. Schweizer and T. von Ungern-Sternberg. Sealed bid auctions and the search for better information. *Economica*, 50(197):79–85, February 1983.

J. R. Searle. *Speech Acts*. Cambridge University Press, 1969.

S. Seifert. *Posted Price Offers in Internet Auction Markets*. PhD thesis, Universität Karlsruhe (TH), 2005.

S. Seifert and K.-M. Ehrhart. Design of the 3g spectrum auctions in the UK and germany: An experimental investigation. *German Economic Review*, 6(2): 229–248, 2005.

S. Sen and G. Weiss. Learning in multiagent systems. In G. Weiss, editor, *Multiagent Systems*, pages 259–298, Cambridge (Massachusetts), London (England), 1999. The MIT Press.

A. Serenko and B. Detlor. *Agent Toolkits: A General Overview of the Market and an Assessment of Instructor Satisfaction with Utilizing Toolkits in the Classroom*. Michael G. DeGroote School of Busness, McMaster University, Hamilton, Ontario, 2002. Working Paper 445.

S. S. Shapiro and M. B. Wilk. An analysis of variance test for normality (complete samples). *Biometrika*, 52(3 and 4):591–611, 1965.

L. S. Shapley. Stochastic games. *Proceedings of the National Academy of Sciences of the United States of America*, 39(10):1095–1100, October 1953.

A. Sloman and R. Poli. SIM AGENT: A toolkit for exploring agent designs. In M. Wooldridge, J. Müller, and M. Tambe, editors, *Intelligent Agents Vol II (ATAL-95)*, pages 392–407, Heidelberg, 1996. Springer.

A. Smith. *The Wealth of Nations*. University of Chicago Press, Chicago, 1776.

V. L. Smith. Microeconomic systems as an experimental science. *American Economic Review*, 72(5):923–955, 1982.

M. Sonnessa. Java agent-based simulation library. In *SwarmFest*, Notre Dame, April 2003.

K. Steiglitz, M. Honig, and L. Cohen. A computational market model based on individual action. In S. Clearwater, editor, *Market-Based Control: A Paradigm for Distributed Resource Allocation*, Hong Kong, 1996. World Scientific. http://www.cs.princeton.edu/ ken/scott.ps (abgerufen am 11.02.2002).

S. Strecker. *Multiattribute Auctions in Electronic Procurement - Theory and Experiment*. PhD thesis, Universität Karlsruhe (TH), Germany, June 2004.

M. Ströbel and C. Weinhardt. The montreal taxonomy for electronic negotiations. *Journal of Group Decision and Negotiation*, 12(2):143–164, 2003.

R. S. Sutton and A. G. Barto. *Reinforcement Learning: An Introduction*. MIT Press, Cambridge, MA, 2002.

P. Terna. *How to Use the Java Enterprise Simulator (jES) Program*. Dipartimento di Scienze economiche e finanziarie G. Prato, Università di Torino, Italy, 2004.

L. Tesfatsion. Agent-based computational economics: Growing economies from the bottom-up. ISU Economics Working Paper No. 1, February 2002. http://www.econ.iastate.edu/tesfatsi/.

G. Tewari and P. Maes. Design and implementation of an agent-based intermediary infrastructure for electronic markets. In *EC '00: Proceedings of the 2nd ACM conference on Electronic commerce*, pages 86–94, New York, NY, USA, 2000. ACM Press. doi: http://doi.acm.org/10.1145/352871.352881.

E. L. Thorndike. *The Human Nature Club; an Introduction to the Study of Mental Life*. Longman, Green and Co., New York, 2nd, enl. edition, 1901.

E. L. Thorndike. *The Elements of Psychology*. A.G. Seiler, New York, 2nd edition, January, 1st 1907.

E. L. Thorndike. Darwin's contribution to psychology. *University of California Chronicle*, 12:65–80, 1909.

E. L. Thorndike. *Animal Intelligence: Experimental Studies*. The Animal Behavior Series. Macmillan, New York, 1911.

E. L. Thorndike. Animal intelligence: An experimental study of the associative processes in animals. *Psyhological Review Monograph Supplement*, II(4, Whole No. 8), June 1898.

S. Tisue and U. Wilensky. NetLogo: A simple environment for modeling complexity. In *Proceedings of the International Conference on Complex Systems*, Boston, May 2004.

R. Tobias and C. Hofmann. Evaluation of free java-libraries for social-scientific agent based simulation. *Journal of Artificial Societies and Social Simulation*, 7 (1), January 2004.

U. M. Ünver. *Internet Auctions with Artificial Adaptive Agents: On Evolution of Late Bidding*. Koc University Istanbul, Istanbul, 2003. Working Paper.

M. Valente. *Evolutionary Economics and Computer Simulations - A Model for the Evolution of Markets, Volume II, Laboratory for Simulation Development - A Proposal for Simulation Models in Social Sciences*. PhD thesis, University of Aalborg, Denmark, 1999.

H. R. Varian. When economics shifts from science to engineering. *The New York Times*, 29, 29. August 2002.

S. Vincent. Input data analysis. In J. Banks, editor, *Handbook of Simulation. Principles, Methodology, Advances, Applications, and Practice*, pages 55–91, New York, 1998. Wiley-Interscience, John Wiley & Sons, Inc.

J. von Neumann. *Theory of Self-Reproducing Automata*. University of Illinois Press, Urbana and London, 1966.

N. J. Vriend. An illustration of the essential difference between individual and social learning, and its consequences for computational analysis. *Journal of economic dynamics and control*, 24:1–19, 2000.

L. Walras. *Elements of Pure Economic Theory*. Allen and Unwin, London, 1874. This English Edition was published 1954.

C. J. Watkins. *Learning from Delayed Rewards*. PhD thesis, University of Camebridge, England, 1989.

C. J. Watkins and P. Dayan. Q-learning. *Machine Learning*, 8(3-4):279–292, May 1992.

I. Weber. Online auctions: Insights into the first bidder discount. In *The 2005 International Symposium on Applications and the Internet (SAINT2005)*, Washington, 2005. IEEE Computer Society.

I. Weber, C. Czernohous, and C. Weinhardt. Simulation of ending rules in online auctions. In S. Klein, editor, *Proceedings of the 11th Research Symposium on Emerging Electronic Markets (RSEEM)*, University College Dublin, Ireland, 2004.

C. Weinhardt and P. Gomber. Softwareagenten. Technical report, BWL-Wirtschaftsinformatik, Justus-Liebig-Universität Gießen, June 1999. http://www.iw.uni-karlsruhe.de/Forschung/Papers/ (abgerufen am 28.11.2001).

C. Weinhardt, C. Holtmann, and D. Neumann. Market engineering. *Wirtschaftsinformatik*, 45(6):635–640, 2003.

C. Weinhardt, C. van Dinther, K. Kolitz, J. Mäkiö, and I. Weber. Meet2trade: A generic electronic trading platform. In *Proceedings of the 4th Workshop on e-Business (Web2005), December 10, Las Vegas*, 2005.

G. Weiss. *Multiagent Systems*, volume 1. The MIT Press, Cambridge (Massachusetts), London (England), 1999.

P. D. Welch. On the problem of the initial transient in steady-state simulation, 1981. IBM Watson Research Center, Yorktown Heights, New York.

P. D. Welch. The statistical analysis of simulation results. In S. S. Lavenberg, editor, *The Computer Performance Modeling Handbook*, New York, 1983. Academic Press.

Whitestein Technologies. LS/TS product brochure. http://www.whitestein.com/pages/downloads/docs.html, 2005.

F. Wilcoxon. Individual comparisons by ranking methods. *Biometrics*, 1:80–83, 1945.

U. Wilensky. *NetLogo User Manual*. Northwestern University, 1999. http://ccl.northwestern.edu/netlogo/.

E. G. Wolfstetter. *Topics in Microeconomics - Industrial Organizations, Auctions and Incentives*. Cambridge University Press, 2002 2nd edition, 1999.

M. Wooldridge. Intelligent agents. In G. Weiss, editor, *Multi Agent Systems*, volume 1, pages 27–77, Cambridge (Massachusetts), London (England), 1999. MIT Press.

M. Wooldridge and P. Ciancarini. Agent-oriented software engineering: The state of the art. In P. Ciancarini and M. Wooldridge, editors, *Agent-Oriented Software Engineering: First International Workshop, AOSE 2000 Limerick, Ireland, June 10, 2000, Revised Papers, Lecture Notes in Computer Science, Vol. 1957*, pages 1–28, Heidelberg, 2001. Springer Verlag.

M. Wooldridge and N. R. Jennings. Intelligent agents: Theory and practice. *Knowledge Engineering Review*, 10(2), 1995.

P. R. Wurman, M. P. Wellman, and W. E. Walsh. The michigan internet auctionbot: A configurable auction server for human and software agents. In K. P. Sycara and M. Wooldridge, editors, *Proceedings of the 2nd International Conference on Autonomous Agents (Agents'98)*, pages 301–308, New York, 9–13 1998. ACM Press. ISBN 0-89791-983-1. URL citeseer.nj.nec.com/wurman98michigan.html.

P. R. Wurman, M. P. Wellman, and W. E. Walsh. A parametrization of the auction design space. *Journal of Economic Literature*, 2000.

P. R. Wurman, M. P. Wellman, and W. E. Walsh. A parametrization of the auction design space. *Games and Economic Behavior*, 35:304–338, 2001.

F. Zambonelli, N. R. Jennings, and M. Wooldridge. Organisational abstractions for the analysis and design of multi-agent systems. *International Journal of Software Engineering and Knowledge Engineering*, 11(3):303–328, 2001.

Abbreviations

AA	open-cry second-price ascending auction
ABLE	Agent Building and Learning Environment
ACC	Agent Communication Channel
ACE	Agent-based Computational Economics
ACL	Agent Communication Language
AGR	Agent Group Role
AHC	Adaptive Heuristic Critic
AID	Agent Identifier
AMASE	Agent-based Simulation Environment
AMM	Atomic Market Model
AMS	Agent Management System
AP	Agent Platform
API	Application Program Interface
B.C.	Before Christ
C	certain agent
CAME	Computer Aided Market Engineering
CDA	Continuous Double Auction
CDMM	Cascading Dynamic Market Model
CE	Computational Economics
CERN	Conseil Europen pour la Recherche Nuclaire
CM	Call Market
CMM	Cascading Market Model
Cougaar	Cognitive Agent Architecture
CP	Conversation Policy
csv	comma separated values
DA	Dummy Agent
DAI	Distributed Artificial Intelligence
DARPA	Defense Advanced Research Projects Agency
DF	Directory Facilitator

df	degree of freedom
DMM	Dynamic Market Model
DPSS	Distributed Problem Solving Systems
EJB	Enterprise Java Bean
ENS	e-negotiation system
ER	Erev-Roth learning mechanism
FIPA	Foundation for Intelligent Physical Agents
FMM	Flexible Market Model
FSM	Finite State Machine
GA	Genetic Algorithm
GEE	Generic Experimentation Engine
GEM	Global Electronic Market
GIS	Geographic Information System
GNP	Generic Negotiation Platform
GUI	Graphical User Interface
H	honest agents
HE	early stationary agent
HL	late stationary agent
HP	price signalling agent
HR	random agent
i.e.	id est (Latin: that is)
IIASA	International Institute for Applied Systems Analysis
iid	independent identically distributed
IT	information technology
J2EE	Java 2 Platform, Enterprise Edition
J2ME	Java 2 Platform, Micro Edition
J2SE	Java 2 Platform, Standard Edition
JADE	Java Agent DEvelopment Framework
JAS	Java Agent-based Simulation library
JASA	Java Auction Simulator API
jES	Java Enterprise Simulator
JMS	Java Message Service
KISS	Keep It Simple Stupid
KQML	Knowledge Query and Manipulation Language
KSE	Knowledge Sharing Effort
LIRMM	Laboratoire d'Informatique, de Robotique et de Microlectronique de Montpellier
LS/TS	Living Systems Technology Suite

Lsd	Laboratory for Simulation Development
MABS	Multi Agent-based Simulation
MadKit	Multi Agent Development Kit
MAML	Multi-Agent Modelling Language
MAS	Multi Agent System
MASON	Multi-Agent Simulator of Neighborhoods
MC	Monte Carlo
MDP	Markov Decision Process
ME	Market Engineering
MES	meet2trade Experimental System
MG	Markov Games
MIMOSE	Mikro- und Mehrebenenmodellierungs-Software
MML	Market Modelling Language
MMM	Market-Maker Market
MRM	Media Reference Model
MT	Montreal Taxonomy
MTP	Message Transport Protocol
MTS	Message Transport System
NYSE	New York Stock Exchange
P2P	Peer to Peer
RePast	Recursive Porous Agent Simulation Toolkit
RL	Reinforcement Learning
RMI	Remote Method Invocation
RMI	Remote Monitoring Agent
RNG	Random Number Generator
SACB	Simulation Agent Control Behaviour
SB	second-price sealed-bid auction
SCA	Simulation Control Agent
SDML	a Strictly Declarative Modeling Language
SeSAm	Shell for Simulated Agent Systems
SG	Stochastic Game
SimPy	Simulation in Python
SMB	Simulation Management Behaviour
TAC	Trading Agent Competition
TCP/IP	Transmission Control Protocol/Internet Protocol
TILAB	Telecom Italia Lab
U	uncertain agent
VAT	Visual Agent Talk

VM	Virtual Machine
VSEit	Versatile Simulation Environment for the internet
XML	Extensible Markup Language
z-Tree	Zurich Toolbox for Readymade Economic Experiments
ZI	zero intelligence